# VAN GOGH

ANNE SEFRIOUI

# VAN GOGH
## THE BIGGER PICTURE

**PRESTEL**
**MUNICH · LONDON · NEW YORK**

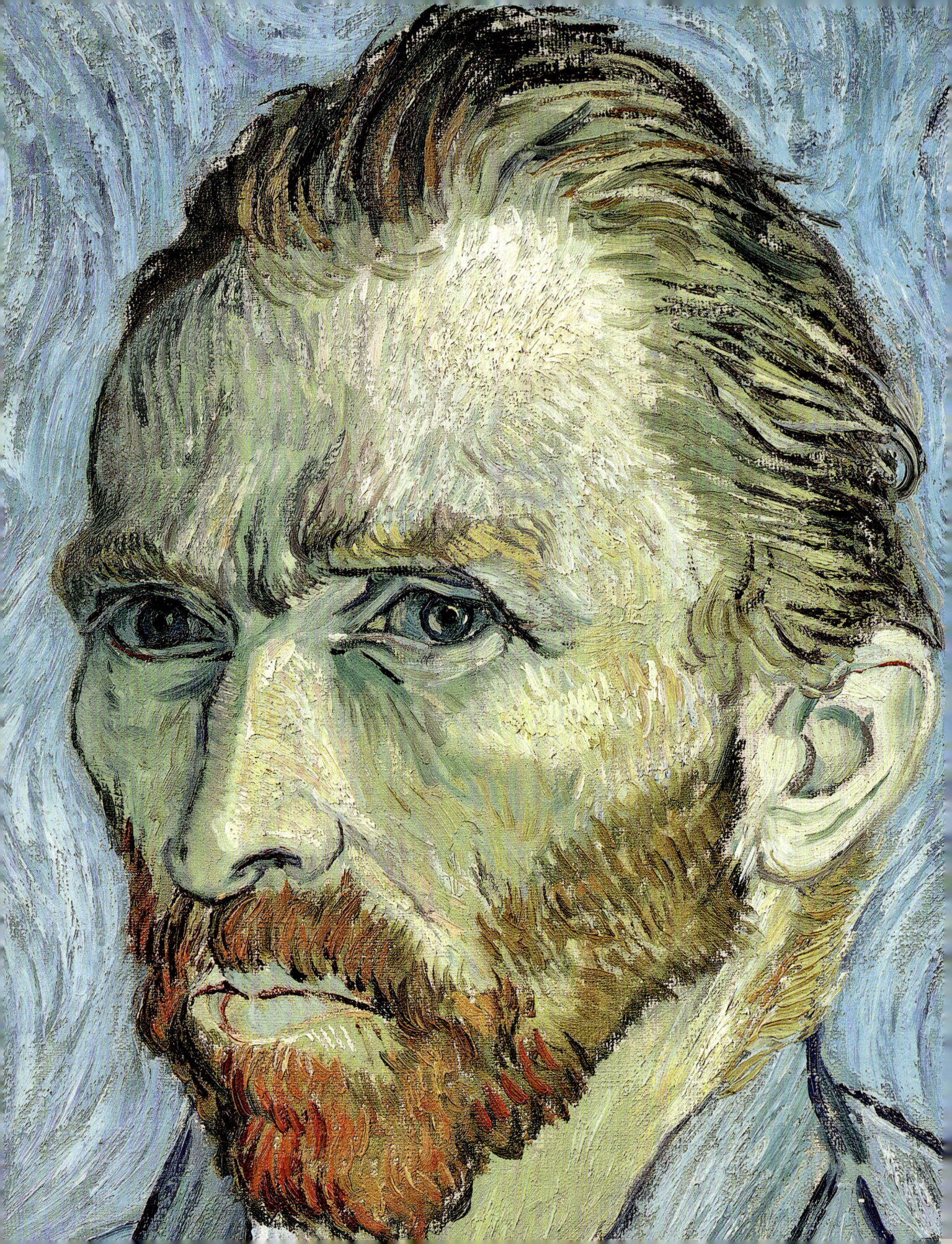

October 1885. Vincent Van Gogh painted a still life – "in one day", he wrote to his brother Theo. The work features a large open Bible, a candlestick with an extinguished candle and, in the foreground, a popular edition of Émile Zola's novel *La joie de vivre* (see pp. 22-23). Two books, two metaphors: a big, dark, heavy book, rife with prohibitions, threats and curses, symbolising his past, his struggles and his dramas; and, in the foreground, a little novel featuring a bright yellow cover, whose title alone speaks volumes. Produced precisely in the middle of Van Gogh's artistic career – which, in reality, only spanned the course of ten years –, this work admirably summarises the turning point that the painter had reached at the time. A page was being turned, and Van Gogh's yearning for renewal and for freedom would become a reality a few months later when he left the Netherlands. This impetus would drive him to forsake his dark palette and soon let colours resound in a vibrant light.

> *I have a more or less irresistible passion for books and the constant need to improve my mind – to study, if you like – just as I have a need to eat bread.*

This emblematic painting also testifies to the essential role that books would hold throughout Van Gogh's life. The first book to come to his attention was, of course, the Bible, and he would read it every day. His father, Theodorus van Gogh, was a Calvinist pastor in the small village of Groot-Zundert in the Province of Brabant, where Vincent Willem was born on 30 March 1853. Van Gogh was born one year to the day after the birth of a first stillborn child, who bore the same name as him – a strange coincidence that would not be devoid of consequences for the child. According to his father, however, there was one book that carried answers to all forms of human anguish: the Bible, which reminds us all that we are God's creatures and that we must obey His will.

Believing in the word of God was a given, in the world where Vincent grew up. However, submission was hardly the temperament of this solitary, taciturn youth, who was prone to sudden temper tantrums. He liked to take long walks in the countryside, a taste for nature that would never leave him. He also enjoyed drawing, and was encouraged by his mother, who was quite talented herself. Vincent did not deal well with school discipline; he attended a variety of institutions,

**Self-portrait** (detail)
September 1889, oil on canvas, 65 × 54.5 cm, Paris, Musée d'Orsay

with no remarkable results, apart from learning foreign languages. On the other hand, he devoured books of all kinds – treatises on philosophy, theology and novels –, and fuelled by a singular particular passion for Dickens. This reading frenzy would last throughout his life.

Growing up, his social relationships remained difficult, and he needed affection and the presence of his brothers and sisters (five children were born after him); for their part, his brethren were concerned about this unpredictable boy. It was with Theo, four years his junior, that Vincent would develop the most intimate relationship. He penned over six hundred and fifty letters to him over the course of his life, once again testifying to his passion for the written word; these would establish Van Gogh as the most "literary" artist of his time.

When this fraternal correspondence began in 1872, Vincent had been working for three years in The Hague, in a branch of the Parisian gallery Goupil & Cie, thanks to recommendations by his paternal uncle, who had himself made a career in the art trade. His seriousness and eagerness to learn were appreciated. Indeed, immersed in this new world, the young man carefully studied all the works that he had access to, read and learned; he advised Theo to do the same, when his younger brother embraced the same trade as him, first in Brussels, and later in The Hague. He wrote to him, in November 1873: "[...] And if you get the chance, read about art, and especially magazines about art, the *Gazette des Beaux-Arts*, etc." In March the following year, he insisted: "Read about art as much as possible." The gallery mainly presented landscapes painted by artists of the Barbizon school (Camille Corot, Julien Dupré and Charles-François Daubigny), as well as contemporary works by painters of The Hague school, whose realism appealed to Vincent. It also sold many engravings, which allowed Van Gogh to discover the works of Jean-François Millet, whose works immediately captivated and moved him. Millet would remain a model and guide throughout Van Gogh's life (see page 21). "*The Angelus*; that is magnificent, that's poetry," he wrote to Theo. Through his profession, Van Gogh thus acquired a solid culture, which he would continue to develop. The way that he was sometimes later depicted – as a spontaneous painter, feverishly obeying his impulses alone – is a far cry from reality.

At the time, however, becoming an artist was not on Van Gogh's agenda. Vincent was then promoted by his manager, who sent him to work at the London branch. While his time in London came off to a good start, with the thrilling discovery of English painters such as Joshua Reynolds, J. M. W. Turner, and John Constable, and the comfort of Mrs. Loyer's boarding house, it ended dramatically. Vincent fell under the spell of his landlady's daughter, Ursula. He was briskly entranced, and felt a deep and lasting shock when she spurned him.

Goupil & Cie then sent him to Paris, where he resided for three months, from October to December 1874, hardly ever leaving his home, before returning to the London branch, with a heavy heart. Disappointed love had instilled a powerful feeling of guilt in him: he, himself, was the cause of this failure; God had punished him for his sins, and he needed to make amends. He immersed himself in pious reading, encouraging those around him – Theo, in particular – to do the same. In May 1875, the deeply troubled young man returned to Paris, in the Goupil & Cie Gallery, which had passed into the hands of Messrs Boussod and Valadon. This second stay in Paris, which in part planned to distract him from his despair over love, nevertheless enabled him to assiduously frequent the Louvre Museum, where he marvelled at the works of Rembrandt Van Rijn and Jacob van Ruisdael, in particular. He would also be a frequent visitor to the Musée du Luxembourg, which was dedicated to living artists, and attended the exhibition devoted to the recently deceased Camille Corot, whom he considered to be one of the leaders of the "revolution in art", possessing "that which is the eternal quality in the greatest of the great: simplicity and truth". However, he failed to embrace modernity – a trend represented by those painters who were recently named "Impressionists" and who, in the spring of 1874, were featured in an exhibition in the studio of the photographer Félix Nadar. He would finally meet them some ten years later. Van Gogh's reading, at that time, was almost exclusively limited to the Bible, which was, for his father, "a light on his path and a lamp ahead of his feet". However, his mystical preoccupations were such that he neglected his work, and was eventually dismissed in April 1876. This time, his uncle Cent refused to help him, while his father did not hide his deep dissatisfaction. From that moment on, Van Gogh began to feel that he was misunderstood, rejected by all and destined to find redemption only through sacrifice.

> *It is a delightful thought that in the future, wherever I go,*
> *I shall preach the Gospel.*

He then decided to return to England: by means of a classified advertisement, he found a job as a teaching assistant at a primary school in Ramsgate, near London, with Reverend Stokes. In this working-class neighbourhood, Vincent lived "in the world of Dickens", as he wrote in his letters, and developed a deep empathy with the unfortunate folk that he encountered there. He soon aspired to spread the word of God among them. "Blessed are those who mourn, for they shall be comforted," says the Gospel. Two months later, he moved to nearby Isleworth, where he was hired by a Methodist minister, Reverend Jones. Van Gogh would assist him in his parish, write his first sermons and, at last, preach in the London suburbs. The idea of saving souls, of guiding them, even at the cost of sacrificing his own life, grew in the young man's mind. Van Gogh worked hard, cared for the parishioners, and prayed, barely feeding himself; and when his parents took him in, in December 1876, he was exhausted, but still exalted by the love of God.

He then spent a few months working as a bookshop assistant in Dordrecht, which did not deter him from what he felt was his calling. Furthermore, he proved to be a mediocre employee, and spent his days translating passages from the Bible into French, English and German. He was certain, he would repeat, that he wanted to become a pastor: why would that be unusual, considering his ancestry, where so many men had devoted their lives to God, starting with his father? His family finally agreed, and Vincent began – though not without great difficulty – studying theology in Amsterdam. He also sought to learn mathematics, Latin and Greek; however, theoretical education was hardly suited to a mind like his, and his results were less than adequate, forcing him to give up his exams.

This didn't really matter to Vincent, however; what he really yearned for was to bring the light of God's word to the poor. A few months later, he regained hope when he joined a missionary training school in Laeken, near Brussels, which accepted him as a trainee for three months. Once again, Van Gogh's difficult character, his nervousness and his propensity to all manner of excesses did not work in his favour; at the end of his training, he was not offered a job. Rejected once again, he decided to carry out his apostolate outside any institutional framework, and settled in the Borinage, Belgium's most destitute region. There, he lived among the miners, the better to understand their misery and bear its burden with them. He tended to the sick, taught catechism, barely ate, and slept in a hut on a heap of straw; he exhausted himself, and no longer washed. The local population thought Pastor Vincent to be very strange... and maybe even slightly mad, some whispered. Faced with his excessive ardour, the Evangelical Council attempted to supervise him by sending him to Wasmes. There, he would work with Pastor Bonte, who would quickly grow exasperated with the young man's zeal. And when Vincent sided with the miners during their uprising, to protest against the use of child workers, the Council could no longer stand by him, and refused to renew his contract.

So, in July 1879, Vincent was left to his own devices; he wandered the roads, and met with the miners to whom he preached in the region of Cuesmes, occasionally trading in a sketch for a handful of potatoes or temporary accommodation. However, he no longer had a heart for this life; he doubted his role, his ability to alleviate the misery that surrounded him, which he had likely chosen to bear in vain. The assessment of his life, at the age of twenty-six, reflected an accumulation of failures and disappointments for those around him.

Even Theo, who disapproved of the life that he had chosen for himself, had ceased writing. So Van Gogh took up his pencils, drawing everything around him whenever he could – men and women at work, desolate landscapes and miserable houses. Every day, his interest for the depiction of the reality of the mining world grew stronger. Amidst this profound crisis, art was, for Van Gogh, a consolation that became a passion; the notion of art's soothing power is indeed pervasive throughout his correspondence. This passion would in fact lead him, the following year, to choose a different path and become an artist.

Many reasons can explain why he embraced this new career: from childhood, Vincent showed a remarkable talent for drawing, as can be seen from the few surviving sheets. Later, he never ceased to adorn his letters with pencil drawings and sketches, to the extent that in the 1870s, Theo suggested that he should cultivate his talents more seriously. At the time, however, his elder brother had dismissed this temptation; he was busy with his faith, a priority far greater to him than what he considered to be selfish pleasure. It wasn't until ten years later, depicting miners and peasants, that art appeared to him as a new mission, another way of loving humanity. And indeed, he would commit himself to it with the same thirst for the absolute as when he embraced evangelisation.

In fact, long before he chose the path of art, Vincent had already been looking at the world with a painter's eye. His correspondence is filled with descriptions of landscapes and references to the great masters. In a letter to his parents in April 1876, he wrote: "At dawn the next morning, on the train from Harwich to London, it was beautiful to see the black fields and green meadows with sheep and lambs, and an occasional thorn bush and a few large oak trees with dark twigs and grey moss-covered trunks; the shimmering blue sky with a few stars still, and a bank of grey clouds at the horizon." Even the bleak Borinage region awakened pictorial memories: "There was snow these last few days, the dark days before Christmas. Then everything was reminiscent of the medieval paintings by Peasant Bruegel, among others, and by so many others who were so good at expressing the singular effect of red and green, black and white."

*That one runs a high risk of going under oneself, that being a painter is like being a forward sentry...*

Van Gogh's correspondence with Theo, which had been on hiatus for almost a year, resumed in July 1880, and Vincent announced his decision to devote himself to painting. His younger brother had a successful career as an art dealer, and was now based in Paris, where he ran one of the two Boussod & Valadon galleries, located in Montmartre.

He would never cease to support his elder brother as he embraced his new path, and from that time on, began to send him money on a regular basis. Thanks to this invaluable support, Vincent could devote himself to his art: he drew tirelessly, and in particular wanted "to do studies of figures, to attempt them and to learn", using miners as models. Seeking to capture the essence of the human condition, he imitated Millet, and practised copying his works, thanks to the engravings that Theo sent him. Aware of his technical shortcomings, Van Gogh immersed himself in Charles Bargue's treatise *Cours de Dessin*; however, despite acquiring some essential basics, he felt the need to have his work corrected: "There are laws of proportion, of light and shadow, of perspective, which one must know in order to be able to draw well."

Vincent left for Brussels and enrolled at the Académie des Beaux-Arts, where he studied anatomy and perspective. He worked hard, hoping to master his drawing well enough to receive commissions for illustrations published in books or newspapers, as he informed his parents to reassure them:

"For a good draughtsman can certainly find work nowadays: such persons are in great demand, and there are positions that are very well paid, [...] but one can't achieve this all at once and I am by no means that far, but it could well come to that [...], but only on the condition that a great deal of work and study is done." This objective no doubt explains why, at this time, he began collecting engravings by Gustave Doré, Paul Gavarni – and, above all, Honoré Daumier, "ten times better than landscapes", in whose studies of manners he discovered "frightening truths". Years later, in Saint-Rémy-de-Provence, he would copy and transpose one of his engravings, *The Drinkers*. This period in Brussels was also marked by his meeting, through Theo, with the Dutch painter Anthon van Rappard. A true artists' conversation took place between the two men, and would continue in the form of a significant correspondence throughout the following years.

> *What is drawing? How does one get there? It's working one's way through an invisible iron wall that seems to stand between what one feels and what one can do.*

In the spring of 1881, Vincent left Brussels to work in Etten, where his parents now lived. Theo joined him for a few days, keen to talk to his brother about his future and the possibilities of turning his activity into a full-fledged profession. He arranged a meeting with Anton Mauve, a renowned painter to whom the Van Gogh family was related, and the master, struck by the vigour of Van Gogh's drawings, encouraged and advised the young man. Vincent took these first lessons on board, and wrote to his brother: "Prompted as well by a thing or two that

Mauve said to me, I've started working again from a live model. [...] Diggers, sowers, ploughers, men and women I must now draw constantly. Examine and draw everything that's part of a peasant's life. Just as many others have done and are doing. I'm no longer so powerless in the face of nature as I used to be." In this letter, he also pointed out that he was varying his techniques, working in Indian ink with a brush and starting to use a bit of colour.

Relations with his parents had become more peaceful, as they at last saw him seriously commit to an honourable trade; they would, however, soon deteriorate. Vincent, who had fallen in love with his cousin Kees, a widow with a child, was spurned by the young woman. However, he persisted and harassed her, to the point where her father asked him to leave the family home. This dispute added to other, deeper disagreements between the pastor and his son, who bluntly criticised his father's life, which was driven by convention and bigotry. It was time for Vincent to leave his parents' home. In January 1882, he moved to The Hague, not far from his cousin Anton Mauven; he would support him financially, and introduce him to oil painting and to the city's artistic scene. It was here that Van Gogh really began his life as a painter.

A long journey awaited him, which would lead him from The Hague to Drenthe, from Nuenen to Antwerp, from Paris to the south of France – and finally, to his tragic end, in Auvers-sur-Oise. Excess, instability, relationship difficulties, and suicide: Vincent van Gogh's troubled personality was the subject of much commentary, and the most extravagant hypotheses about the causes of his alleged "madness" began to spread on the day following his death. The fact remains that he was a phenomenal artist, graced with remarkable culture, and that he was perfectly lucid about his craft, the evolution of his art and his objectives. No one, better than Theo, described the character of this man, who would never experience true happiness: "It appears as if there are two different beings in him; the one, marvellously gifted, fine and delicate, and the other, selfish and heartless. They appear alternately, so that one hears him talk now this way, and then that way, and always with arguments to prove pro and contra. It is a pity that he is his own enemy, for he makes life difficult not only for others, but also for himself."

# The founding years

## Painting reality

In January 1882, Vincent moved with Anthon Mauve to The Hague, where he would stay for almost two years. With the fierce determination that characterised everything that he did, he practised painting with watercolour, whilst learning oil painting; these explorations would lead him to tackle the question of colour. His technique improved swiftly, enriched by his frequent visits to the Pulchri Studio, which provided him with the opportunity to mingle with the local art scene. This "Hague School of painters" included not only Anthon Mauve, but also Jozef Israëls, Jacob Maris, Willem Roelofs and Anthon Van Rappard – all painters whose slightly grey works, imbued with a certain romanticism, delivered an idealised vision of the life of fishermen and peasants. While their themes were similar to Van Gogh's, the latter interpreted them with a very personal form of harshness and realism. The artist would constantly keep his brother informed of his progress and plans, including drawings in the letters that he sent him: "I've tackled that old giant of a pollard willow, and I believe that I made it the best of my watercolours. [...] This is just about the effect of the pollard willow, but there is no black, in the watercolour itself, only graded black." (See page 25.)

Shortly after arriving in The Hague, he met Clasina Hoornik, known as Sien – an alcoholic, pregnant prostitute who already had a child. He took her as his model and, moved by her distress, took her to give birth in Leiden. Soon, they were living together in dismal conditions, which alienated Van Gogh from the people around him. Under pressure from Theo and his family – and, above all, because it hindered his work –, Vincent finally gave up this precarious home in the autumn of 1883. He then moved to Drenthe, an agricultural region in the north-east of the Netherlands. Amidst these wild, melancholic landscapes, he painted thatched cottages on the moors, peasants harvesting potatoes and the extraction of peat. After three months, ill and tired of solitude, he returned to his parents' home in Nuenen.

Determined to paint rural life, like Jean-François Millet did, Van Gogh chose weavers and farmers as his subjects. As he had in the Borinage, he accompanied them in their daily occupations (p. 21), drew and painted them, and undertook a series of head studies (p. 20), predominantly in tones of blue and brown. This series this led him to compose *The Potato Eaters* (pp. 18-19), which Van Gogh always considered to be his first painting. Inspired by the great Dutch masters, particularly Rembrandt's use of *chiaroscuro*, the artist depicted peasants gathered around a plate, seated under the light of a lamp. Although the subject had already been depicted by contemporaries such as Jozef Israëls, Henry De Groux and Léon Lhermitte, Van Gogh infused it with realism and expressiveness, with the aim of extolling "manual labour and the fact that they have thus honestly earned their food". This dark, dull canvas did not appeal to Theo, who rather praised the bright palette of the Impressionists; nor did it appeal to Anthon Van Rappard, whose harsh criticism put an end to his friendship with Van Gogh.

When he tried his hand at painting the reddish autumn trees, Vincent realised that he still had a lot to learn about the effects of sunlight and movement, which his brother said the "Impressionists" had mastered magnificently. This would require him to discover how they proceeded; to do so, Van Gogh would need to leave Nuenen, where he felt beset by boredom, and missed the world of painting. Bidding farewell to the region became inevitable when Van Gogh's father died of a heart attack on 26 March 1885, forcing the family to leave the village.

One of Van Gogh's last paintings in Brabant was *Still Life with a Bible* (pp. 22-23), which perfectly summarises his state of mind at the time. He needed to leave, but where to? Van Gogh settled for Antwerp, the home of Peter Paul Rubens, the master of colour; the city might also provide an opportunity for him to meet some merchants. Vincent gathered a few paintings, and left the Netherlands at the end of November; he would never return.

At the time, Antwerp was an important artistic centre; its Royal Academy of Fine Arts has enjoyed international renown since its foundation, in the seventeenth century. Vincent enrolled on the winter course, in the "Antique" section; as he wrote to Theo, he "very much [would] like to make more studies of the nude". He very soon rebelled against the absurdities of the academic system and clashed with his teachers, but agreed that he had made progress in drawing. Fortunately, there were museums, where Rubens's free use of colour and brushstrokes came as a revelation to Van Gogh. Another fruitful discovery was Japanese prints, of which he covered his bedroom's walls and became an avid collector. He insistently asked his brother to allow him to travel to Paris as soon as possible. However, Theo was hesitant, well aware of Vincent's difficult character.

**Self-Portrait with Grey Felt Hat** (detail, p. 12)
Early 1886, oil on canvas, 41.5 × 32.5 cm, Amsterdam, Van Gogh Museum

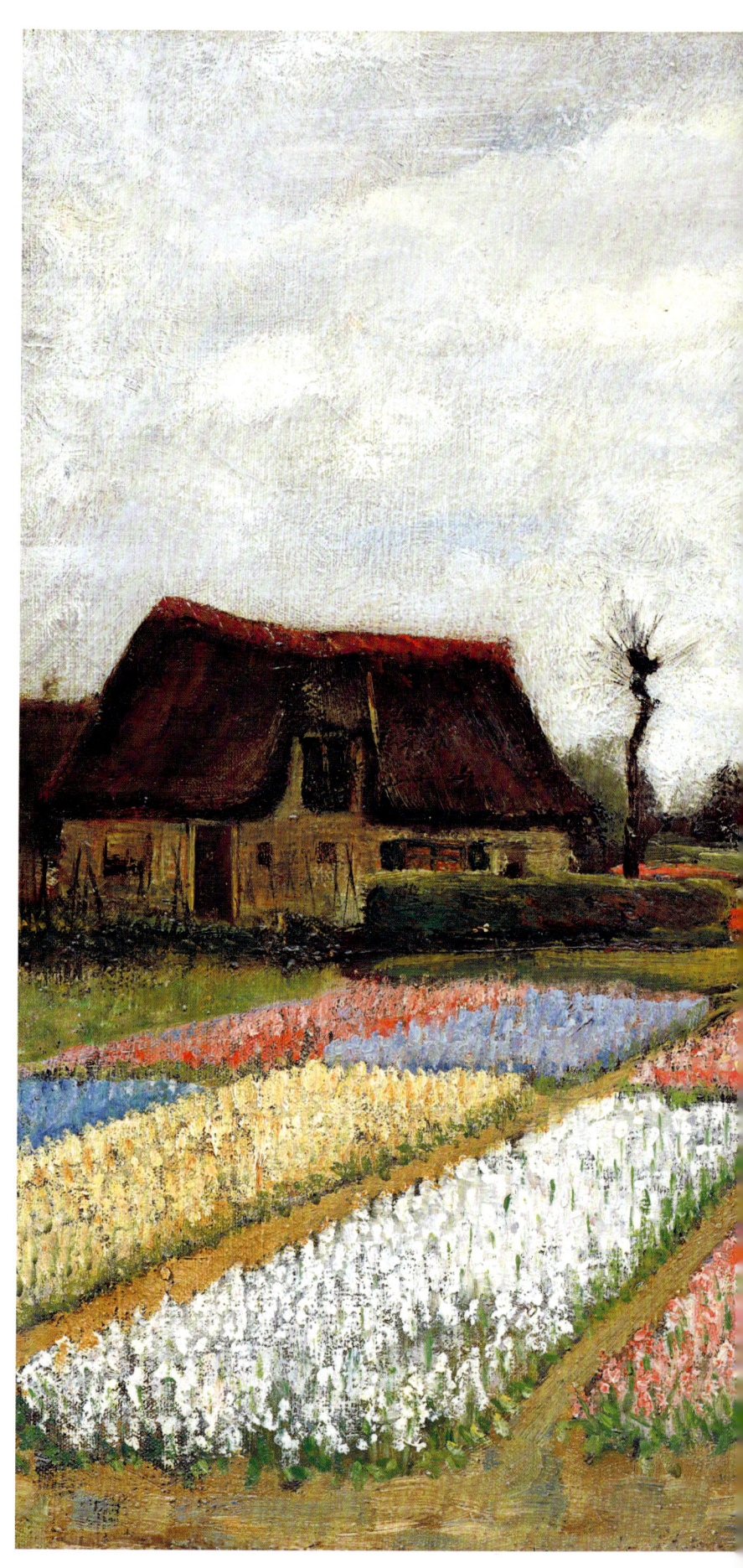

**Bulb Fields (Flower Beds in Holland)**

April 1883
Oil on canvas, 48.9 × 66 cm
Washington, National Gallery of Art

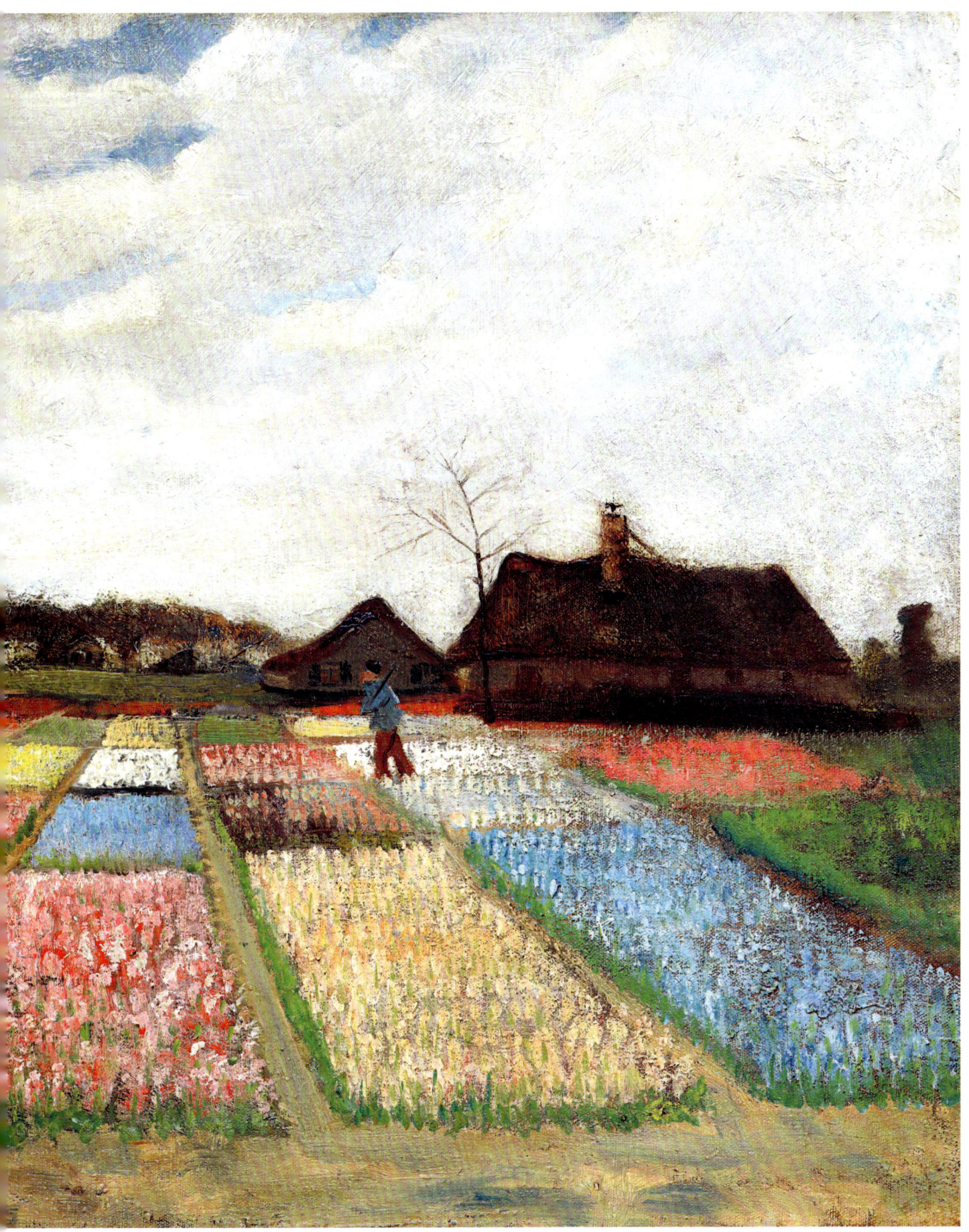

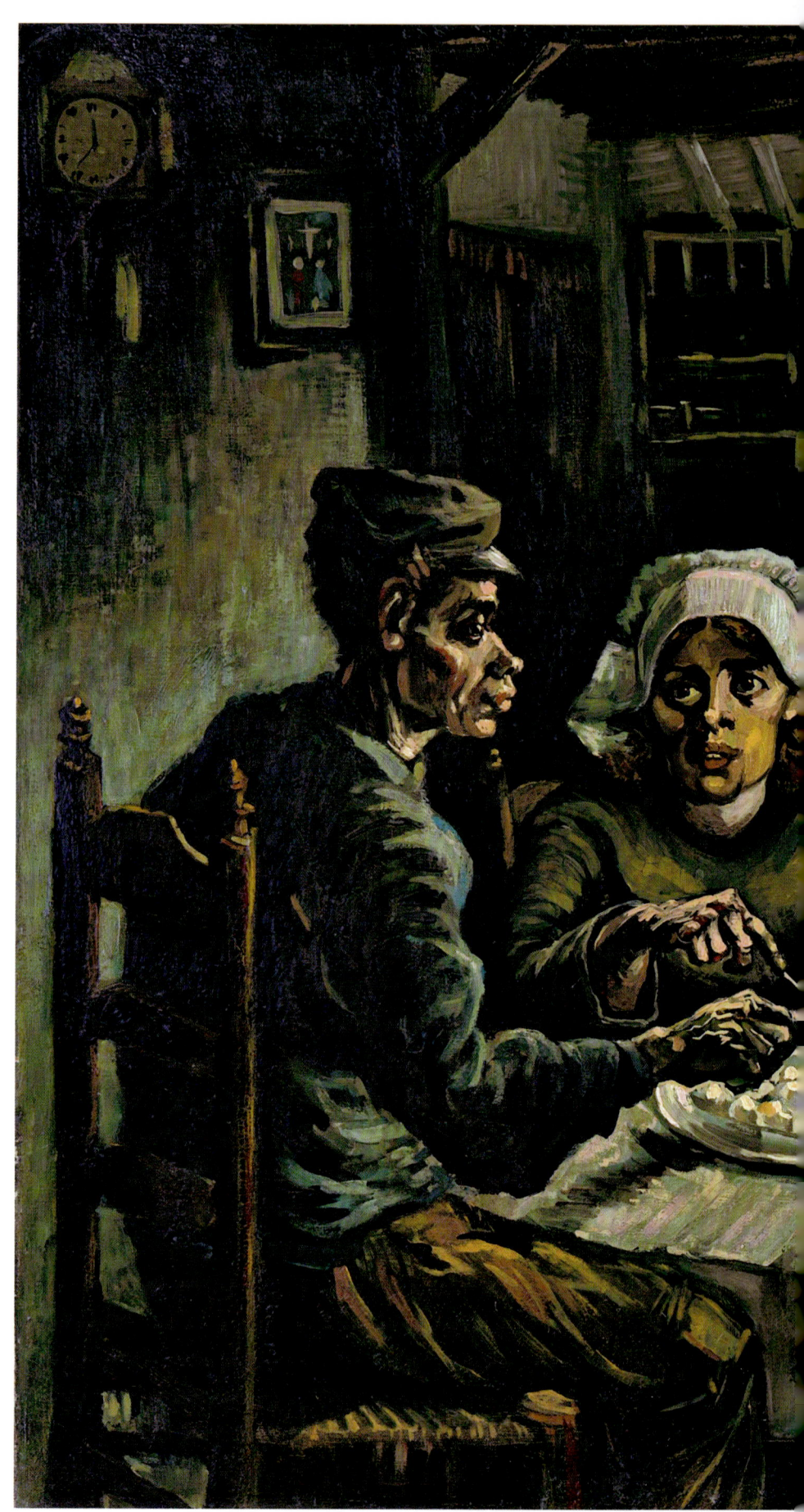

**The Potato Eaters**

April 1885
Oil on canvas, 81.5 × 114.5 cm
Amsterdam, Van Gogh Museum

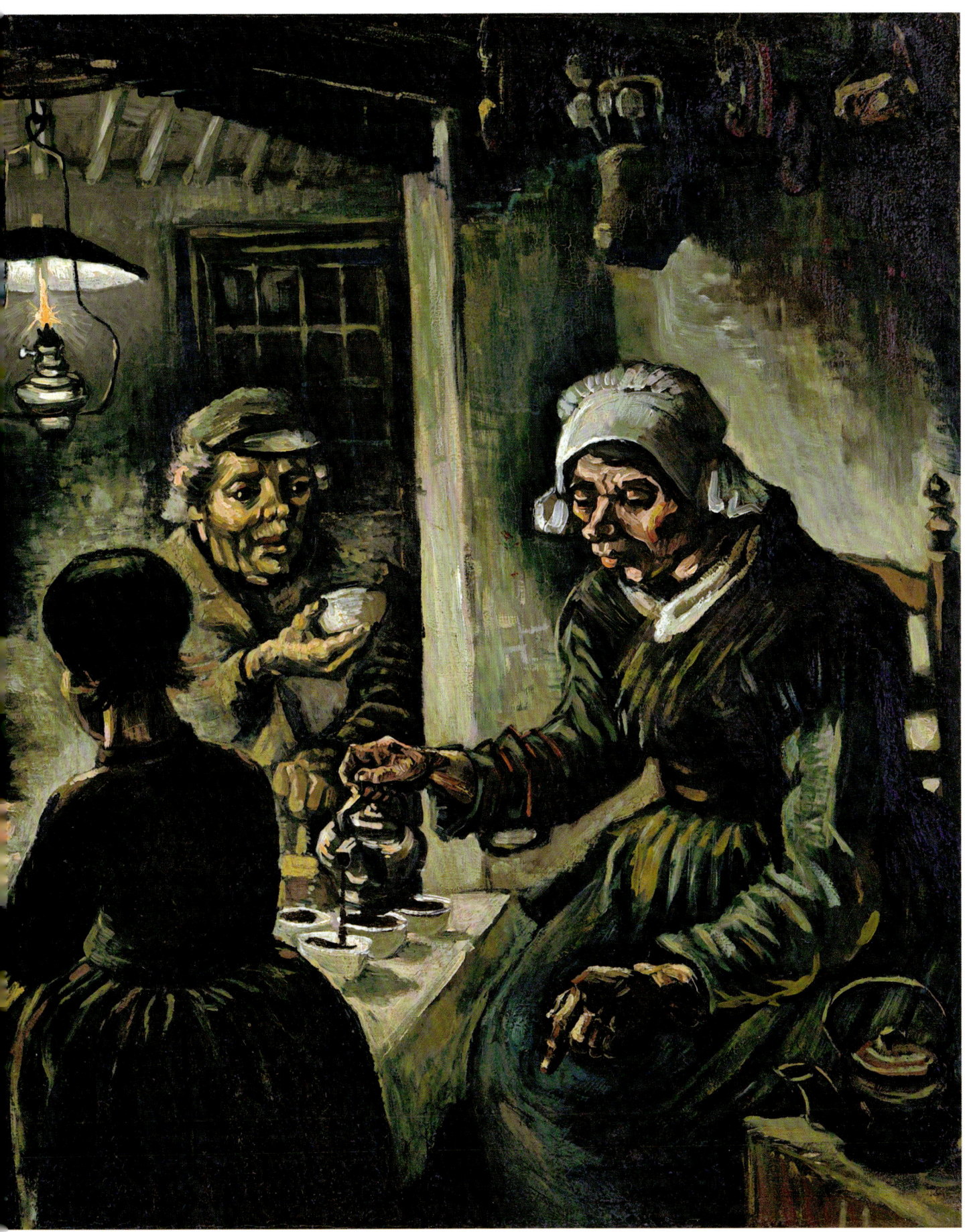

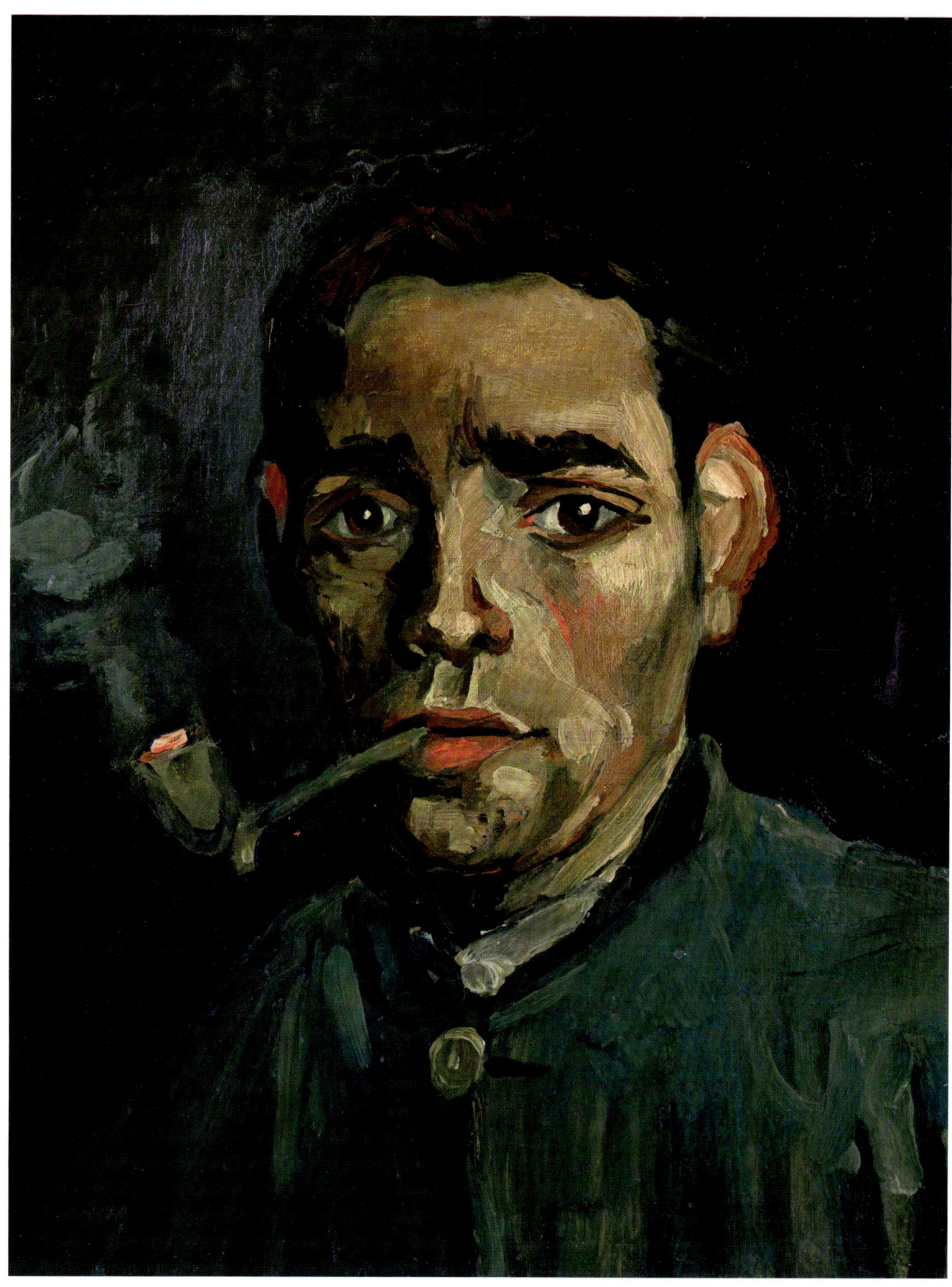

**Head of a Man**, ca. May 1885, oil on canvas, 37.7 × 29.5 cm, Amsterdam, Van Gogh Museum

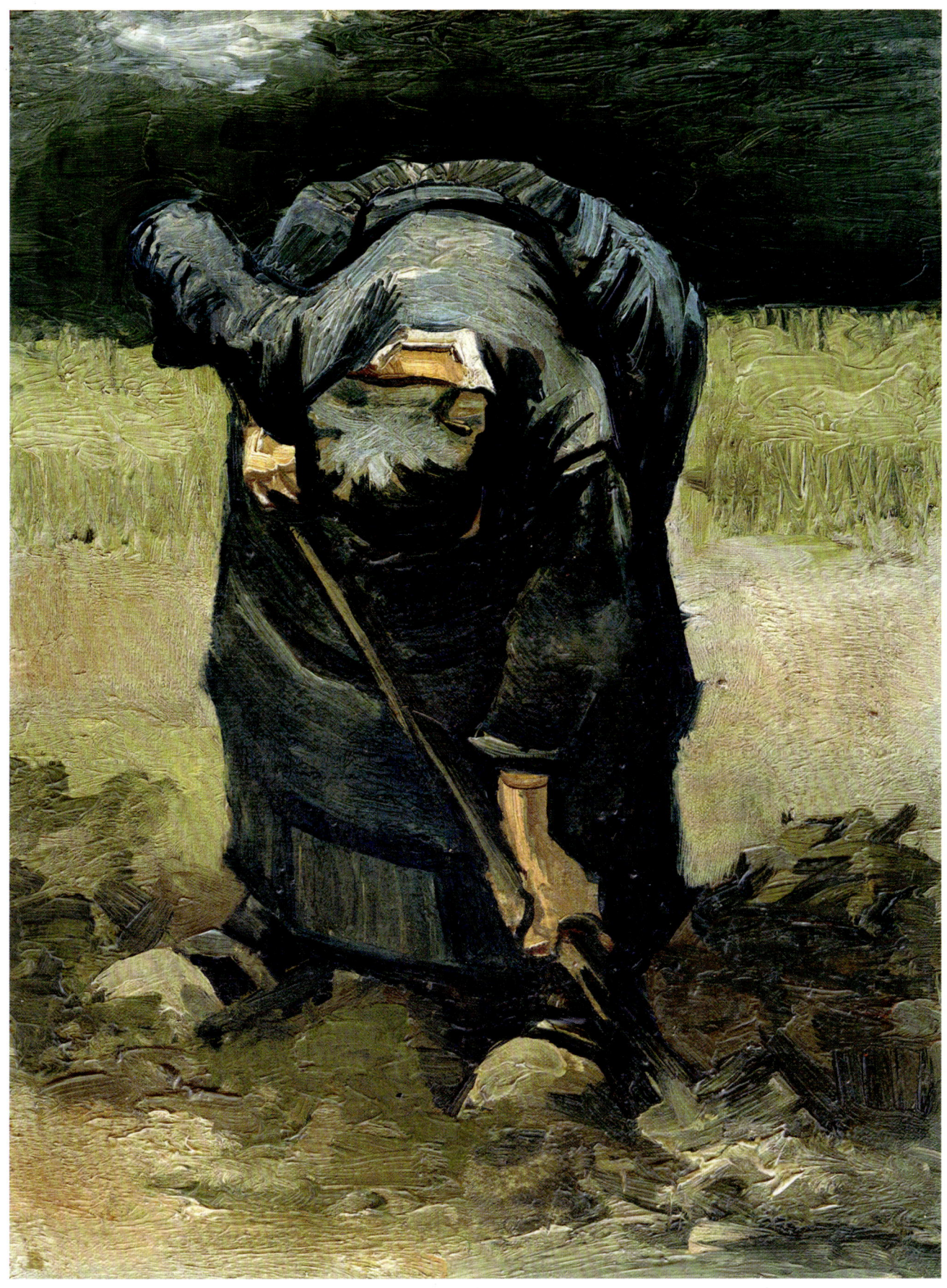

**A Peasant Woman Digging**, April 1885, oil on canvas, 42 × 32 cm, Birmingham, Barber Institute of Fine Arts

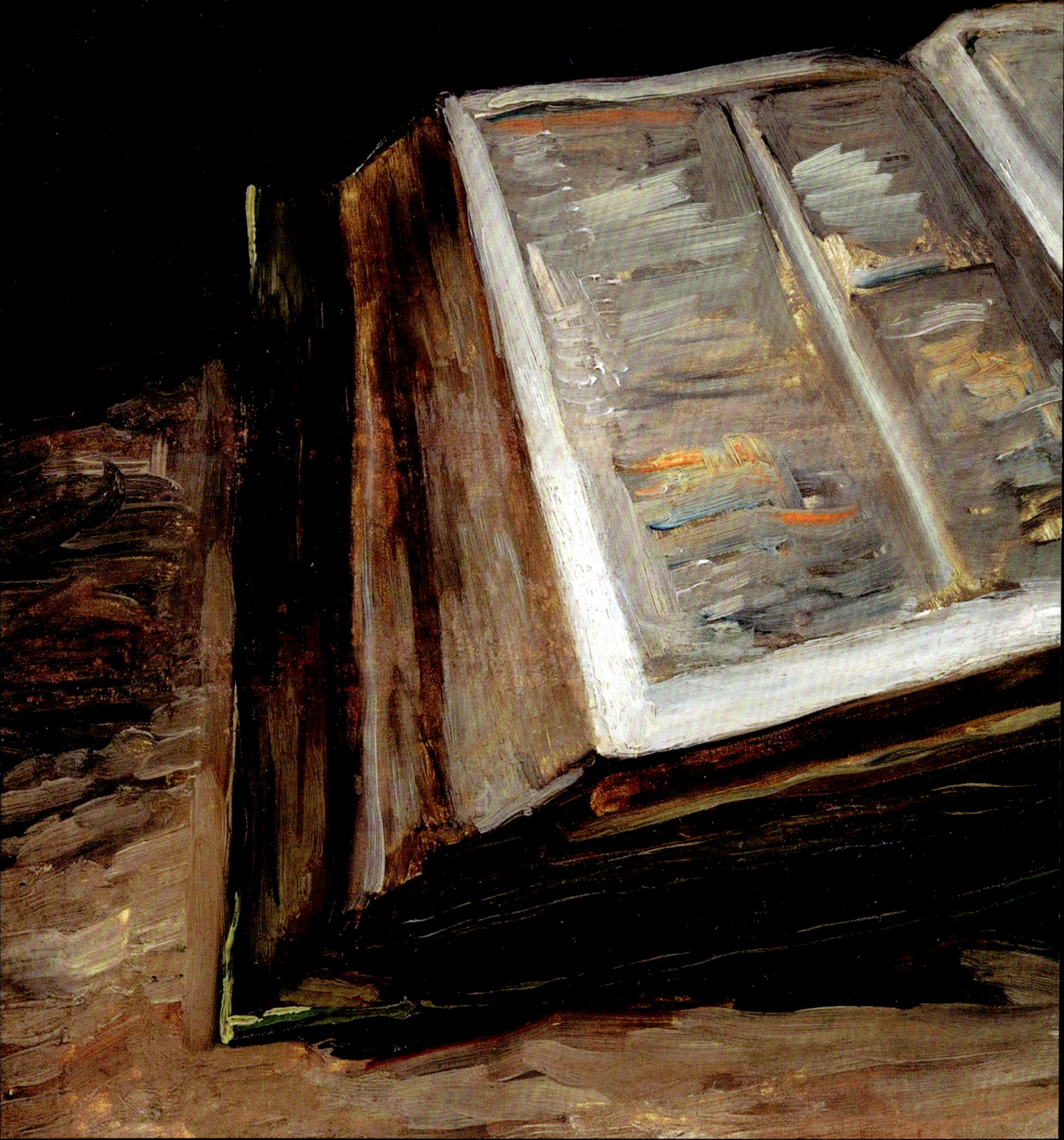

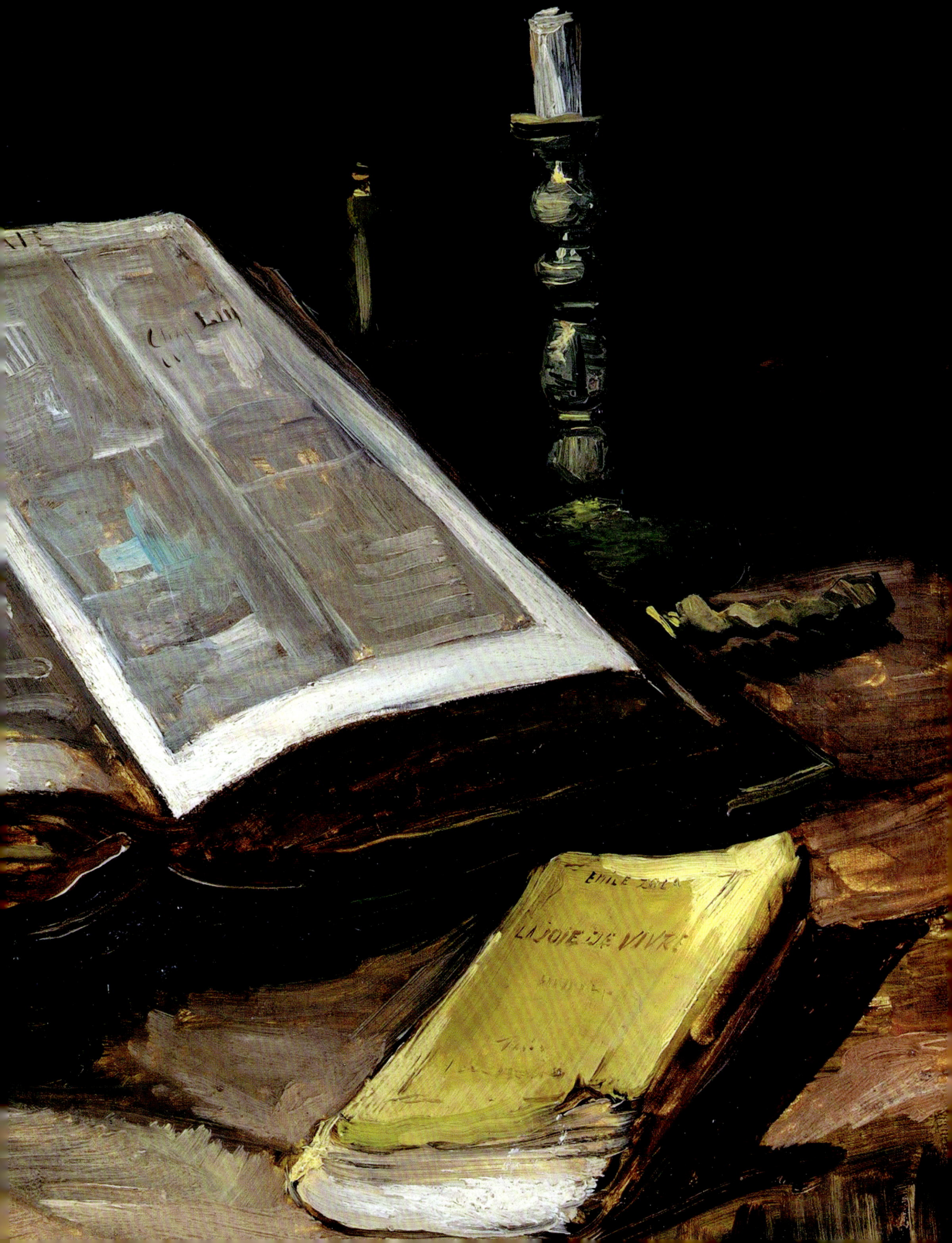

"Art is man added to nature –
nature, reality, truth, [...]
with an interpretation, with a
character that the artist brings
out and to which he gives
expression, which he sets free,
which he unravels, releases,
elucidates."

Vincent Van Gogh Letter to Theo,
June 1879

dat schetsje het zwart 't donkerst is zitten de
in na de aquarel. — donkergroen bru
w. Nu adieu, en geloof me dat sommy
artelyk om lach dat de lui my die eyge
ders ben dan een vriend van de natuur v
van werk — ook van menschen vooral
iverse kwaadaardigheden en absurditeiten waaro
van op myn hoofd denkt. Enfin — tot
een handdruk b.a.b. —

Vincent

221

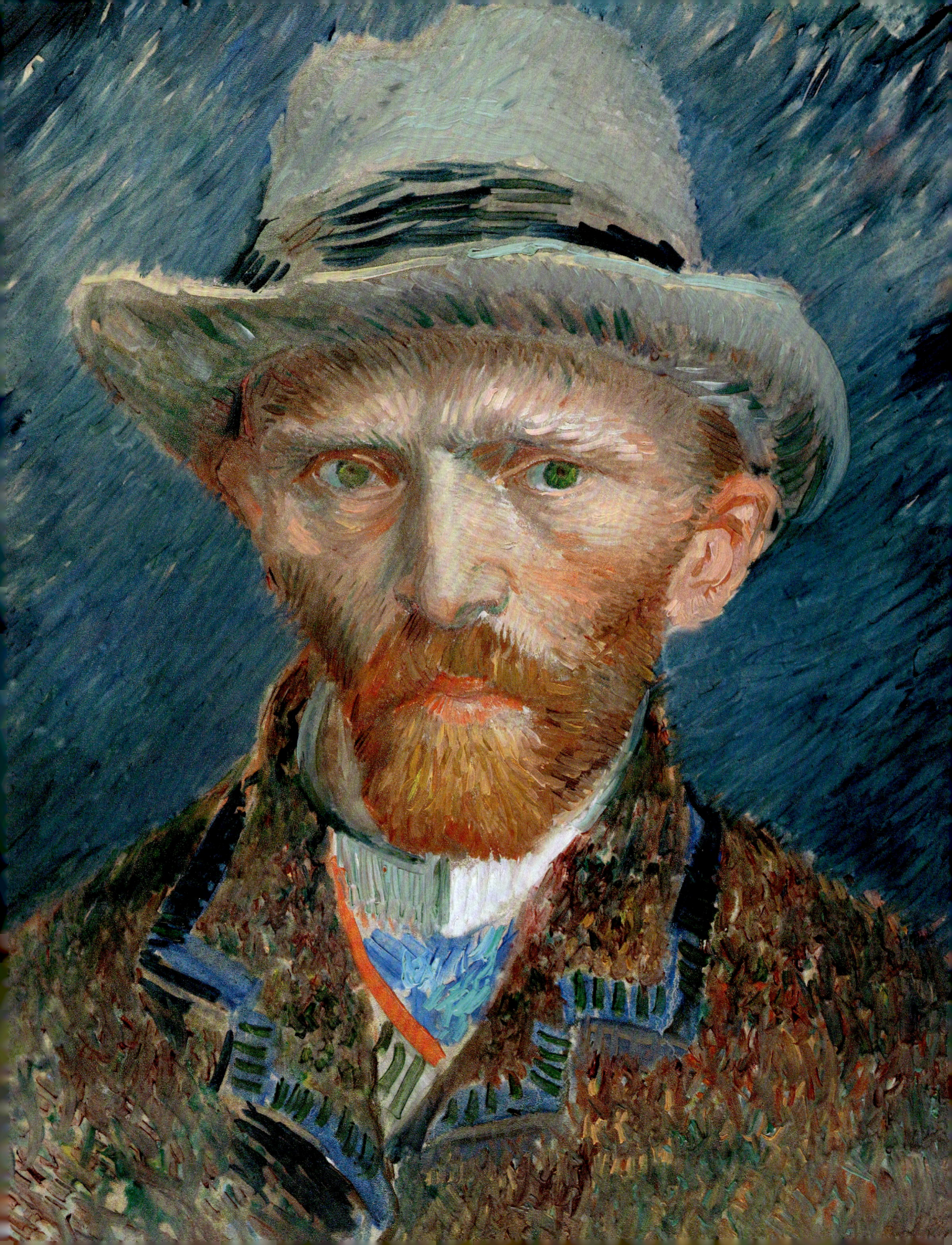

# Paris

## The quest for light

At the beginning of March 1886, without even warning him, Vincent joined Theo in Paris. For almost two years, the brothers lived together; first, on Rue Laval and then, from June onwards, on Rue Lepic, at the foot of the Butte-Montmartre. The absence of correspondence with Vincent's brother during this period deprives us of direct impressions of the artist. However, it is certain that this time was for him – at the beginning, at least – a privileged moment, since he could finally escape solitude and material precariousness. The Parisian art scene also offered him the opportunity to meet his peers and exchange ideas; it also drove him to take his art in a new direction, by encouraging him to broaden his palette.

Although his arrival was impromptu, it had been preceded by a number of letters written in Antwerp, in which Vincent asked his brother for permission to settle in Paris. The main reason behind this was that he wished to join the studio of the painter Fernand Cormon, who was known for his liberalism. Vincent enrolled there shortly after his arrival in Paris, where he stayed for around three months, distinguishing himself by the intensity of his work. The drawings that have survived clearly testify to the speed of his progress in the academic vein.

However, there was another reason why Vincent moved to Paris: the desire to broaden his subjects, including city life. While he painted the Luxembourg Gardens and the Louvre – his only known painting of a monument –, he focused on his neighbourhood: views of the rooftops from his bedroom on Rue Lepic (p. 35), the nearby Boulevard de Clichy (p. 47), the Buttes-Montmartre (which was still a rural area, with its vegetable gardens, windmills and dance halls (pp. 32-33), or the heterogenous area of the fortifications, near the Porte de Clichy. But soon, as a tireless walker, he went to the suburbs, to Courbevoie (pp. 36-37) and especially to Asnières (pp. 38-39 and 46), in the company of the young Émile Bernard and of Paul Signac.

At the same time as he was painting enthusiastically (he produced over two hundred canvases during his stay in Paris), Vincent was, at last, discovering those artists who used bright palettes: his brother had been talking about them for a long time, and they would, in turn, become a source of inspiration for his own work. Indeed, on the ground floor of his gallery, Theo exhibited established names, such as Jean-François Millet and Camille Corot, while on the mezzanine floor, he displayed modern works by Claude Monet, Edgar Degas, Camille Pissarro and Pierre-August Renoir. Thanks to his brother's contacts, Vincent was acquainted with a number of increasingly famous artists, as well as younger artists that he had worked with at Fernard Cormon's studio, such as Henri de Toulouse-Lautrec and Louis Anquetin. Through his network of friends, he also met Paul Gauguin, Paul Signac, Georges Seurat, Armand Guillaumin and Camille Pissarro, with whom he forged ties based on mutual esteem.

Although the chronology of his Parisian works is difficult to establish, it can be noted that for some time, the artist oscillated between the dark, realistic style of the Nuenen period and the bright painting style of the French avant-garde, which he would eventually adopt. His brushwork evolved, sometimes long and thick, other times short and light, sometimes also marked by pointillism, under the influence of Claude Signac and Georges Seurat. However much he borrowed, Van Gogh would never be content with being an imitator: he studied, assimilated and eventually produced a personal synthesis.

Another strong influence on him at this time was Japanese "crépons" (*chirimen-e*), which he had begun to collect in Antwerp, and which he purchased in large numbers in Paris. Fascinated by the clarity of tone and the frank composition of these works, by the use of flat tints and the absence of shadows,

Van Gogh produced copies of Hiroshige; he also drew inspiration from them, painting a handful of magical portraits featuring strong colours, such as *Italian Woman* (p. 41) and *Portrait of Père Tanguy* (p. 49), whom he depicted seated in front of a wall lined with woodblock prints. Faced with the difficulty of finding models, he also painted an impressive series of self-portraits (pp. 26 and 43) – more than twenty-five of them. He perceived these as technical exercises, learning both how to master brushstrokes, which he wanted to imbue with dynamism, and to render human expressions.

His stay in Paris also gave him the opportunity to present his works, for which he hoped to finally find a following. Some would be exhibited in the office of the broker Alphonse Portier, in the shop held by Père Tanguy (a colour merchant and a friend to painters), or on the walls of *Le Tambourin*, a cabaret run by Agostina Segatori (see p. 40), with whom Van Gogh had a brief affair. In November 1887, he organised an exhibition with the "Impressionnistes du Petit Boulevard" (the second generation of Impressionists) at the restaurant *Le Chalet*, on the Avenue de Clichy. He presented his works alongside those of Émile Bernard, Louis Anquetin and Henri de Toulouse-Lautrec; however, none would sell. Finally, in March of the following year, three of Vincent's paintings were sent by Theo to the Salon des Indépendants, including *Parisian Novels (The Yellow Books)* (p. 30-31), evidence of his enduring taste for realist literature, as written by Émile Zola, Guy de Maupassant and authors rewarded by a Prix Goncourt.

The stay in Paris, which had come to an enthusiastic start, ended in a heavy atmosphere. Weakened by years of deprivation, an unhealthy diet and absinthe abuse, Vincent struggled to cope with the harshness of the winter of 1887, and his physical exhaustion was compounded by other wounds: disappointment with humans (*"...so many painters who fill me with disgust as men."*) and the lack of understanding with which his painting was met. So he dreamt of another place, a place of light and warmth – *le Midi*, the south of France: "[...] looking at nature under a brighter sky can give us a more accurate idea of the Japanese way of feeling and drawing". On 20 February 1888, Van Gogh abruptly left Paris for Arles.

**Self-Portrait with Grey Felt Hat** (p. 26)
1887, oil on canvas, 42 × 34 cm, Amsterdam, Rijksmuseum

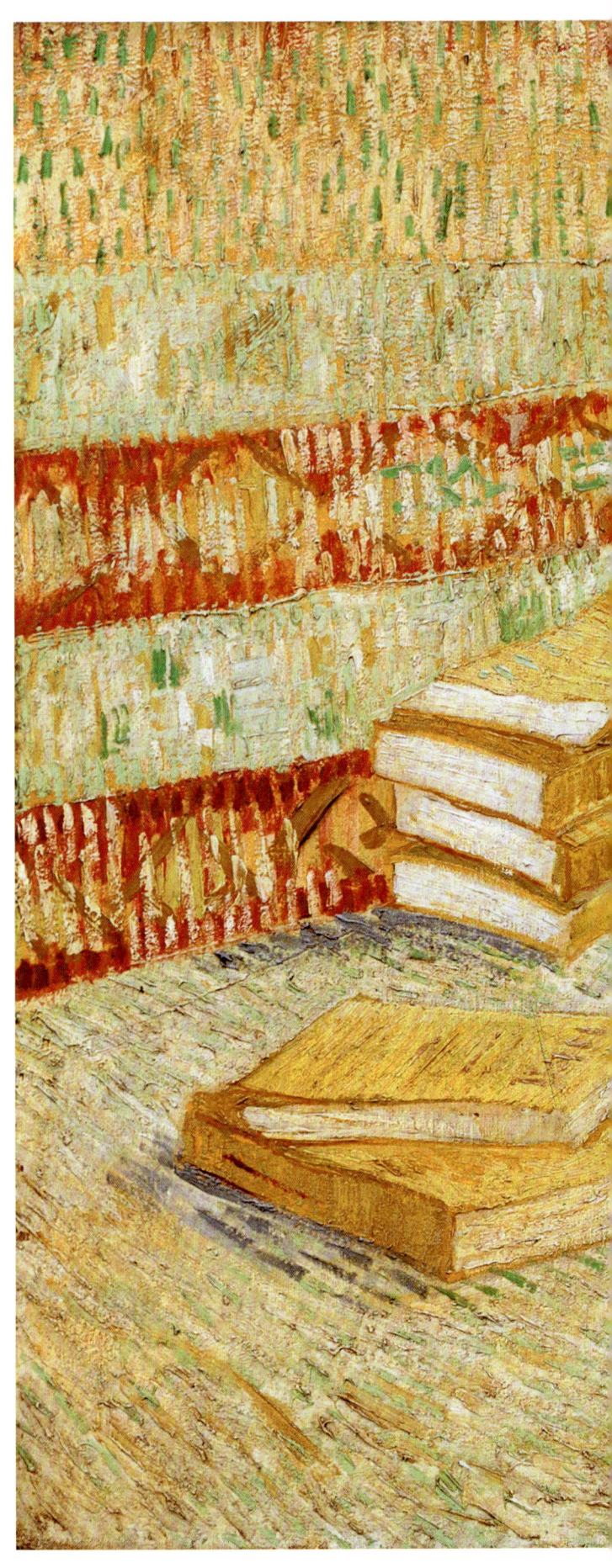

**Parisian Novels (The Yellow Books)**

Autumn 1887
Oil on canvas, 73 × 93 cm
Private collection

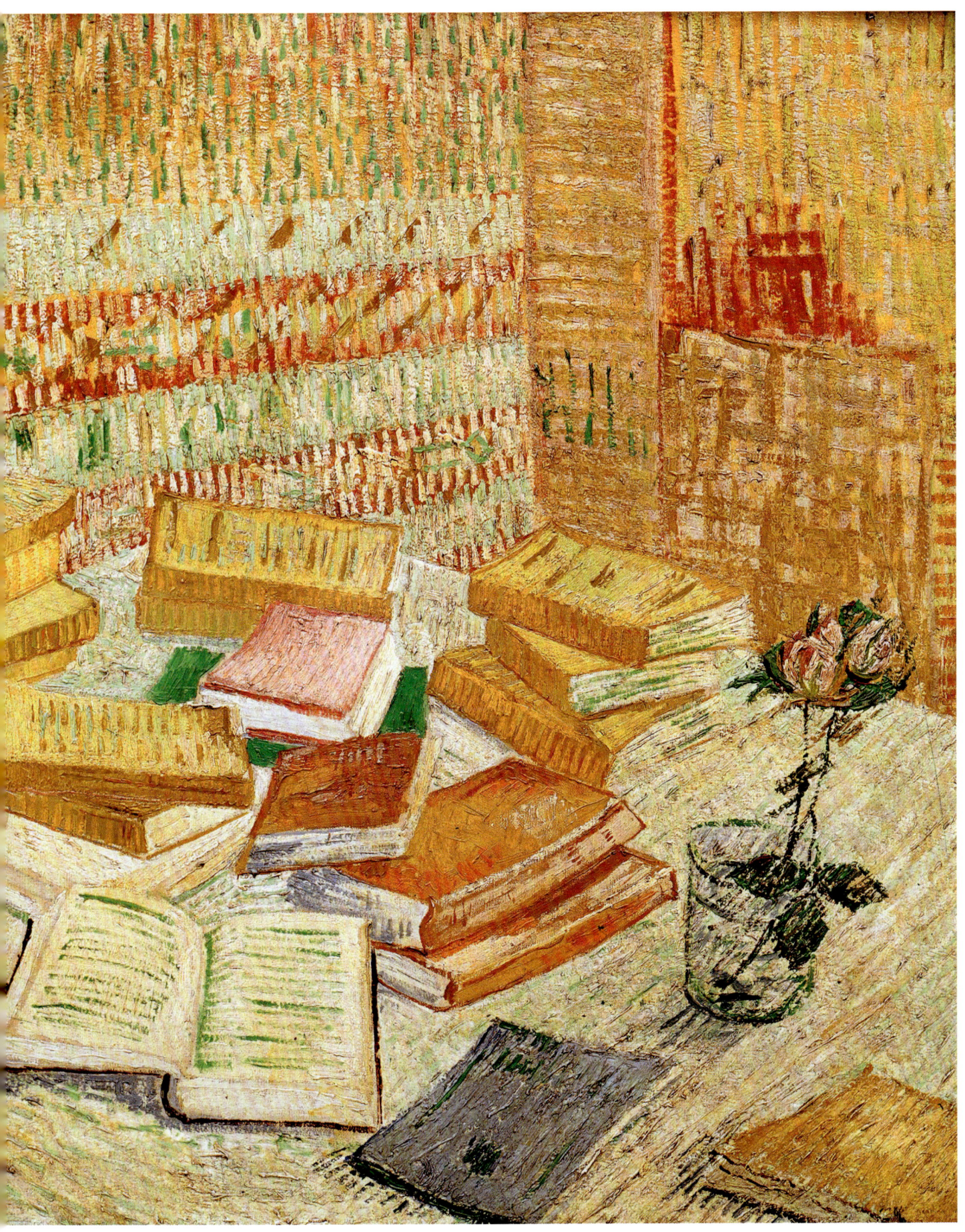

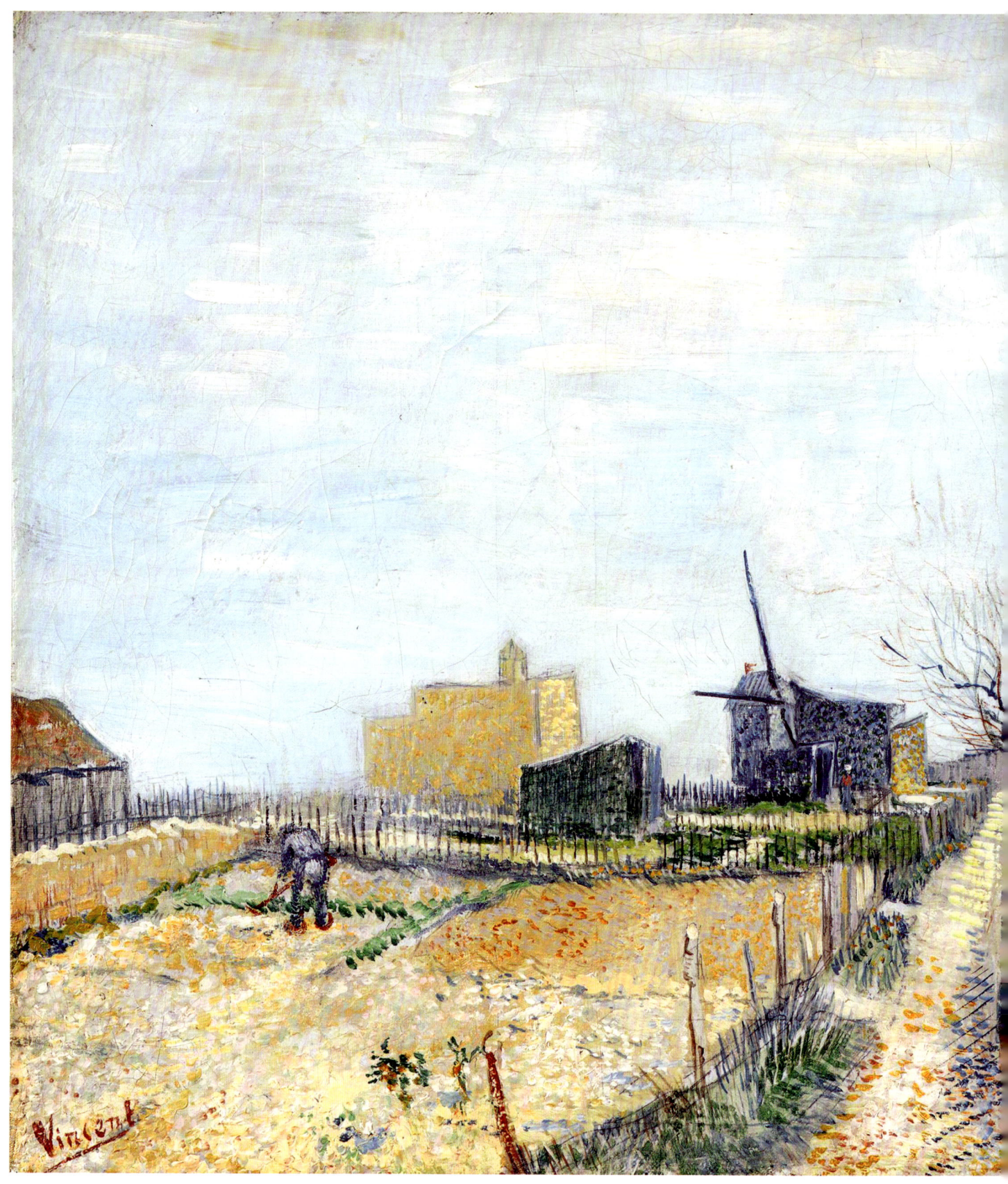

**Montmartre: Windmills and Allotments,** spring 1887, oil on canvas, 45.2 × 81.4 cm, Amsterdam, Van Gogh Museum

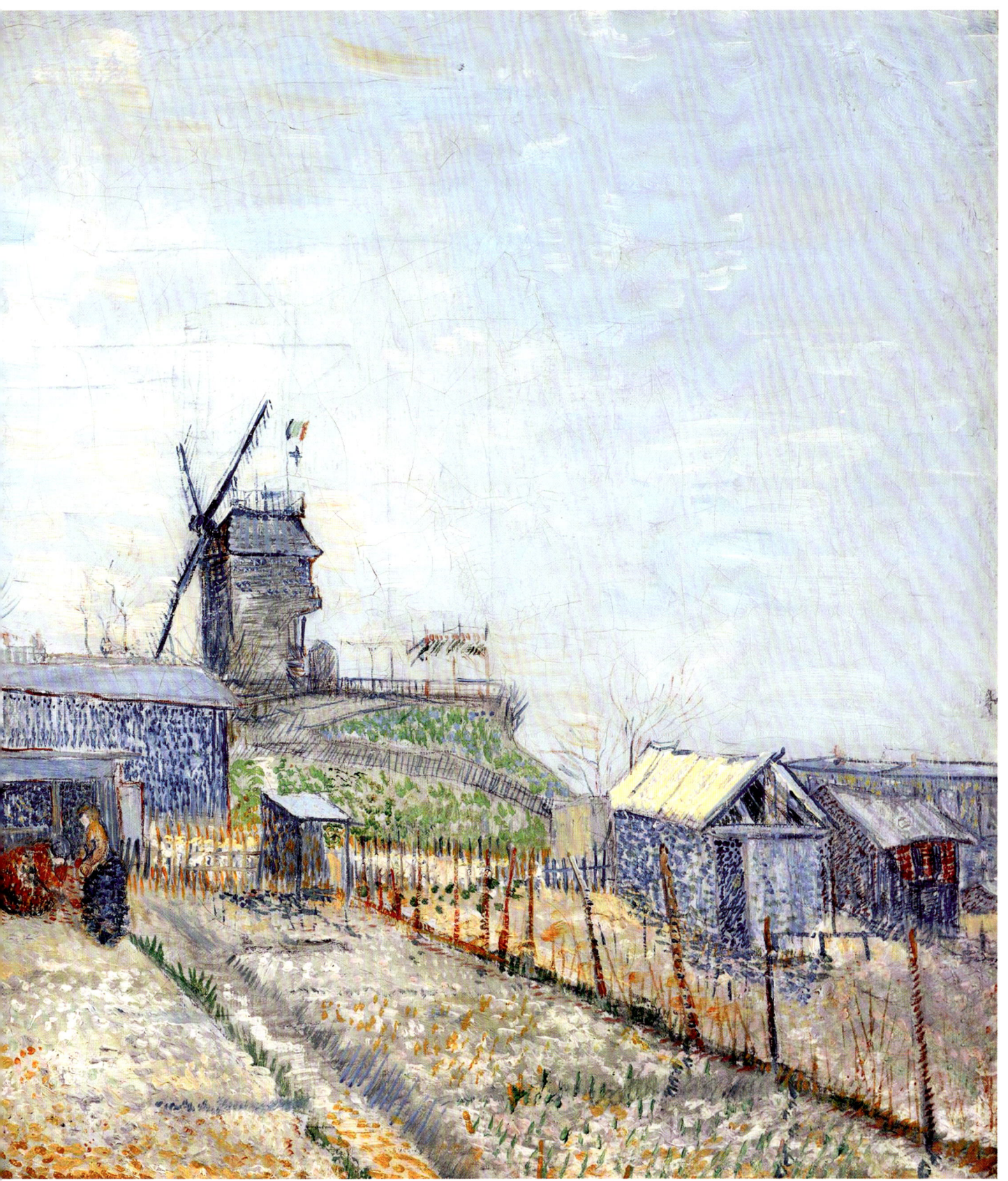

"And mind, my dear fellow, Paris is Paris. There is but one Paris and however hard living may be here, and if it became worse and harder even [...] the French air clears up the brain and does well – a world of good."

Vincent Van Gogh
Letter to Levens, autumn 1886

**View of Paris from Vincent's Room in the Rue Lepic**
Spring 1887
Oil on canvas, 45.9 × 38.1 cm
Amsterdam, Van Gogh Museum

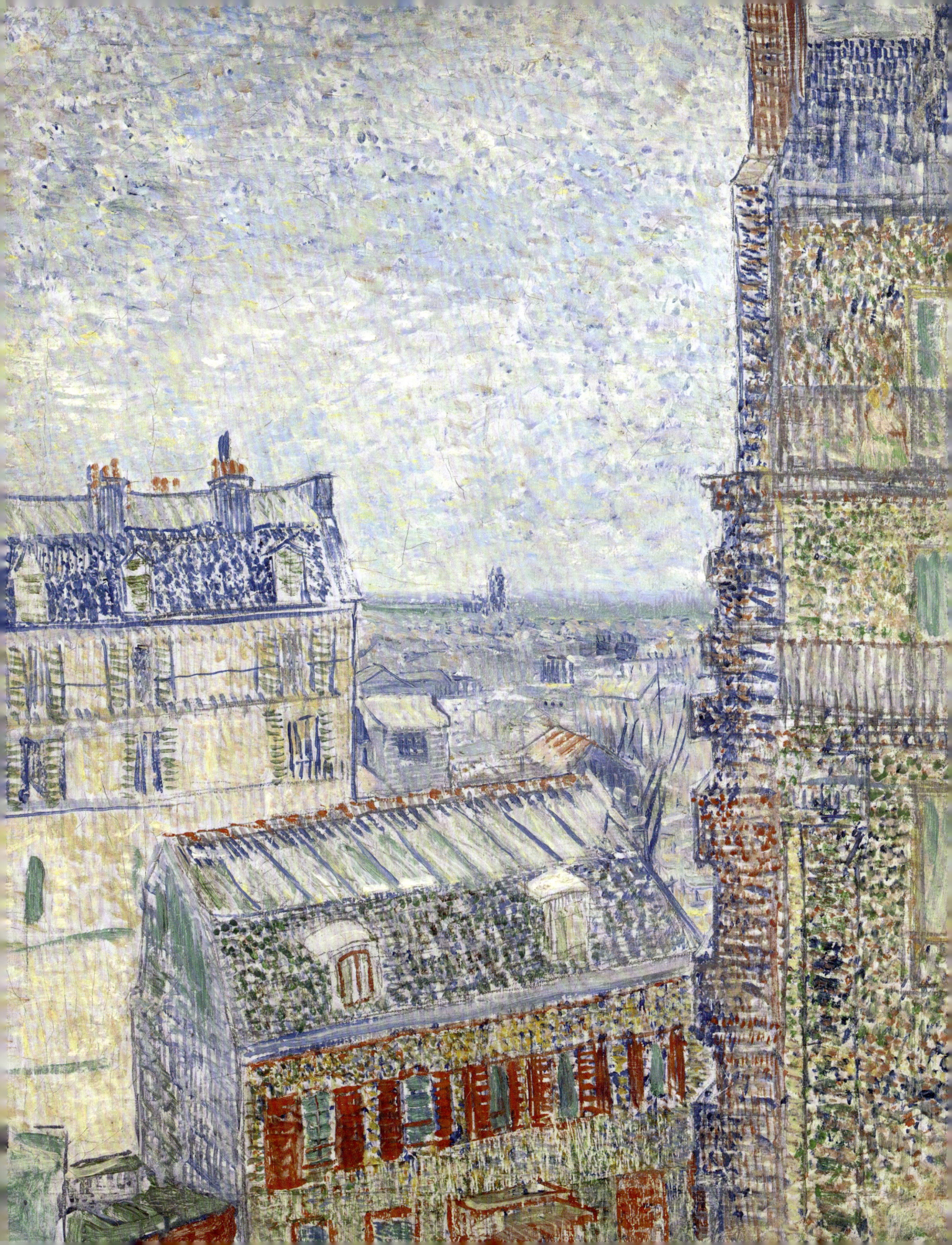

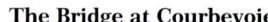

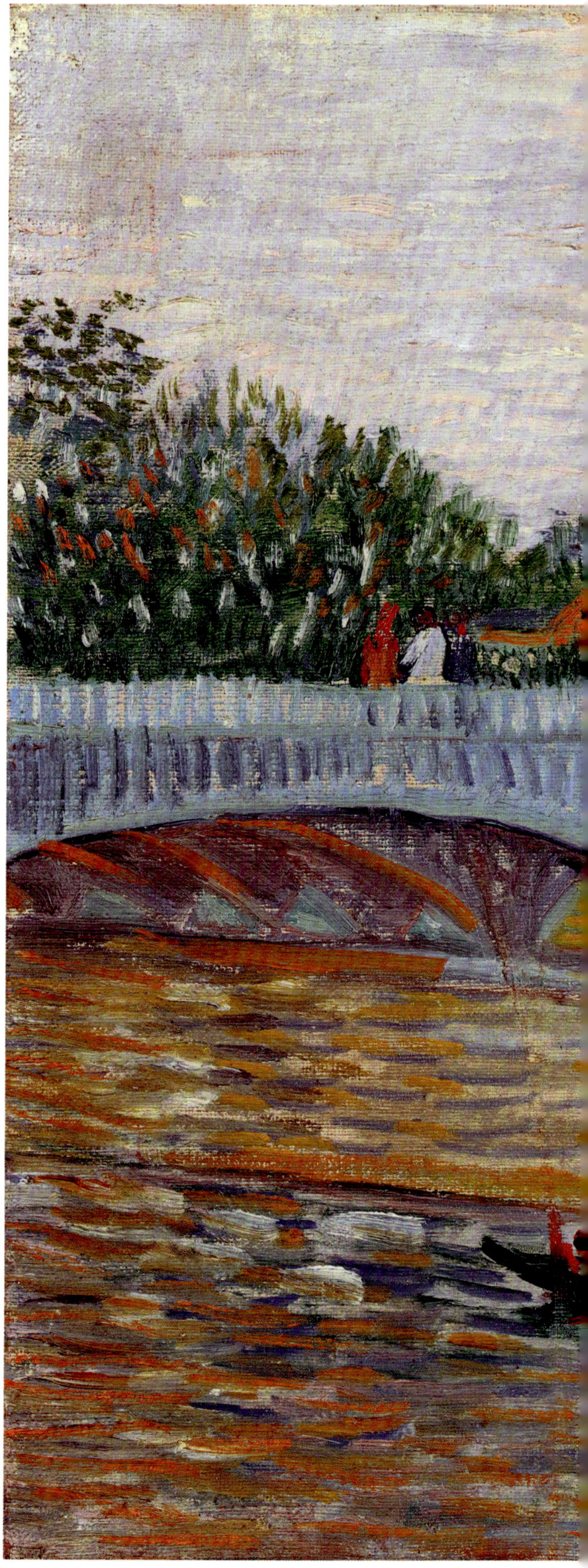

**The Bridge at Courbevoie**

Summer 1887
Oil on canvas, 32.1 × 40.5 cm
Amsterdam, Van Gogh Museum

**Garden with Courting Couples:
Square Saint-Pierre**

Spring 1887
Oil on canvas, 75 × 113 cm
Amsterdam, Van Gogh Museum
(double page below, detail)

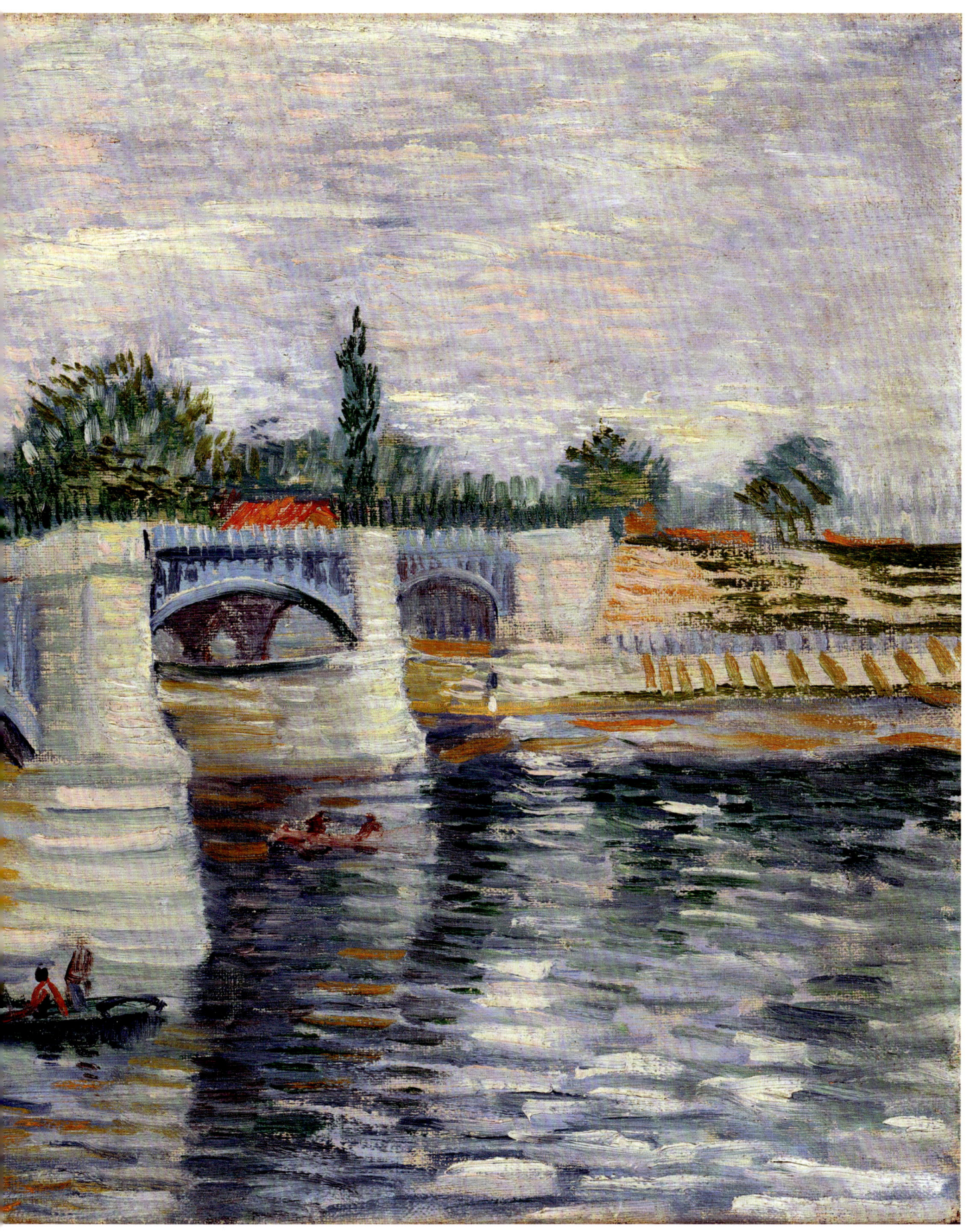

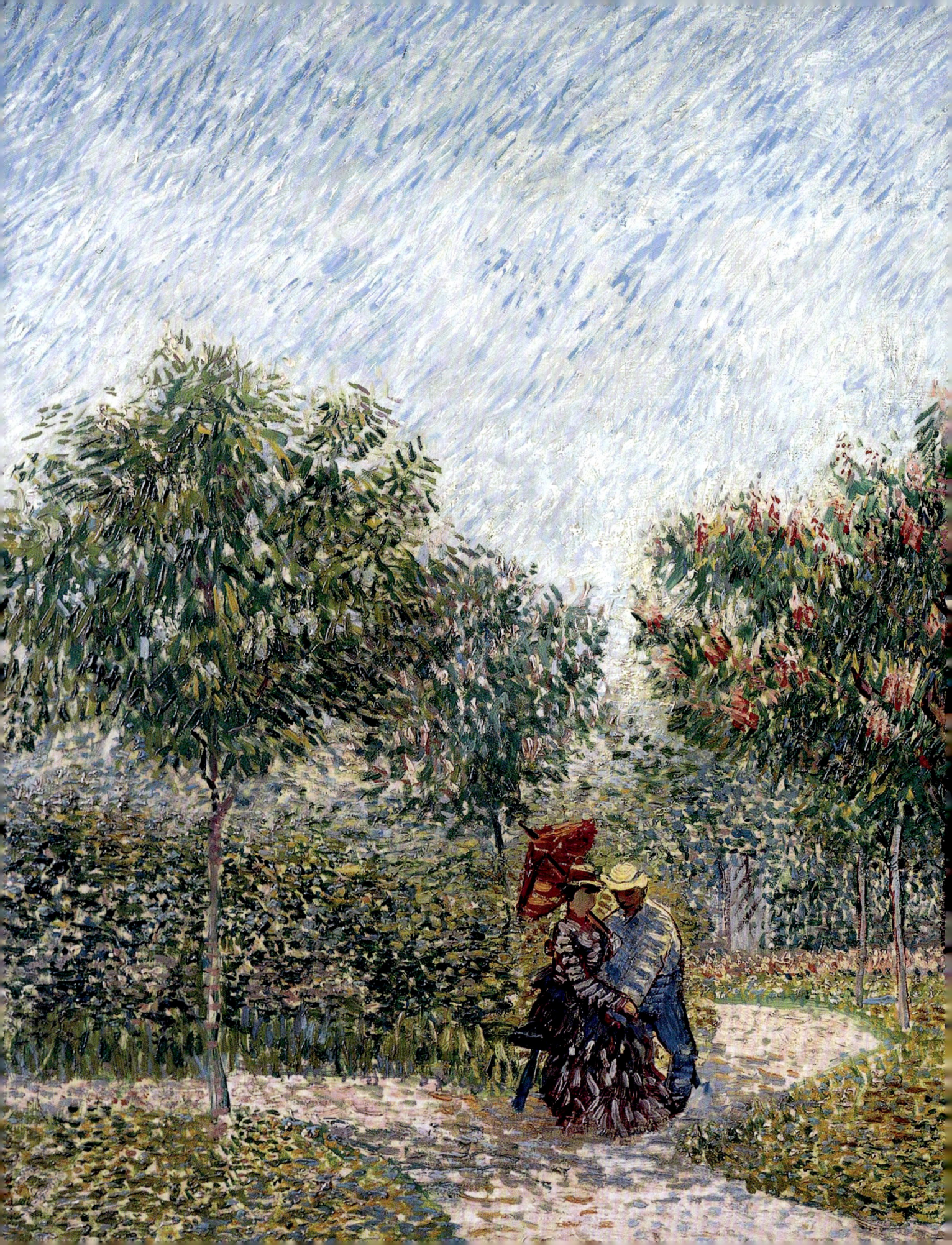

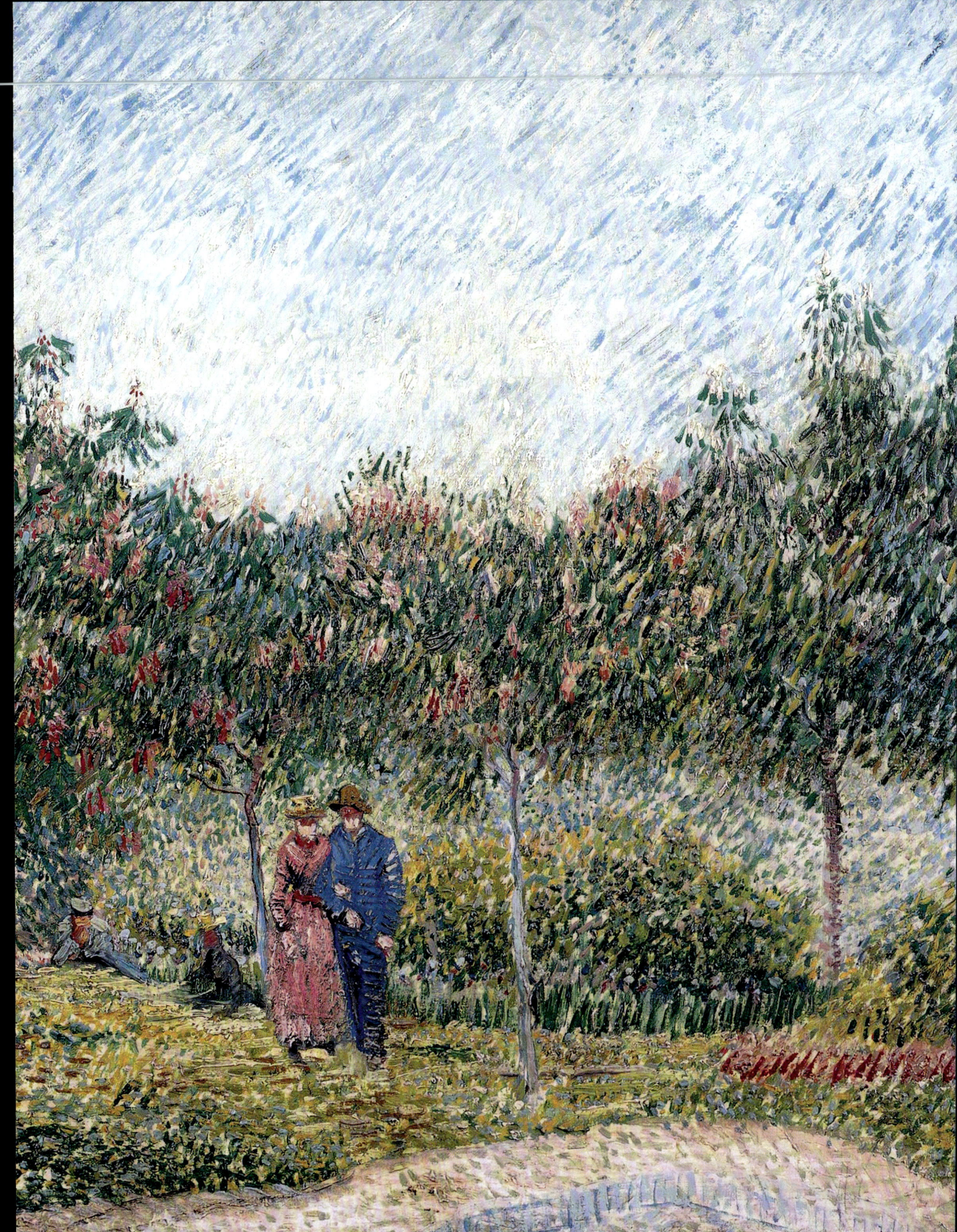

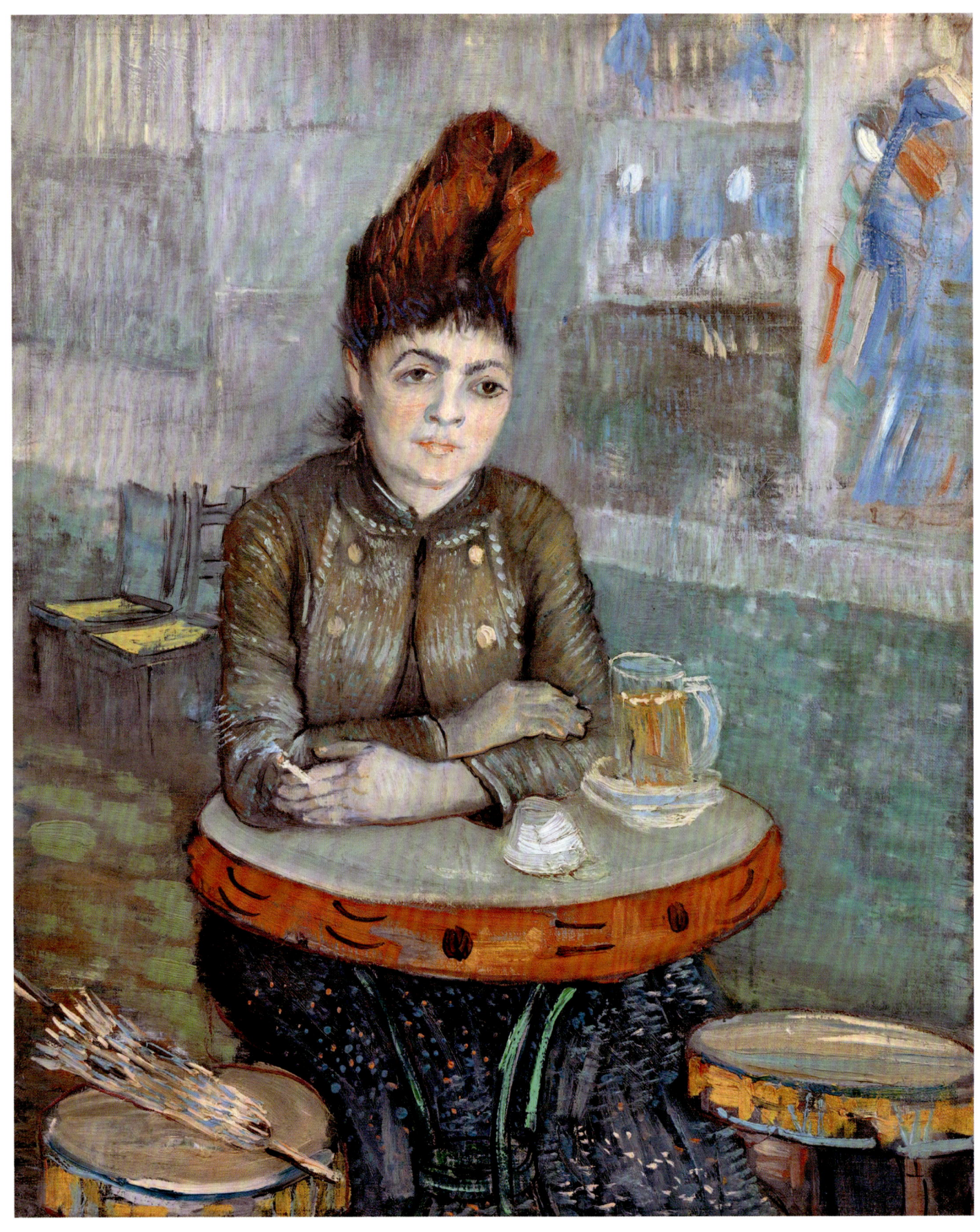

**Agostina Segatori Sitting in the Café du Tambourin,** February 1887, oil on canvas, 55.5 × 47 cm, Amsterdam, Van Gogh Museum

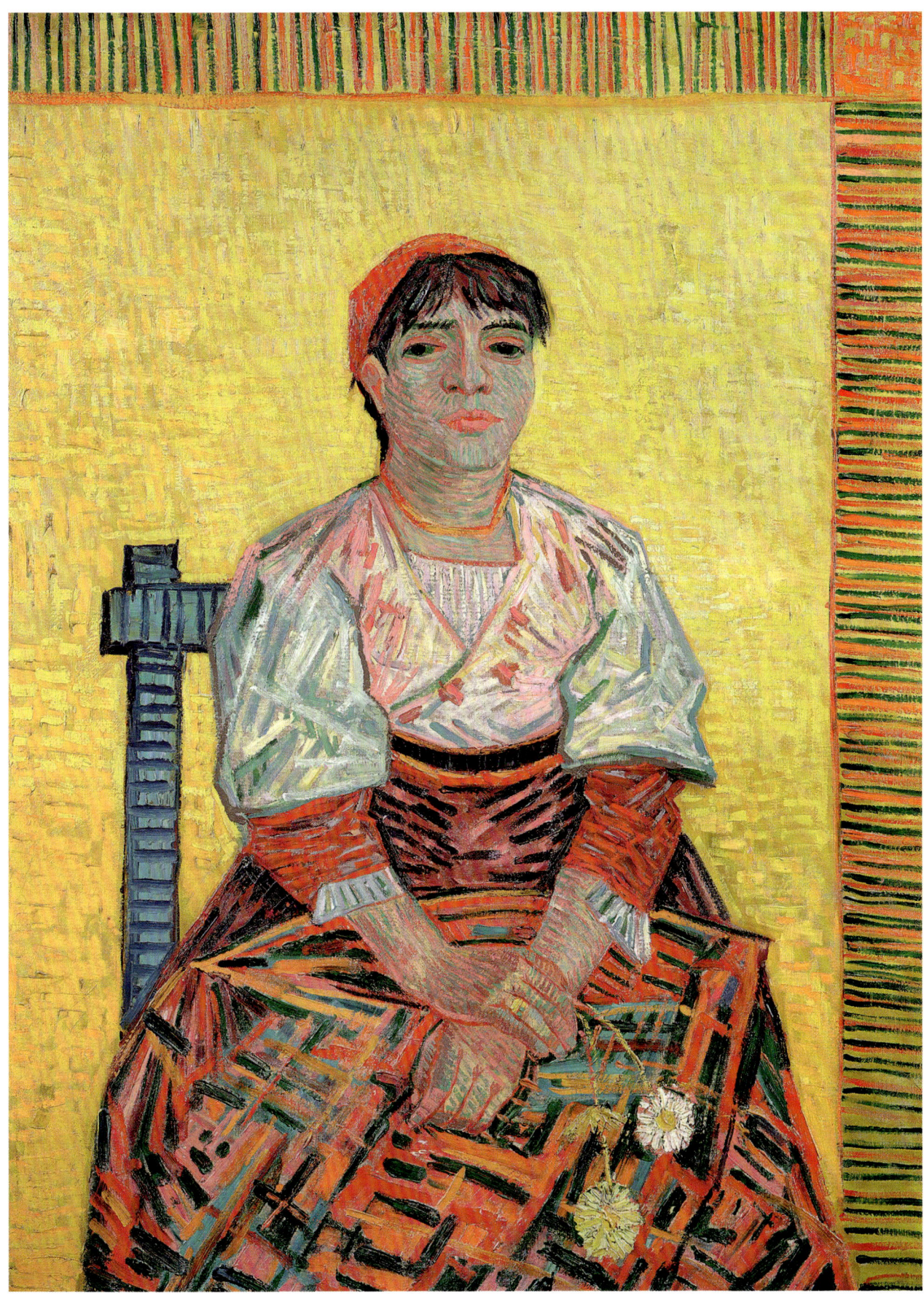

**The Italian Woman (Agostina Segatori?),** late 1887, oil on canvas, 81 × 60 cm, Paris, Musée d'Orsay

"The heart of man is very much like the sea, it has its storms, it has its tides and, in its depths, it has its pearls too."

Vincent Van Gogh Sermon, autumn 1876

**Self-Portrait with a Straw Hat**
Summer 1887
Oil on canvas, 40.6 × 31.8 cm
New York, The Metropolitan Museum of Art

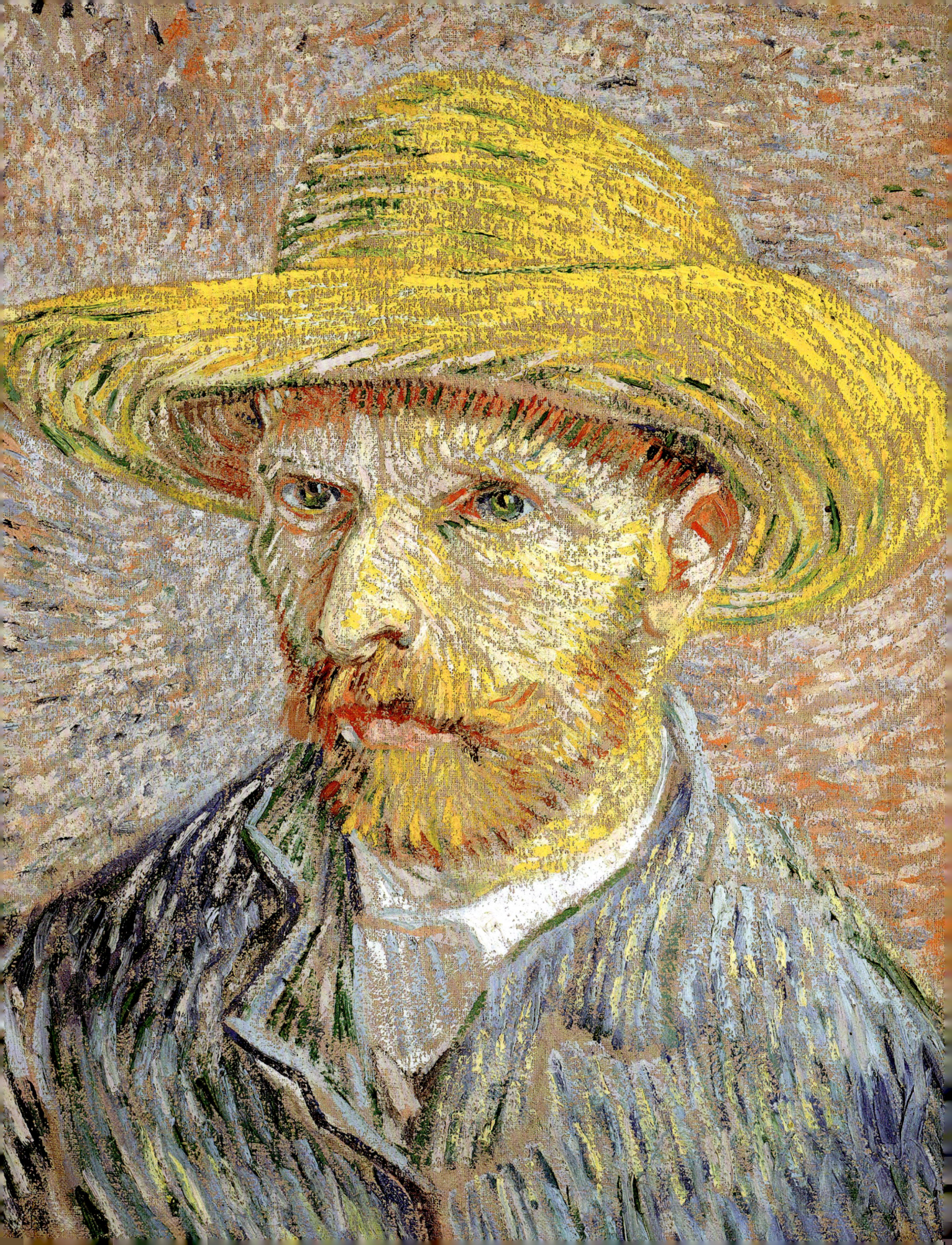

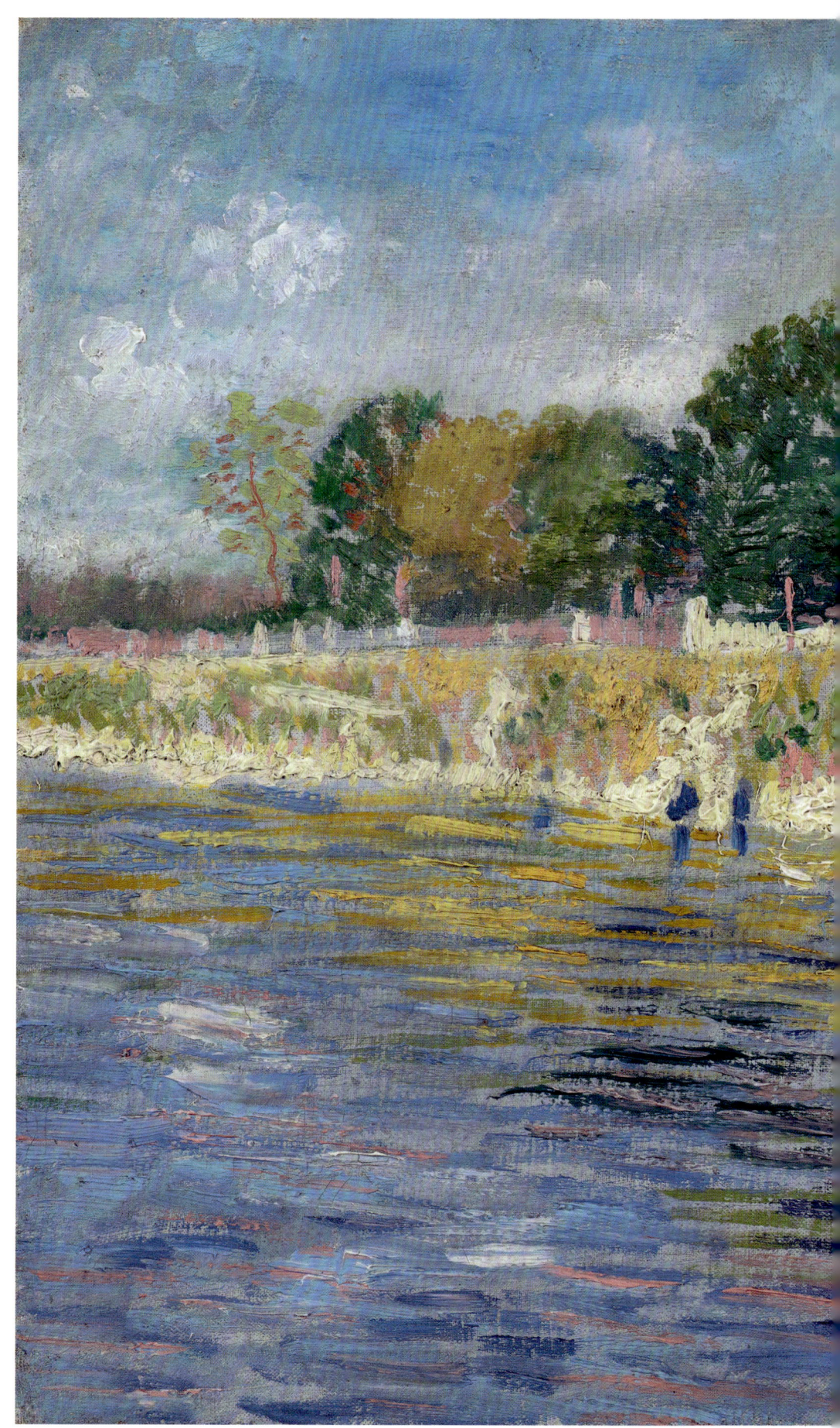

**Bank of the Seine**

Late summer 1887
Oil on canvas, 32 × 46 cm
Amsterdam, Van Gogh Museum

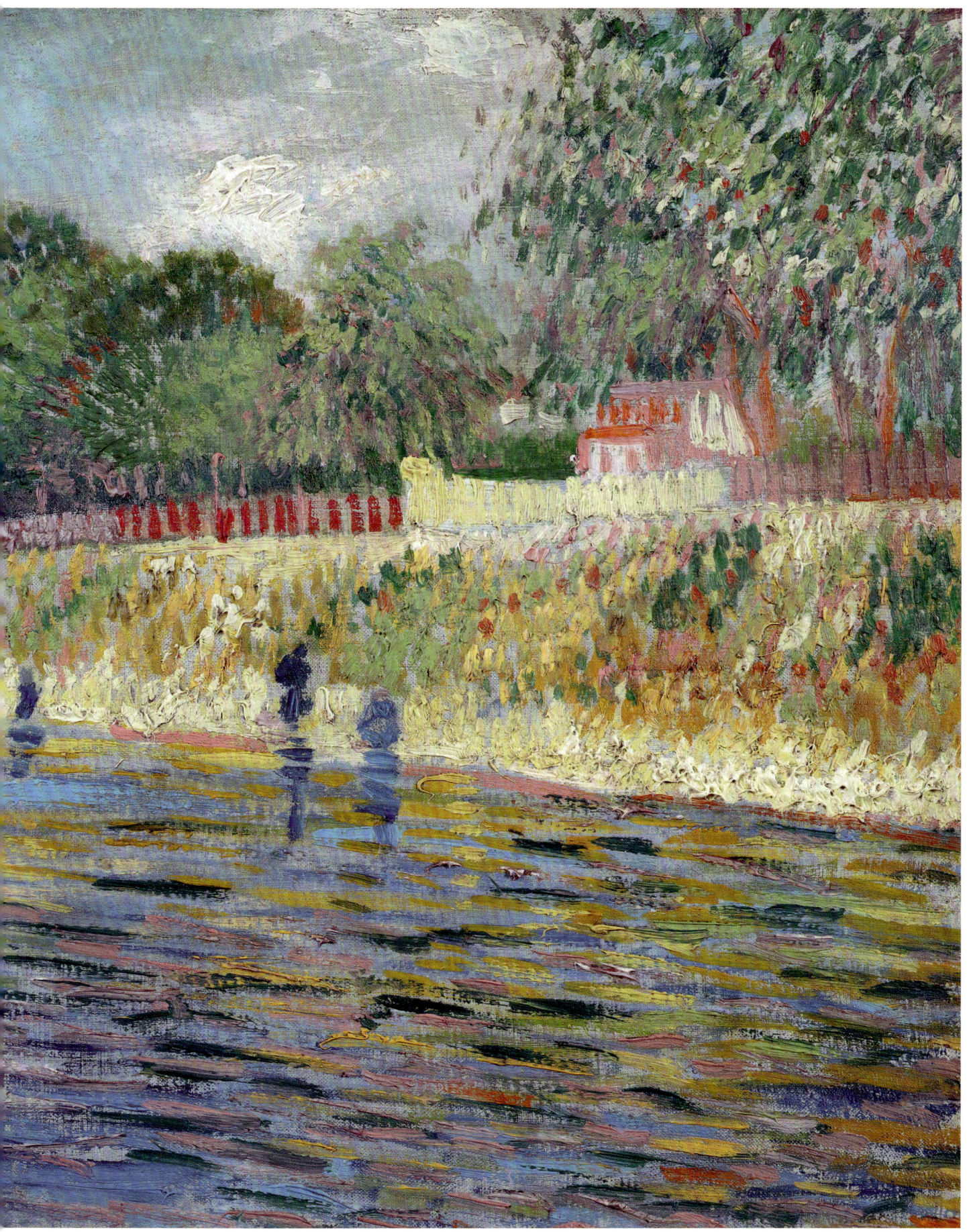

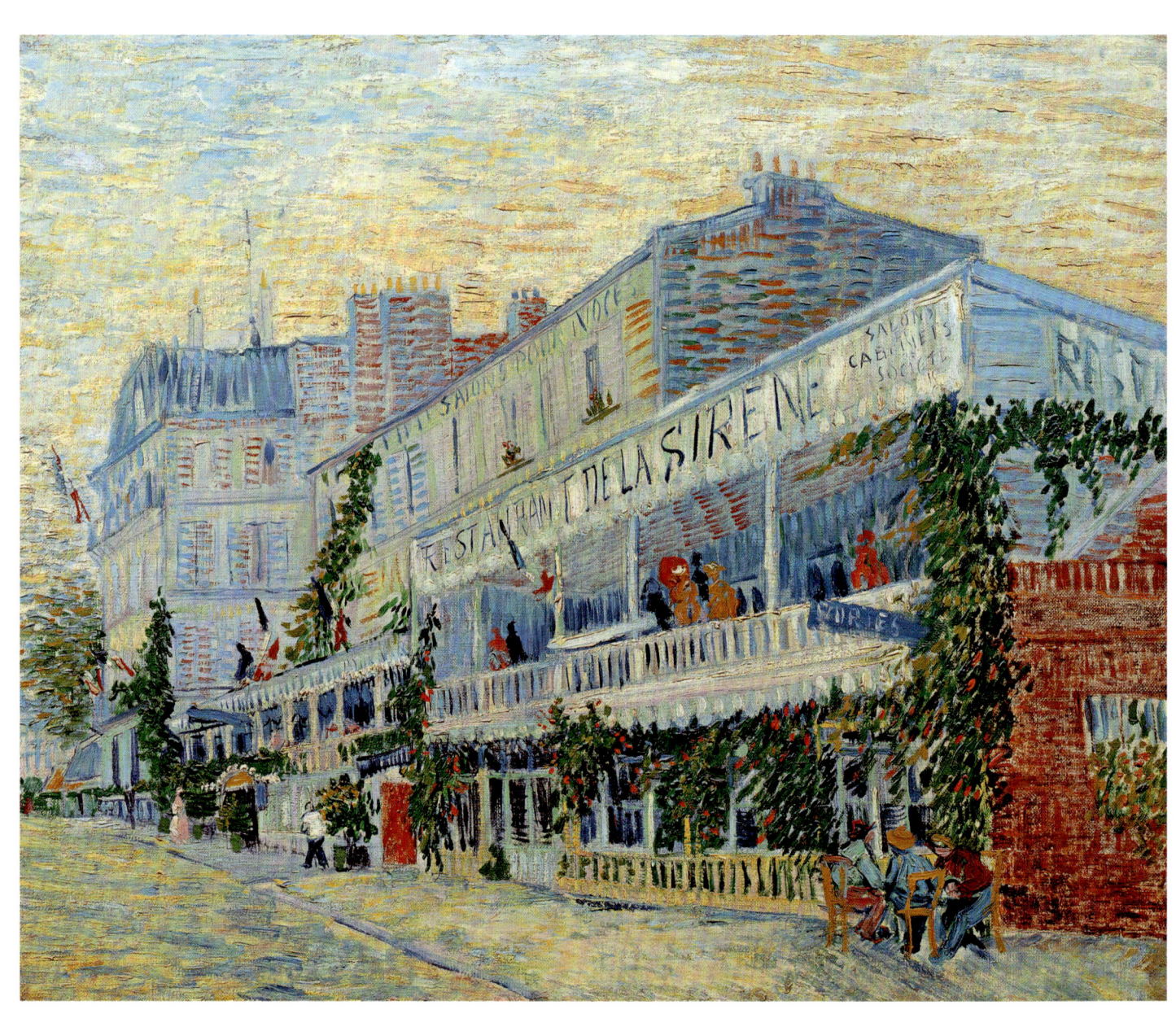

**The Restaurant de la Sirène at Asnières**

Summer 1887
Oil on canvas, 54.5 × 65.5 cm
Paris, Musée d'Orsay

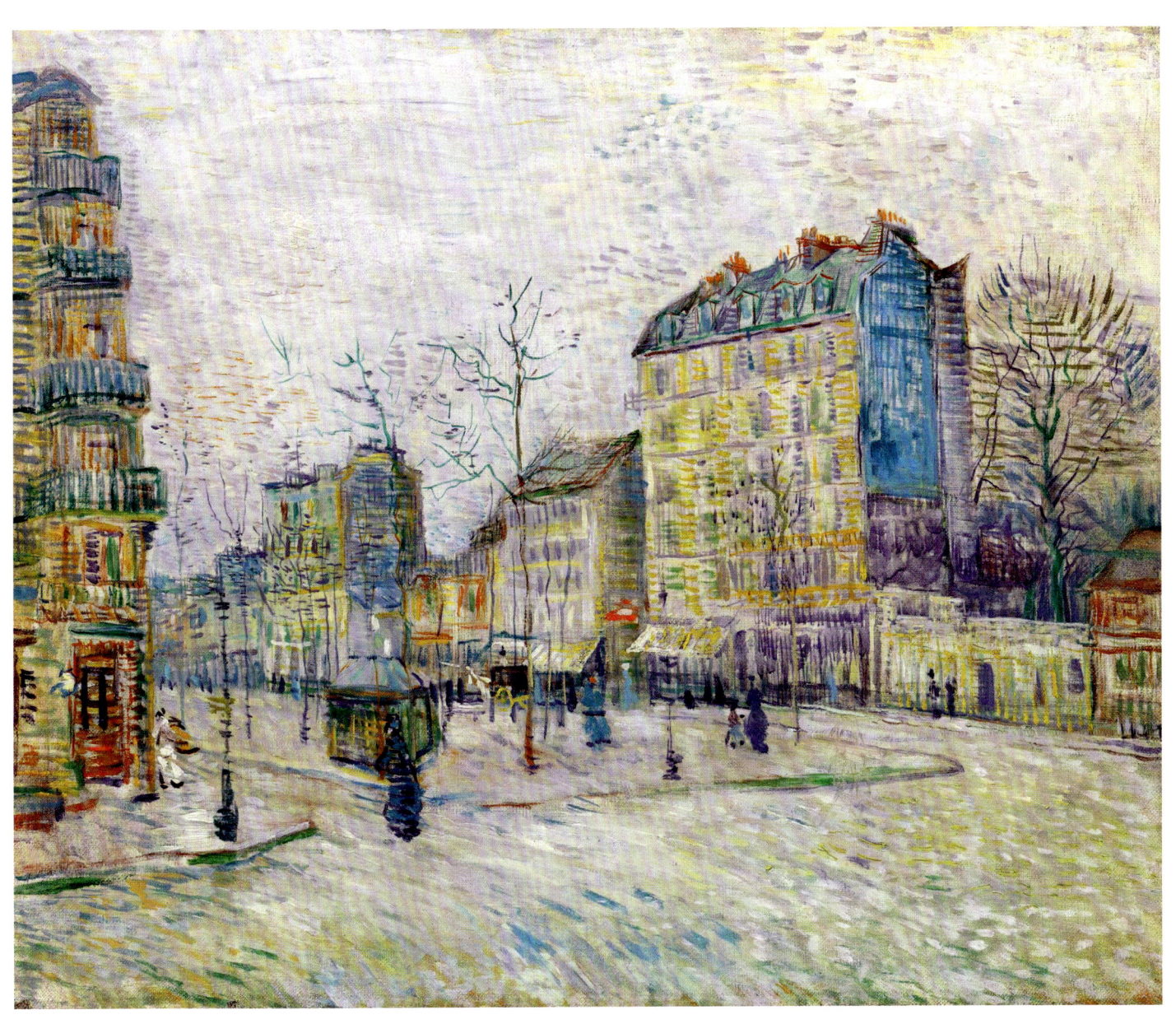

**Boulevard de Clichy**

March-April 1887
Oil on canvas, 46 × 55.5 cm
Amsterdam, Van Gogh Museum

"I saw Tanguy yesterday,
and he put a canvas I had
just done in his window. I've
done four since you left, and
I have a big one on the go.
I'm well aware that these
big, long canvases are hard
to sell, but in time people
will see that there are open-
air and good cheer in them."

Vincent Van Gogh
Letter to Theo, summer 1887

**Portrait of Père Tanguy**

Autumn 1887
Oil on canvas, 92 × 75 cm
Paris, Musée Rodin

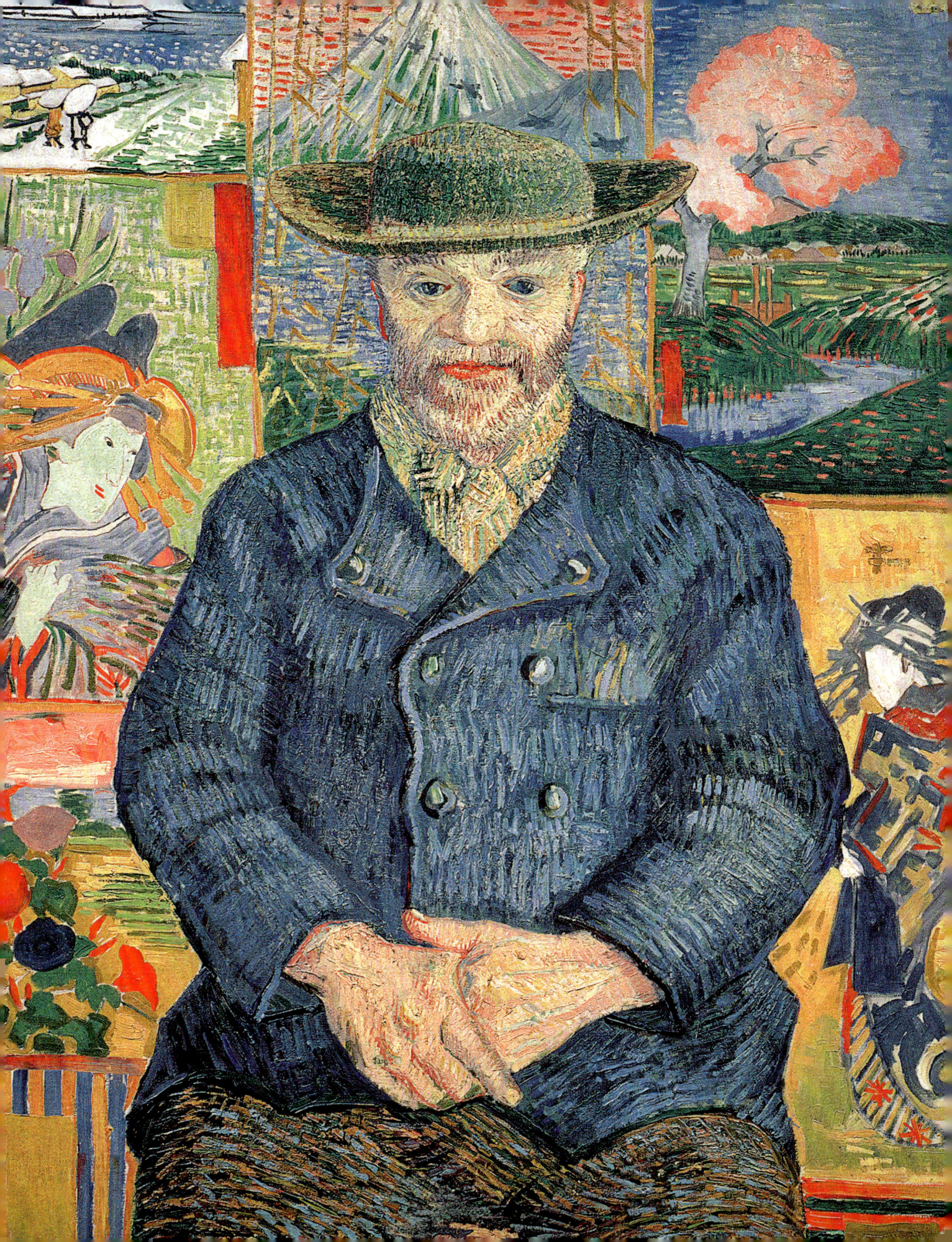

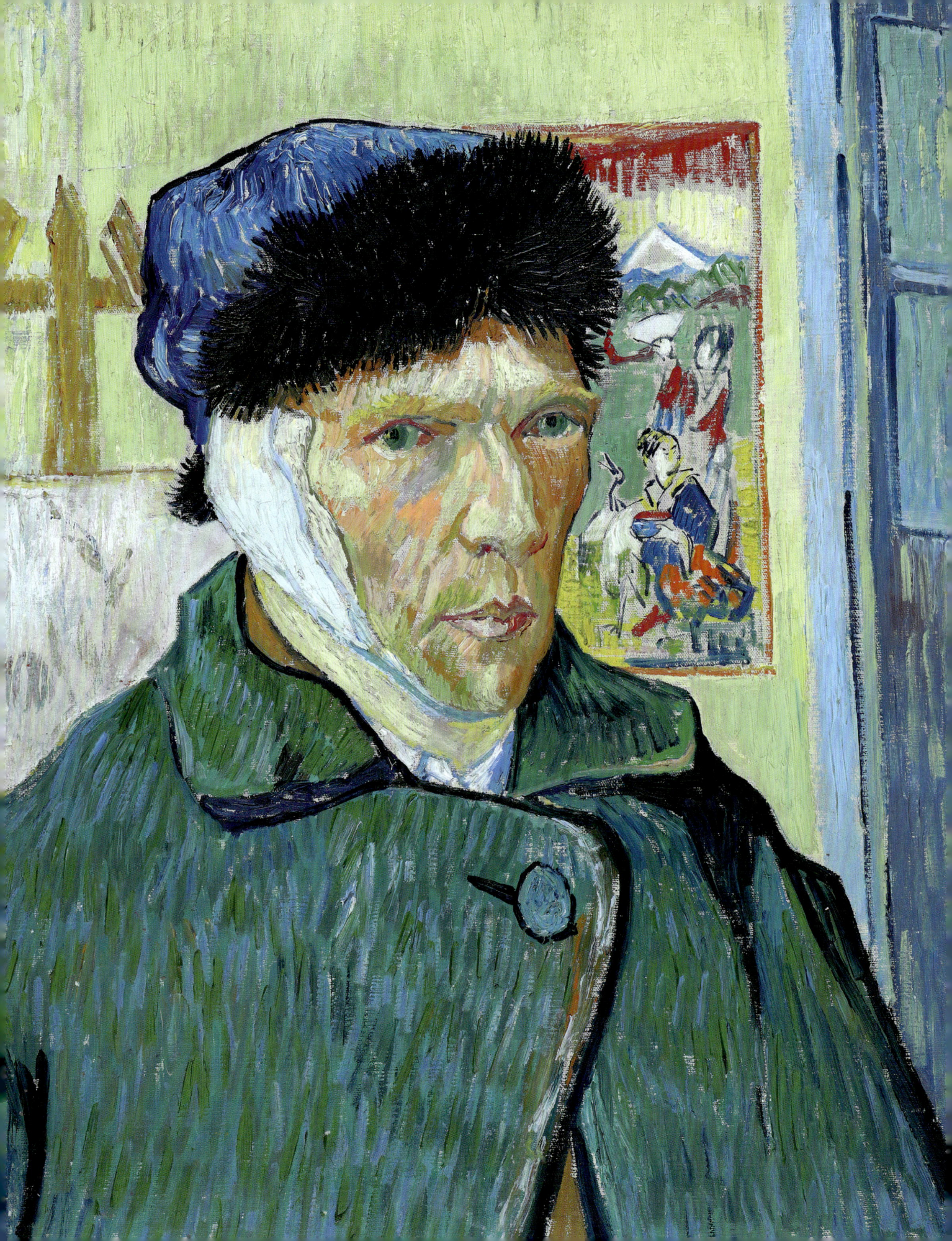

# Arles

## The triumph of colour

The Arles period is often regarded as the culmination of Vincent Van Gogh's creative decade. The two hundred paintings that he produced in Arles, over the course of fourteen months, include some of his most emblematic works, such as *Sunflowers* (p. 64, 65 and foldout), *Bedroom in Arles* (pp. 72-73) and *Starry Night* (pp. 70-71). Having mastered a wide range of techniques, he felt free to express his subjectivity and to exalt colour as he aspired to. On 20 February 1888, when he arrived in Arles, "the homeland of Tartarin", Van Gogh first stayed at the Hôtel Carrel, near the railway station. In May, he rented a room where to work on Place Lamartine, in what would become the famous "Yellow House" (pp. 68-69), but did not move in until September.

His assiduous correspondence with Theo allows us to follow his actions, his projects and his pictorial production almost from day to day, also detailing the emotions that ran through him and the goals that he set himself.

He was enchanted by the region he discovered: "This part of the world seems to me as beautiful as Japan for the clearness of the atmosphere and the gay colour effects," he wrote in March. In the summer, he did not seem bothered by the climate of the south of France: "I feel fine working outside in the hottest part of the day. It's a dry, clean heat." From the very first days, Vincent set to work, painting the snowy countryside, producing a study titled *L'Arlésienne*, and "a view of a stretch of pavement with a butcher's shop". His motifs were very diverse – a trait that would remain present throughout his output during this period, as he painted landscapes as well as portraits, interiors, urban views and still lifes (pp. 60-61). In addition to these works, Van Gogh produced a large number of drawings depicting the same themes, many of them using ink and reeds.

Five weeks after his arrival, the artist also began a series of orchards in bloom (pp. 54 and 55) – a joyous celebration of this spring which, for him, also came as a rebirth. One of these, he dedicated to Anthon Mauve; having just heard of his passing, he wanted to send it to his widow.

Now, he no longer bothered with theories, forgot all about Parisian discussions, and gave himself over entirely to the pleasure of painting freely, as he wrote to Émile Bernard: "I follow no system of brushwork at all; I hit the canvas with irregular strokes which I leave as they are." At the beginning of June, he travelled to Saintes-Maries-de-la-Mer, to see the Mediterranean, at last. In addition to the paintings and drawings that he brought back (pp. 58-59), he came to a significant conclusion: "Now that I have seen the sea here, I am absolutely convinced of the importance of staying in the Midi, and of positively piling it on, exaggerating the colour." Shortly afterwards, he began a series of works dedicated to harvests and public gardens.

In August, his friend Paul Gauguin told him he would be arriving "as soon as possible": Vincent's dream of the famous "Atelier du Midi", which would bring together a brotherhood of artists, would finally come true, and he looked forward to it impatiently. He had his house repainted yellow, both inside and out, purchased some furniture, and began his famous *Sunflowers* series to decorate its walls. When Gauguin arrived on 23 October, Van Gogh wrote to his brother: "He's very, very interesting as a man, and I have every confidence that with him, we'll do a great many things." And indeed, their collaboration came off

to a good start. Both worked a great deal, sometimes on the same motif, such as the Alyscamps, the grape harvest, *L'Arlésienne* (p. 75) or the *Café Terrace at Night* (p. 67), while Vincent worked on the theme of the *Sower* (p. 56 and leaflet), café interiors (pp. 62-63) and starry nights. In November, bad weather deprived them of working outdoors, and Gauguin advised Vincent to compose from memory, which disconcerted him: "I feel that habit is also necessary for works of the imagination." *Memory of the Garden at Etten* (pp. 76-77), however, is an attempt in this direction, as is *The Dance Hall in Arles* (pp. 78-79). Then, returning to the motif, Van Gogh worked on portraits of the Roulin family: the father, a postman by trade, his wife *(Madame Augustine Roulin Rocking a Cradle (La Berceuse),* p. 81), and their children (p. 74). However, relations between the two painters, both with strong personalities, soon deteriorated, as Gauguin wrote to Theo in mid-December: "Vincent and I can absolutely not live side by side without trouble, as a result of incompatibility of temperament," while Van Gogh stated that "the discussion is excessively electric". On 23 December, following a violent argument, Vincent cut off part of his left earlobe, then gave it to a prostitute. He would never explain this act, which he committed while beset by great mental confusion. In the hospital, where he was admitted the next day, he was diagnosed with "acute mania with generalised delirium". Under the supervision of Doctor Rey (p. 80), Vincent returned home in early January, where he painted his *Self-Portrait with Bandaged Ear* (p. 50) and worked on new versions of his work *La Berceuse.*
On 7 February, however, another crisis caused him to return to the hospital for ten days, before being committed on 25 February, following a petition from his neighbours. While he continued to paint a little and draw for the next few months, he was aware of his unstable mental condition, and requested to be transferred to the asylum in Saint-Rémy-de-Provence. He then put his furniture in storage, sent his paintings to Theo, and left Arles on 8 May 1889.

**Self-Portrait with Bandaged Ear** (p. 50)
January 1889, oil on canvas, 60 × 49 cm, London, Courtauld Institute Galleries

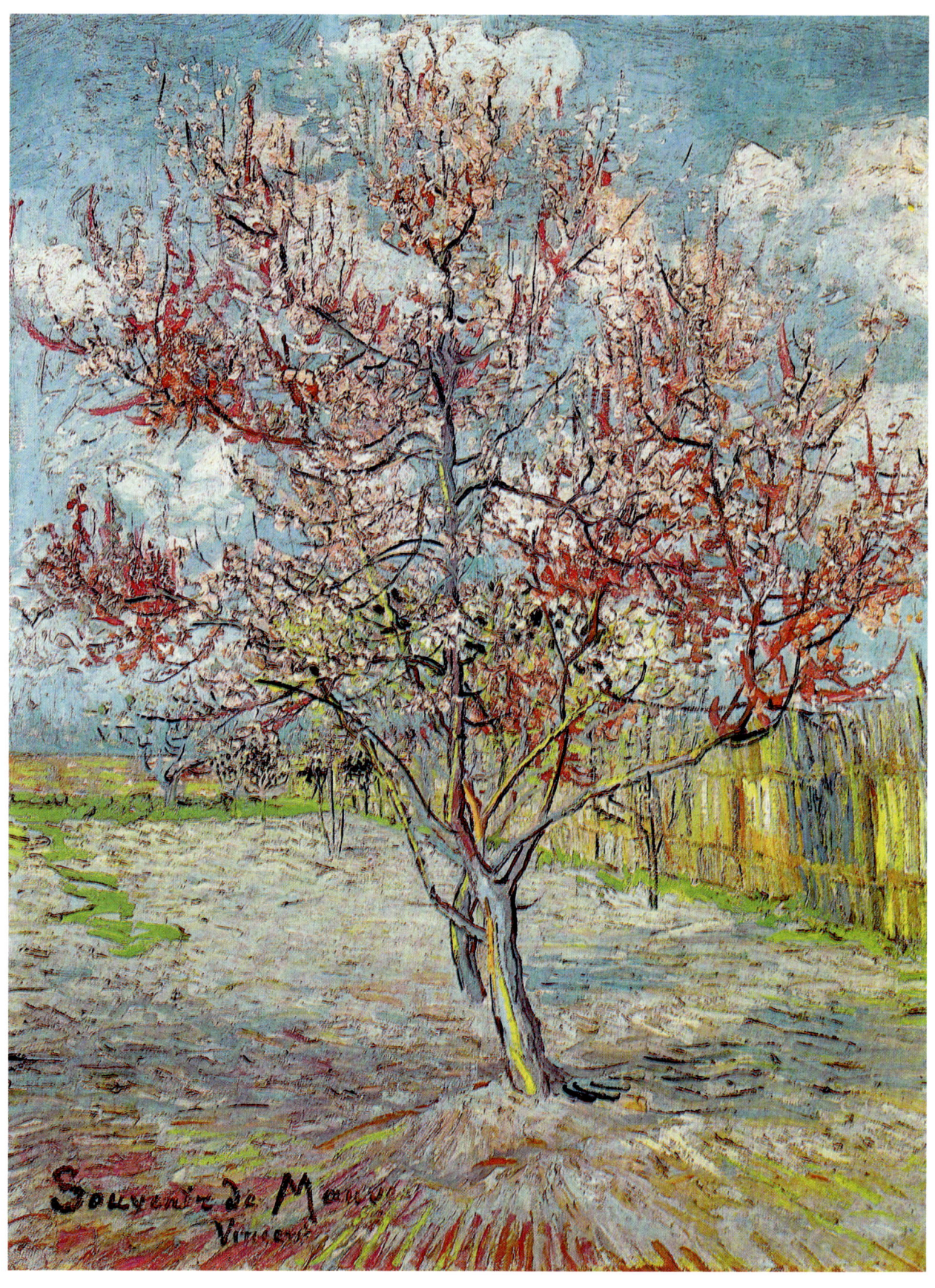

**Pink Peach Trees (Souvenir de Mauve),** March-April 1888, oil on canvas, 73 × 60 cm, Otterlo, Kröller-Müller Museum
**Flowering Orchards,** March-April 1888, oil on canvas, 80.9 × 60.2 cm, Amsterdam, Van Gogh Museum (right, detail)

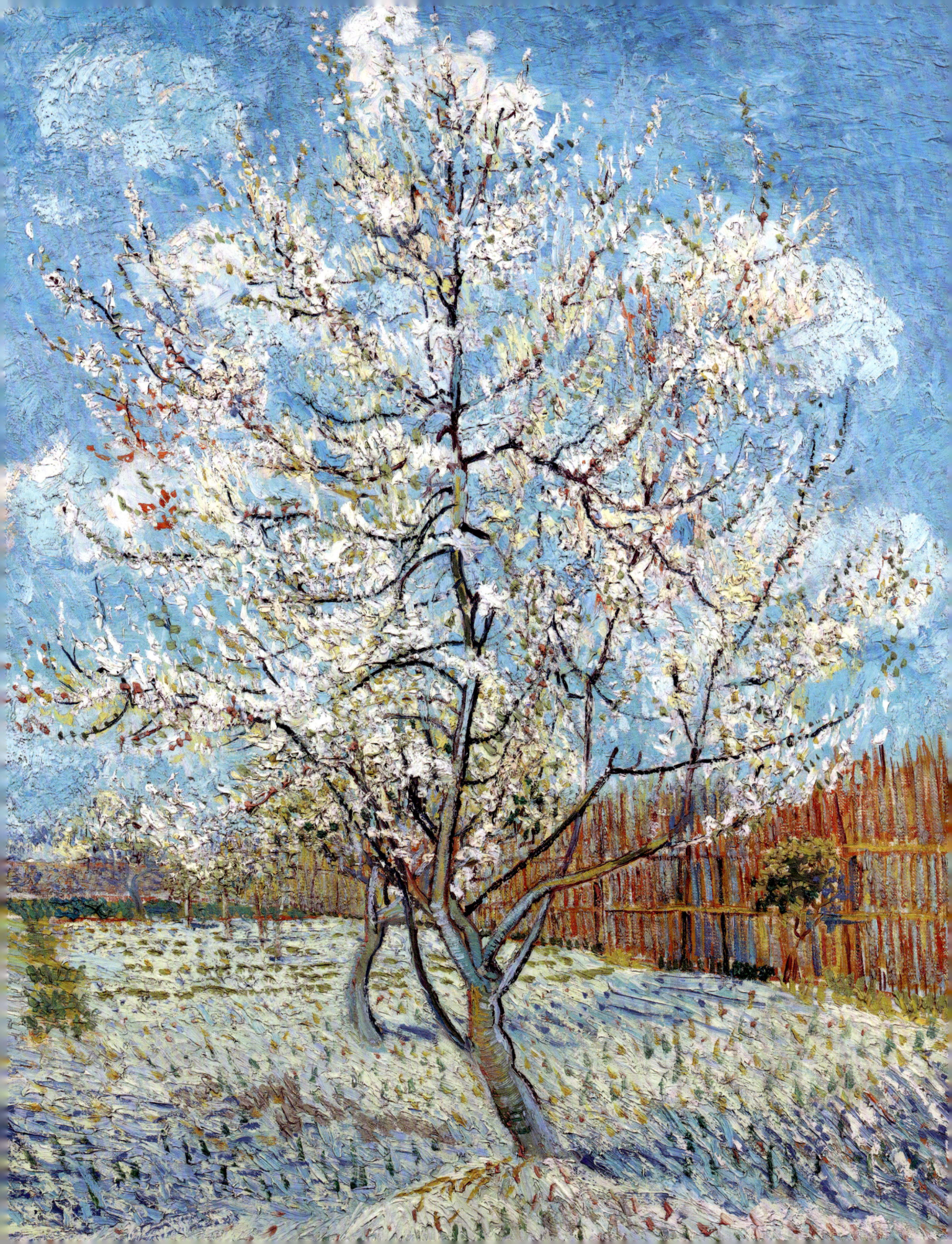

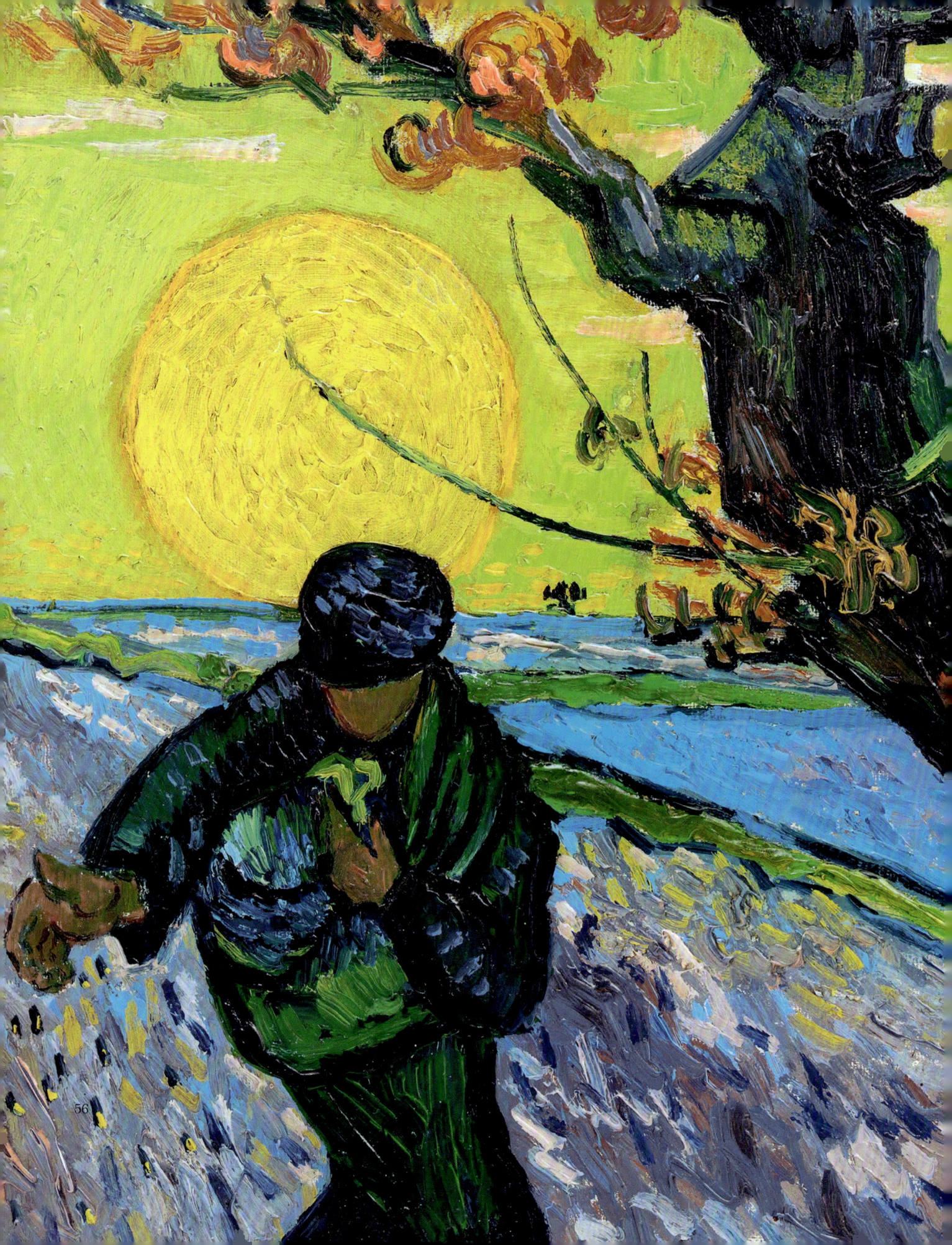

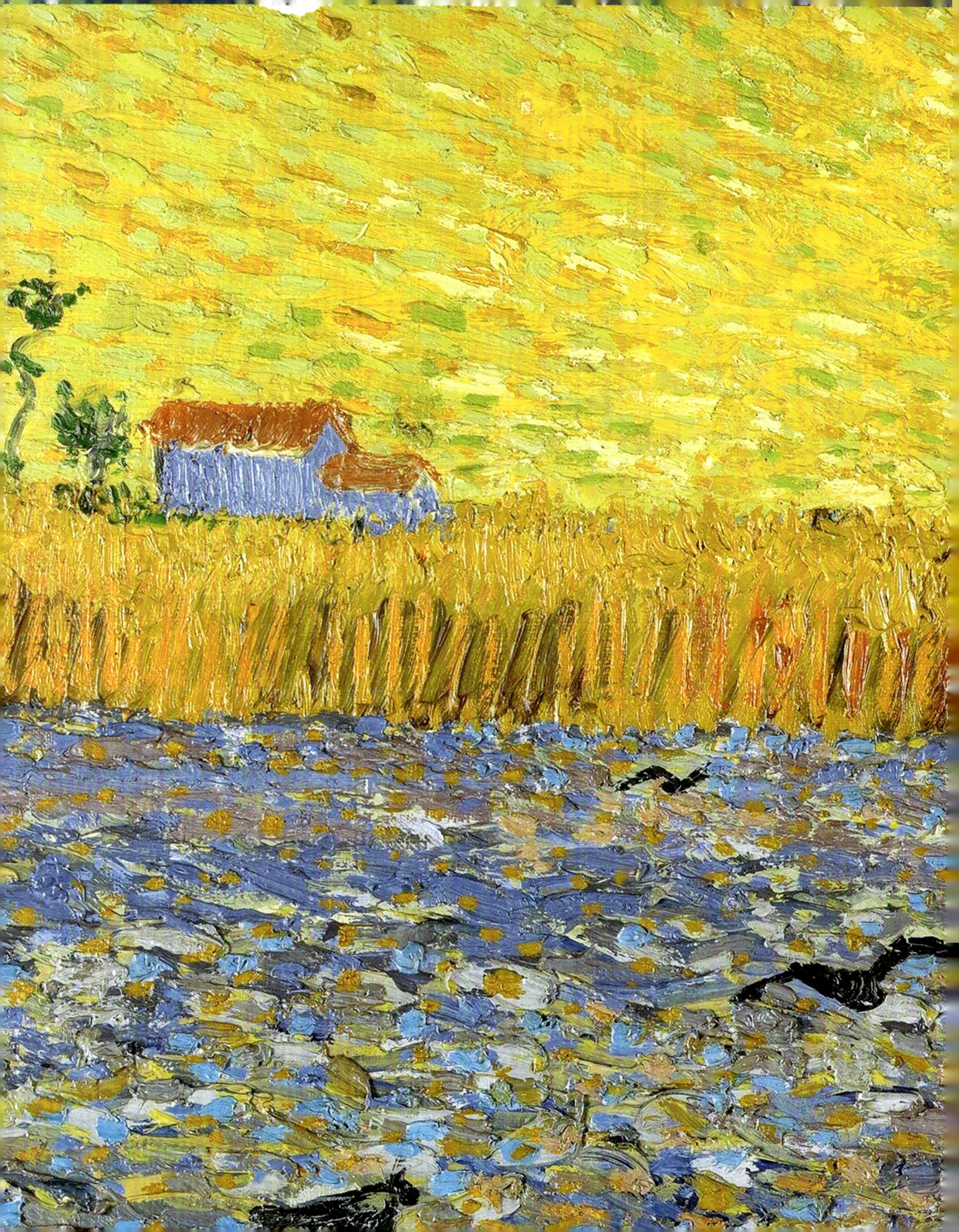

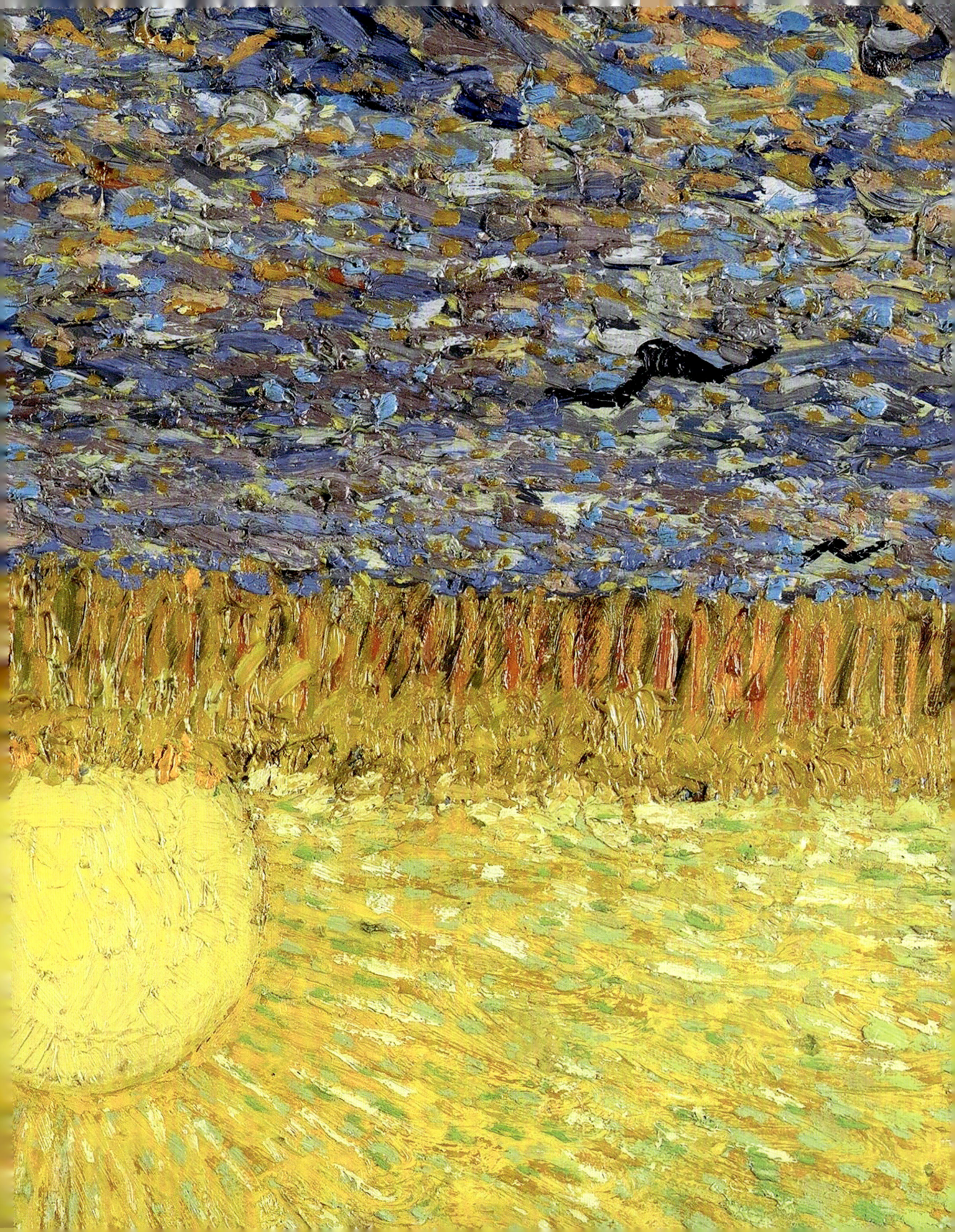

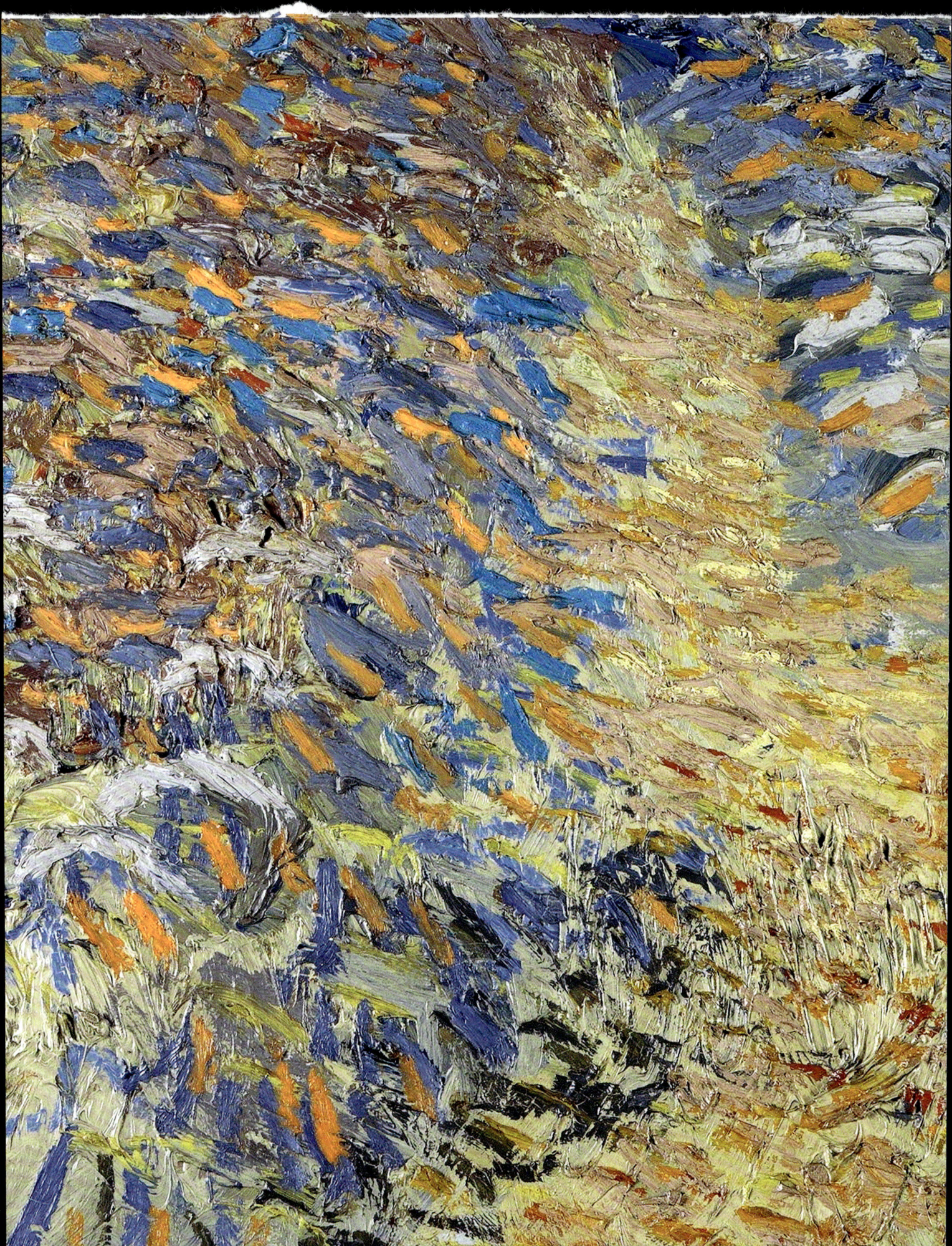

# The Sower

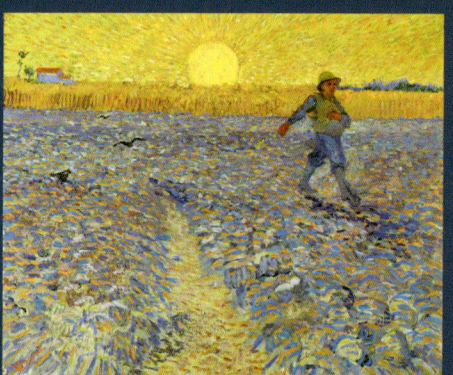

Van Gogh felt a particular admiration for Jean-François Millet's work *The Sower*, which he copied many times, then reinterpreted in June 1888, when he was in Arles. Whereas in variations of *The Sower* that he painted in Holland, the painter remained faithful to Millet's dark palette, here, he used intense colours. Vibrant yellow tones pervade the upper part of the painting, while in the lower part, violet blues and ochres are applied with a thick impasto. As for the motif, which is both realistic and highly symbolic, it has been the subject of numerous interpretations – spiritual, first of all, as the figure of *The Sower* refers to the biblical parable, the divine sower of truth that Christ embodied. The work has also been understood as an image of the cycle of life, of the passage of time; as a celebration of fertile nature, a tribute to the nurturing role of the peasantry; and, sometimes even, as a representation of the artist himself, planting seeds in the hope of seeing them blossom one day.

the big picture

*The Sower*, June 1888, oil on canvas, 64 × 84.5 cm, Otterlo, Kröller-Müller Museum
*The Sower*, November 1888, oil on canvas, 32.5 × 43 cm, Amsterdam, Van Gogh Museum (left, detail)

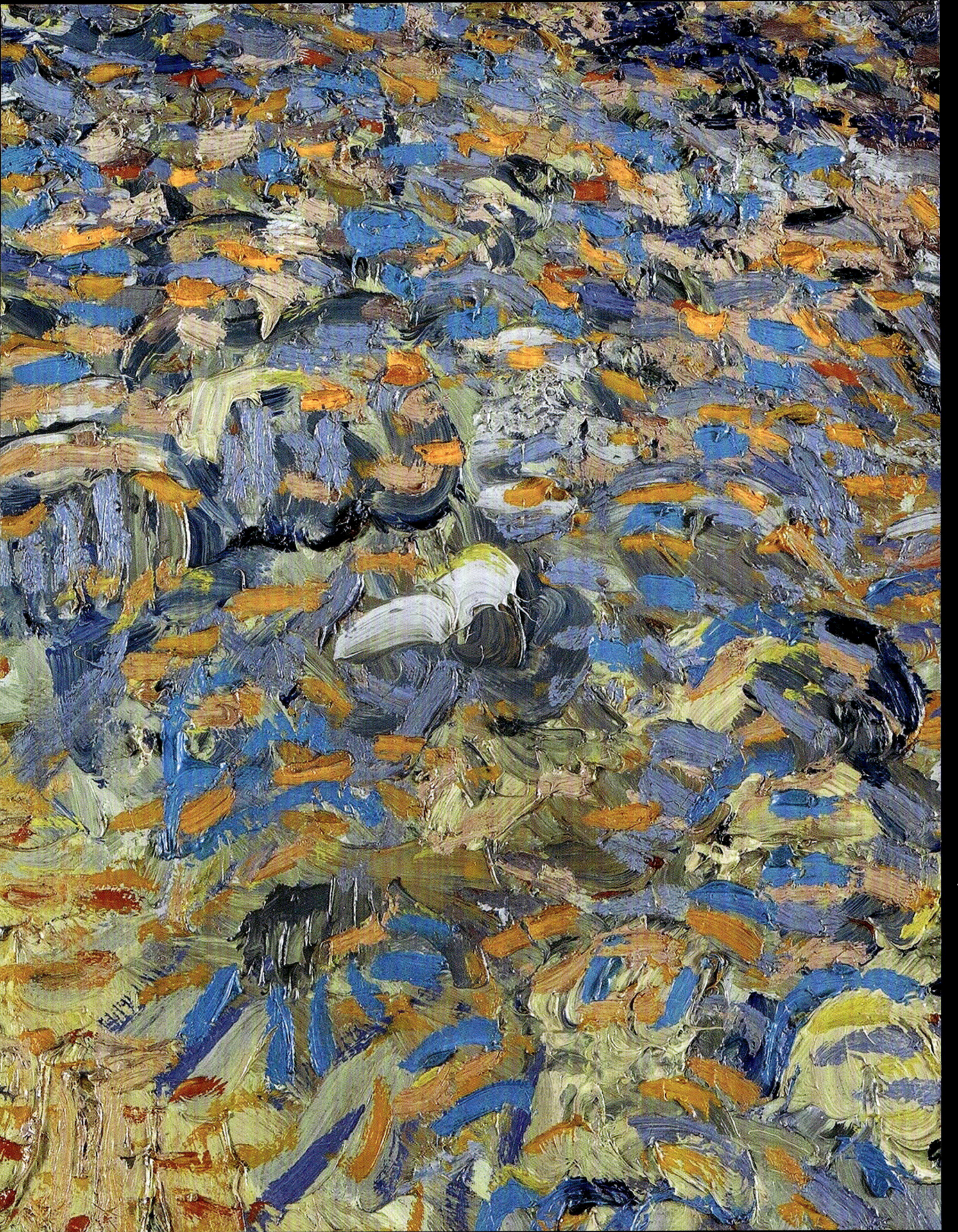

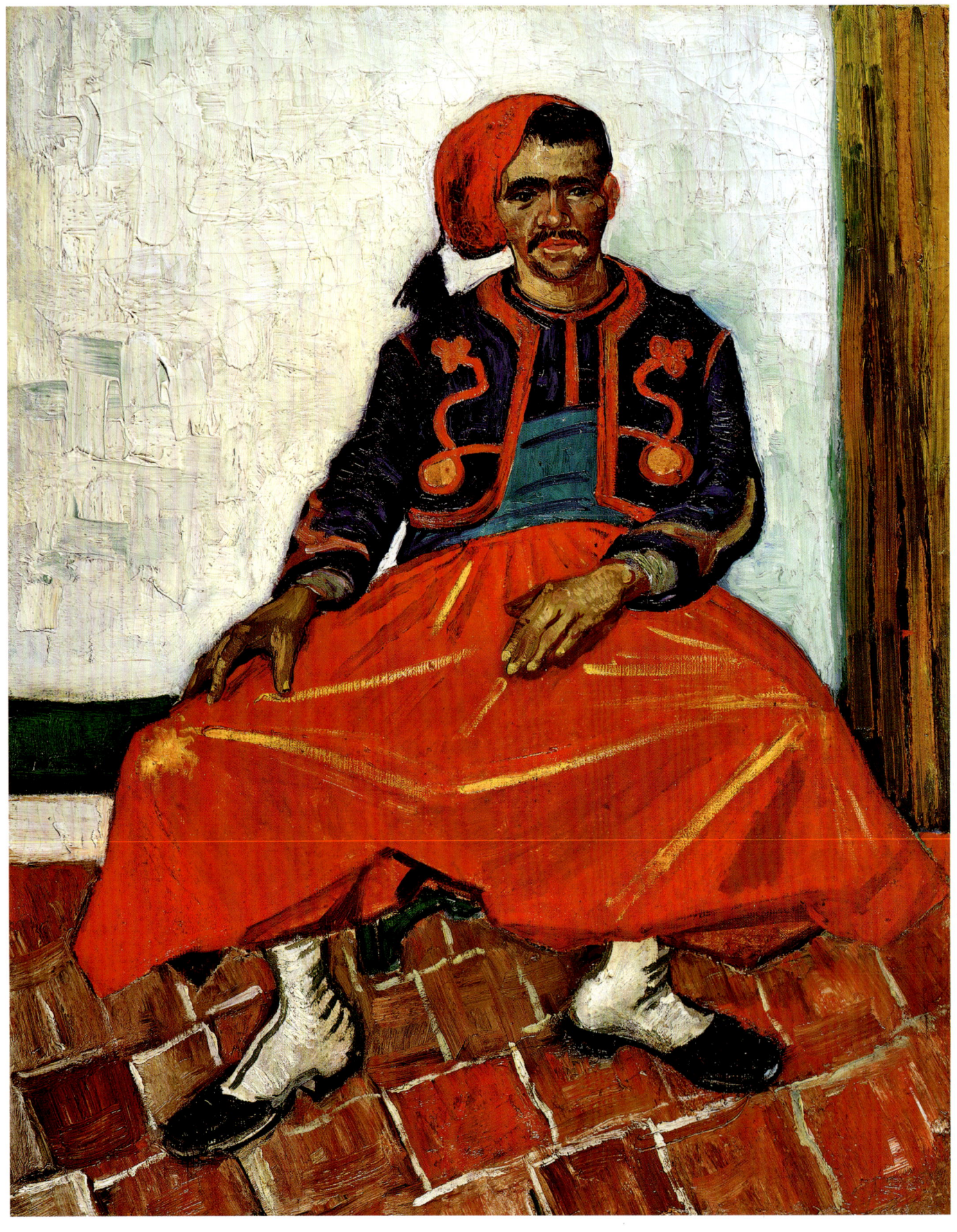

*The Zouave,* 1888, oil on canvas, 81 × 65 cm, private collection

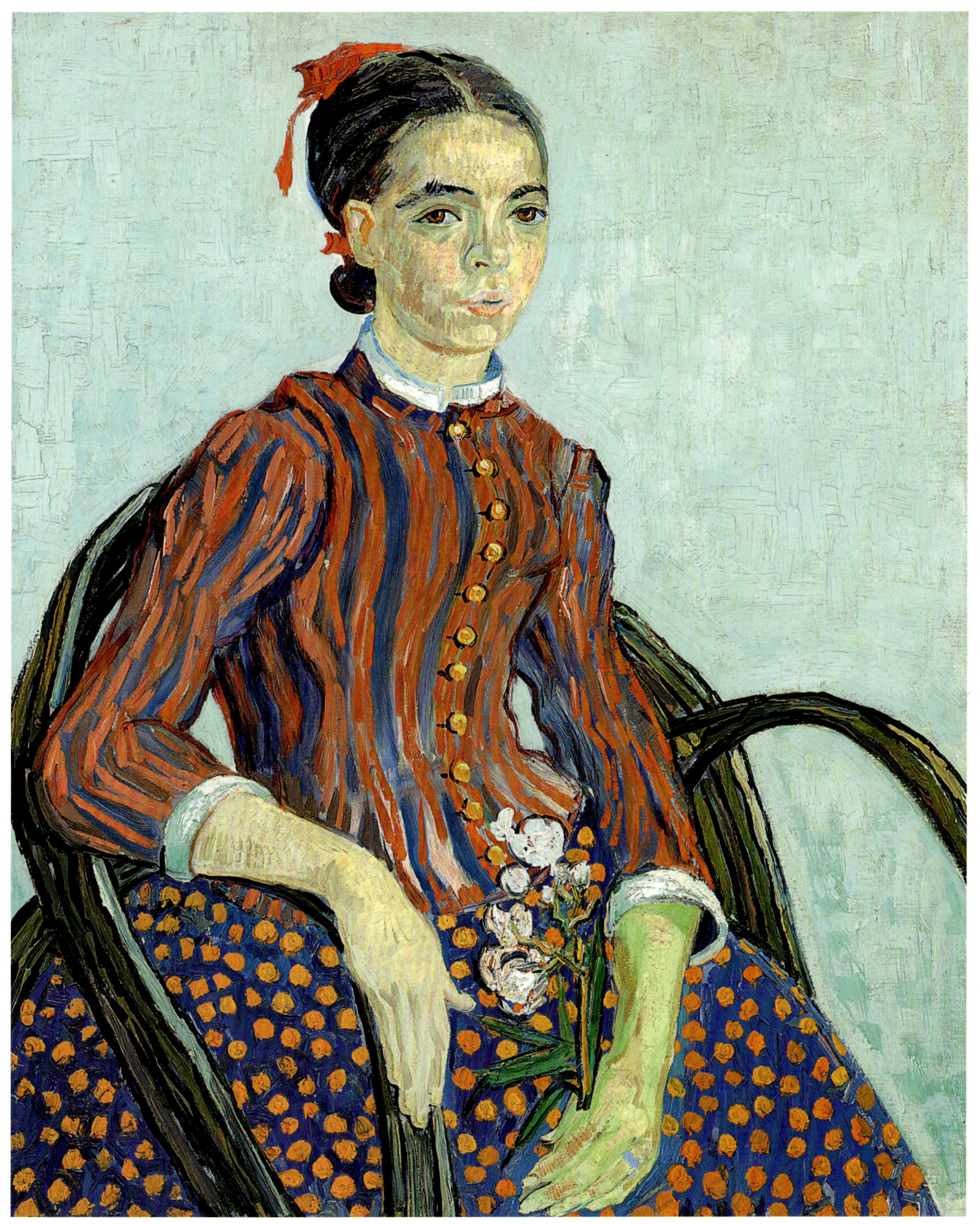

**La Mousmé,** July 1888, oil on canvas, 73.3 × 60.3 cm, Washington, National Gallery of Art

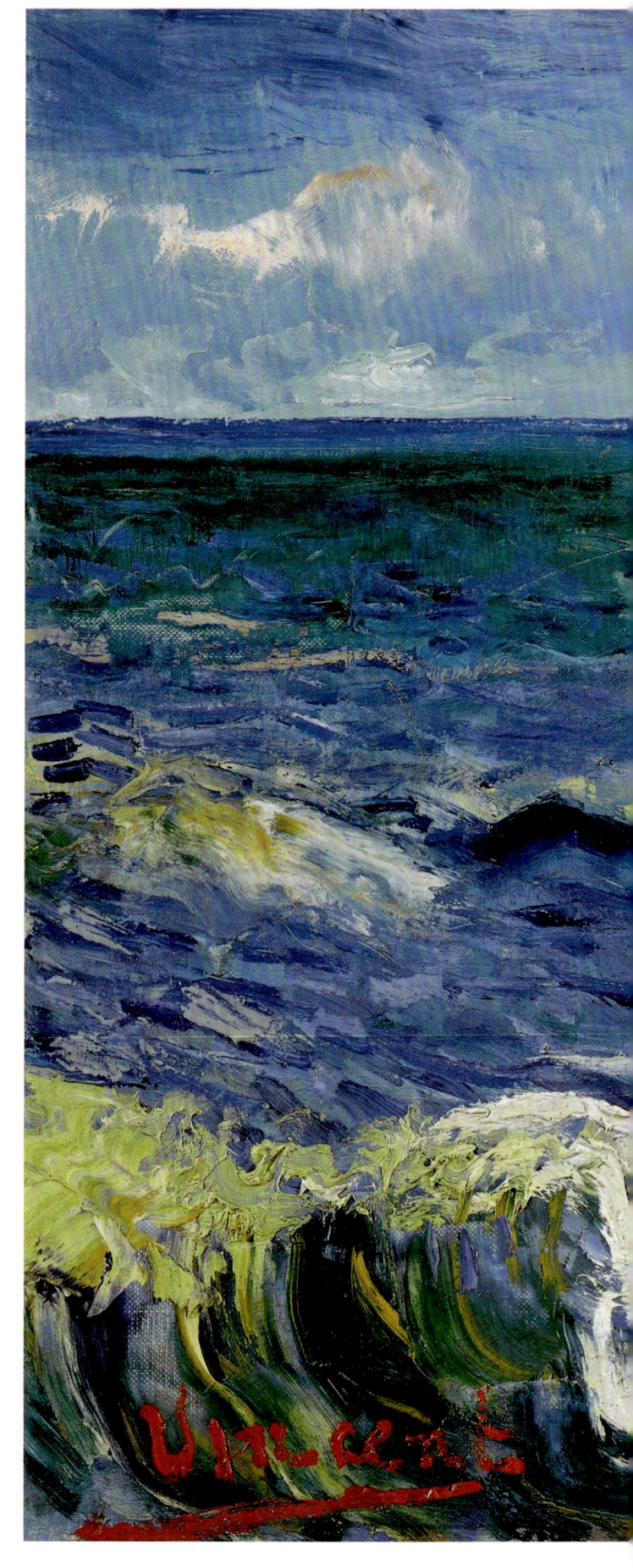

**Seascape near Les Saintes-Maries-de-la-Mer**

June 1888
Oil on canvas, 50.5 × 64.3 cm
Amsterdam, Van Gogh Museum

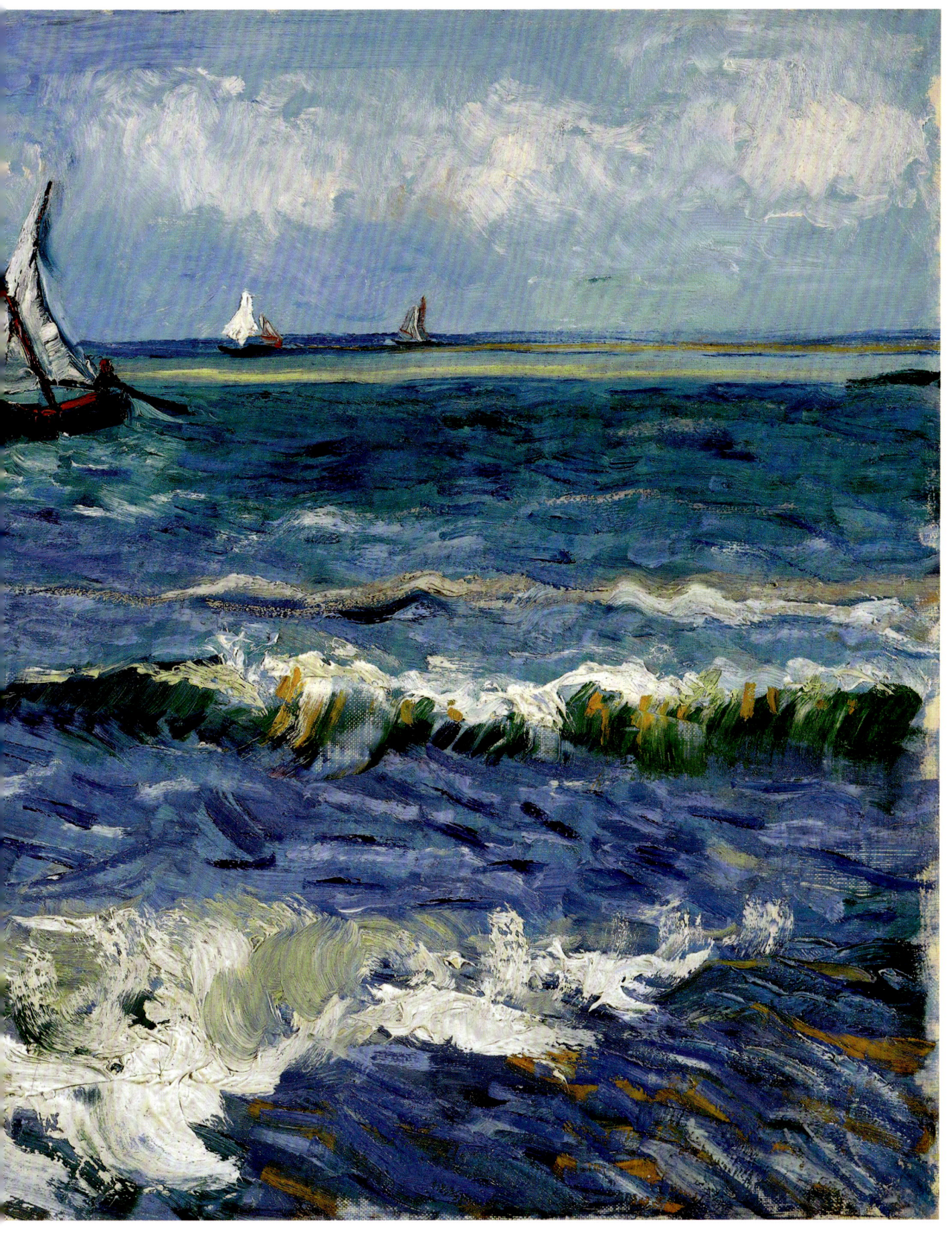

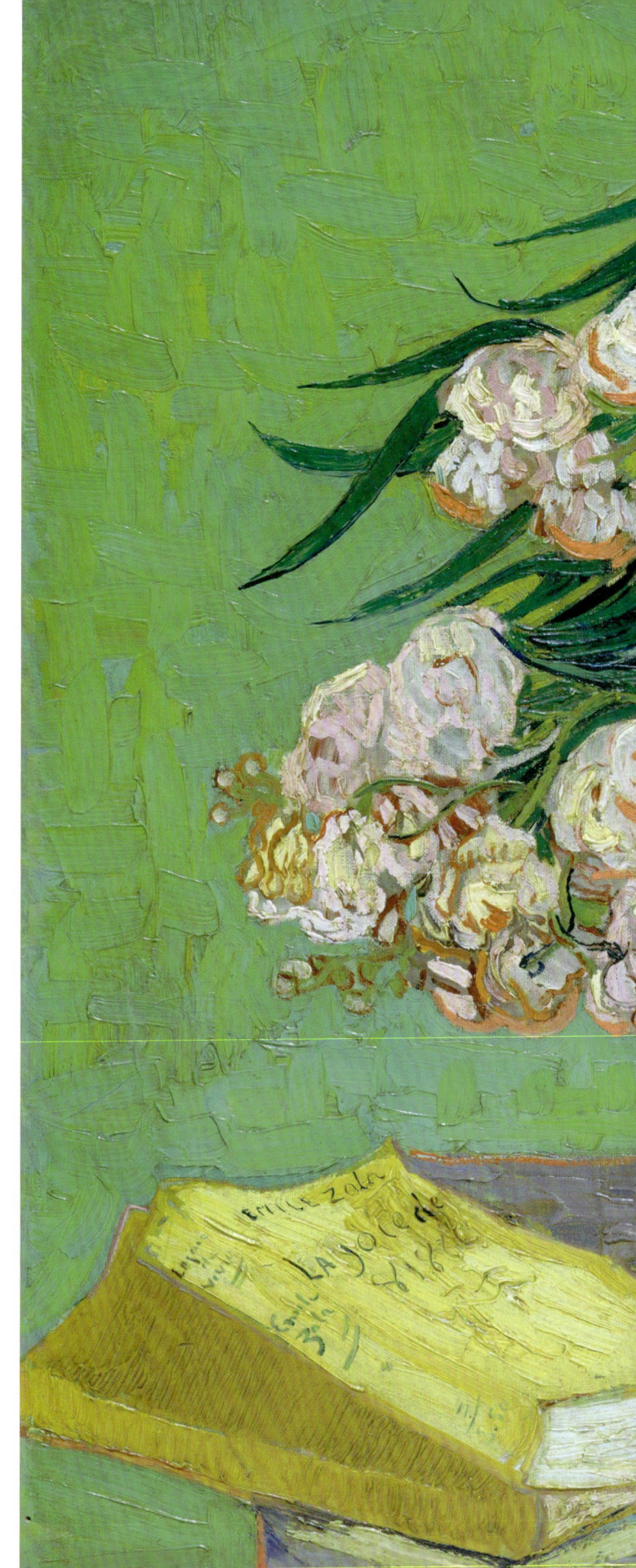

**Oleanders**

August 1888
Oil on canvas, 60.3 × 73.7 cm
New York, The Metropolitan Museum of Art

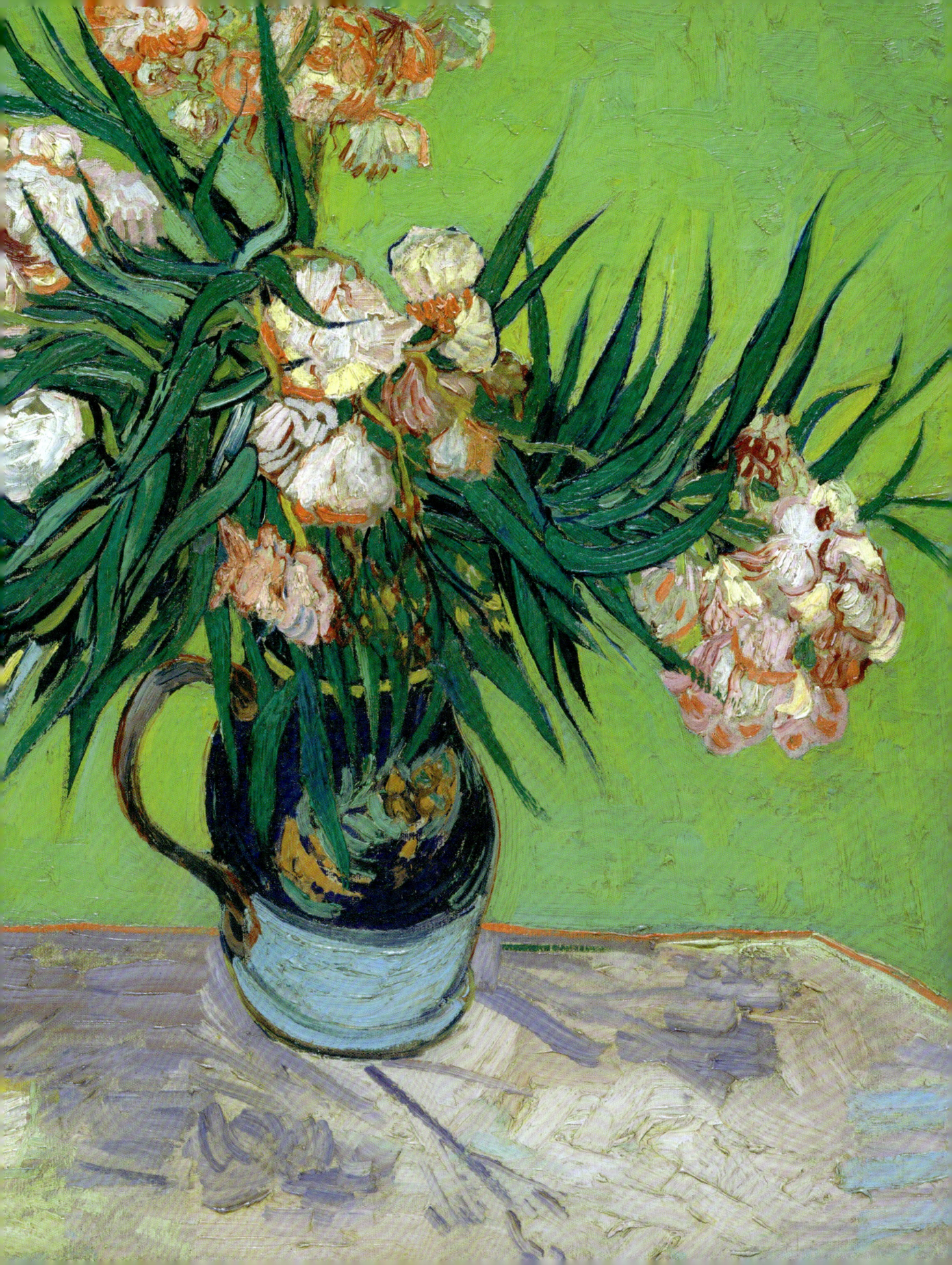

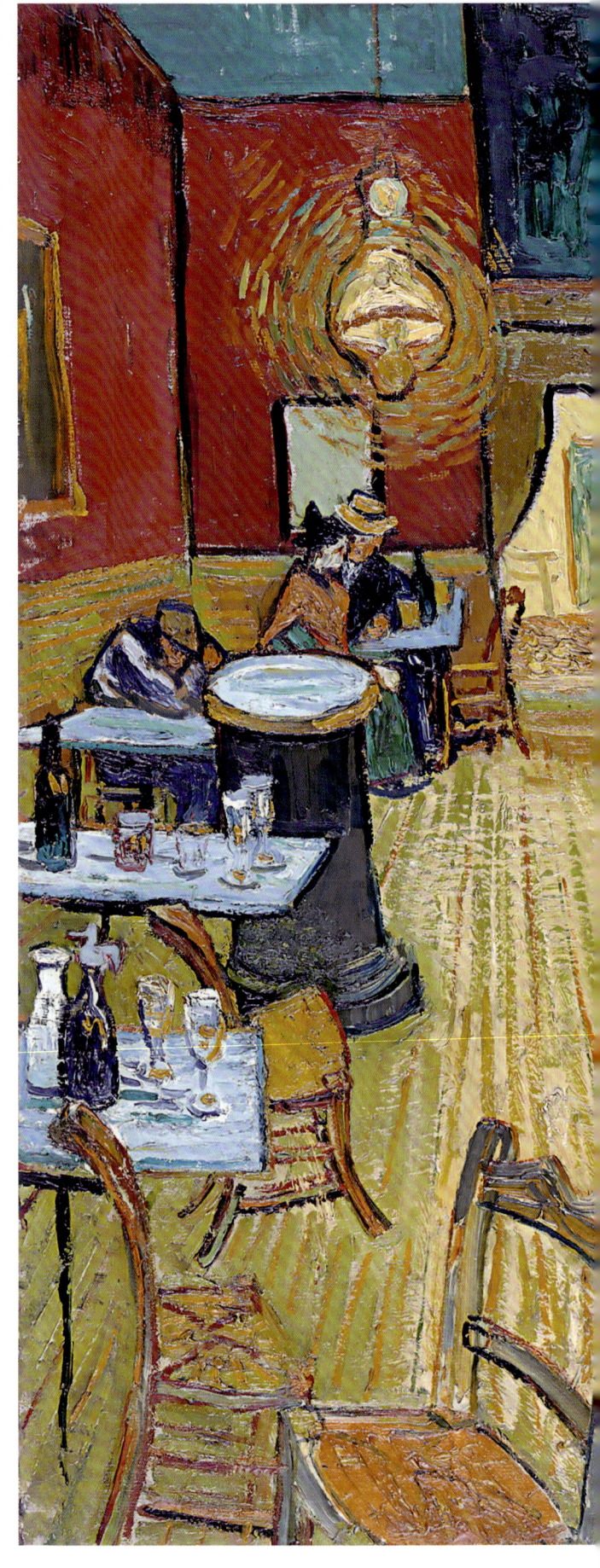

**The Night Café**

September 1888
Oil on canvas, 72.4 × 91.2 cm
New Haven, Yale University Art Gallery

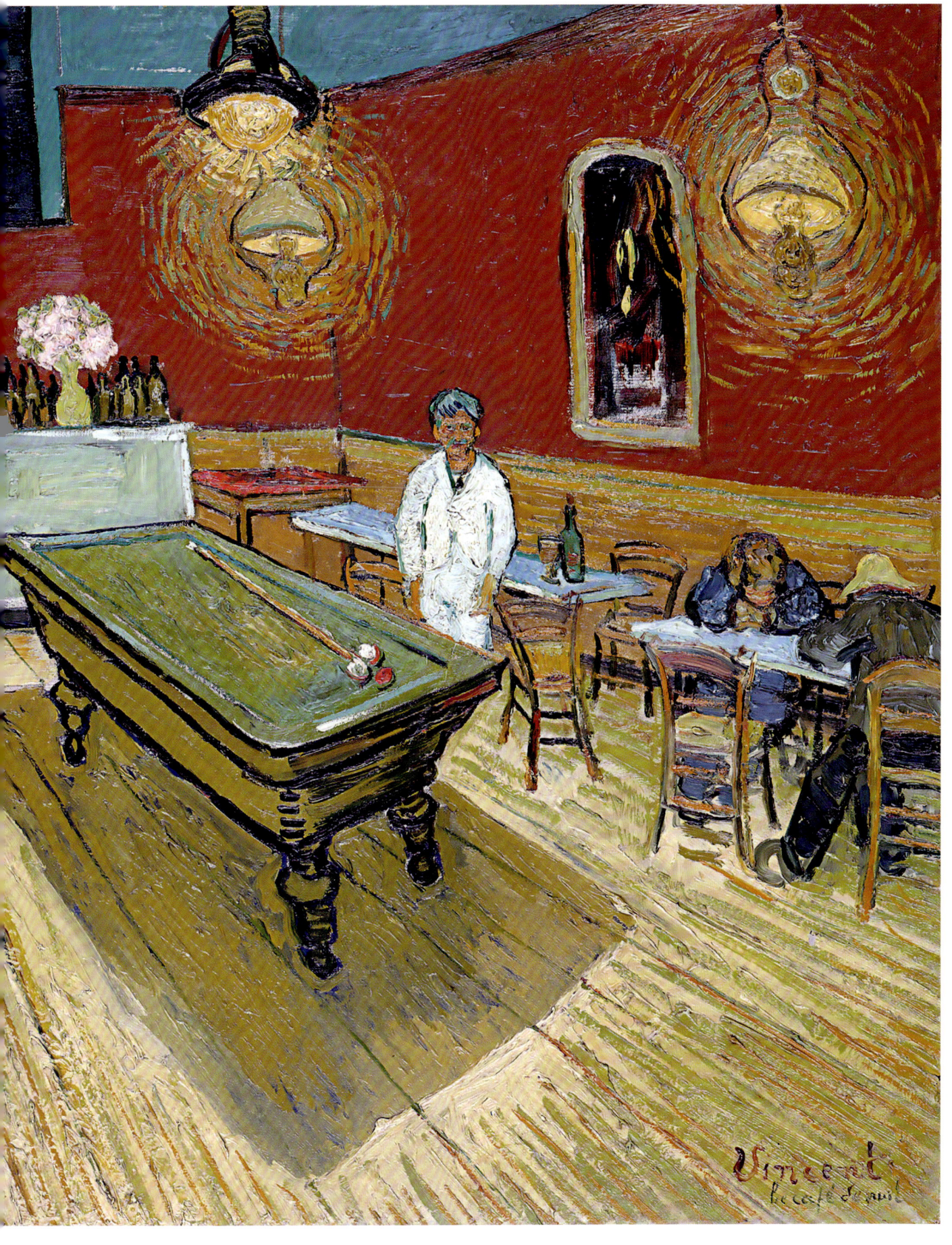

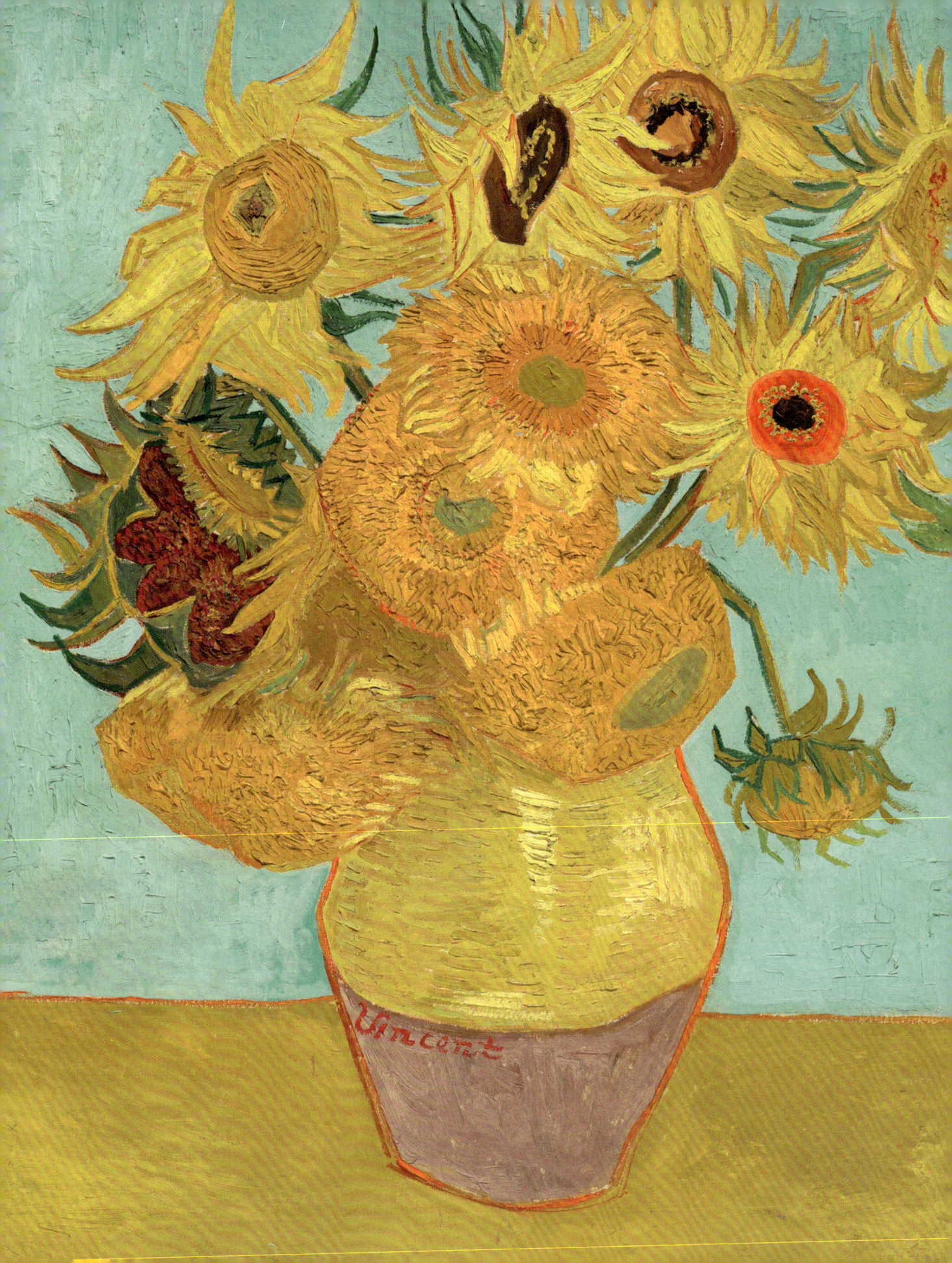

# Sunflowers

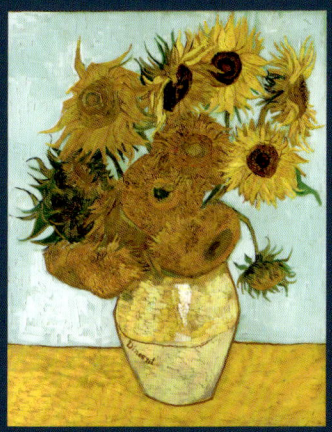

*Sunflowers* are among Vincent Van Gogh's most iconic works. This work was painted in Arles in the summer of 1888, when the artist was waiting for his friend Paul Gauguin, in order to finally fulfil his dream of founding a fraternity of artists, the "Atelier du Midi". He then wrote to his brother Theo: "In the hope of living in a studio of our own with Gauguin, I'd like to do a decoration for the studio. Nothing but large sunflowers. [...] Well, if I carry out this plan there'll be a dozen or so panels." Inspired by Japanese art, he opted for a very simple composition, using contours and colour to define separate spaces, while treating the flowers with meticulous care. Despite a lot of hard work – "I am hard at work, painting with the enthusiasm of a Marseillais eating bouillabaisse", he wrote –, he would paint only four Sunflowers, as the annual flowering season came to an end. Deprived of a model, he produced copies of these two paintings a few months later.

*Vase with Twelve Sunflowers*, August 1888, oil on canvas, 91 × 72 cm, Munich, Neue Pinakothek
*Sunflowers*, August 1888, oil on canvas, 92.4 × 71.1 cm, Philadelphia, Philadelphia Museum of Art (left)

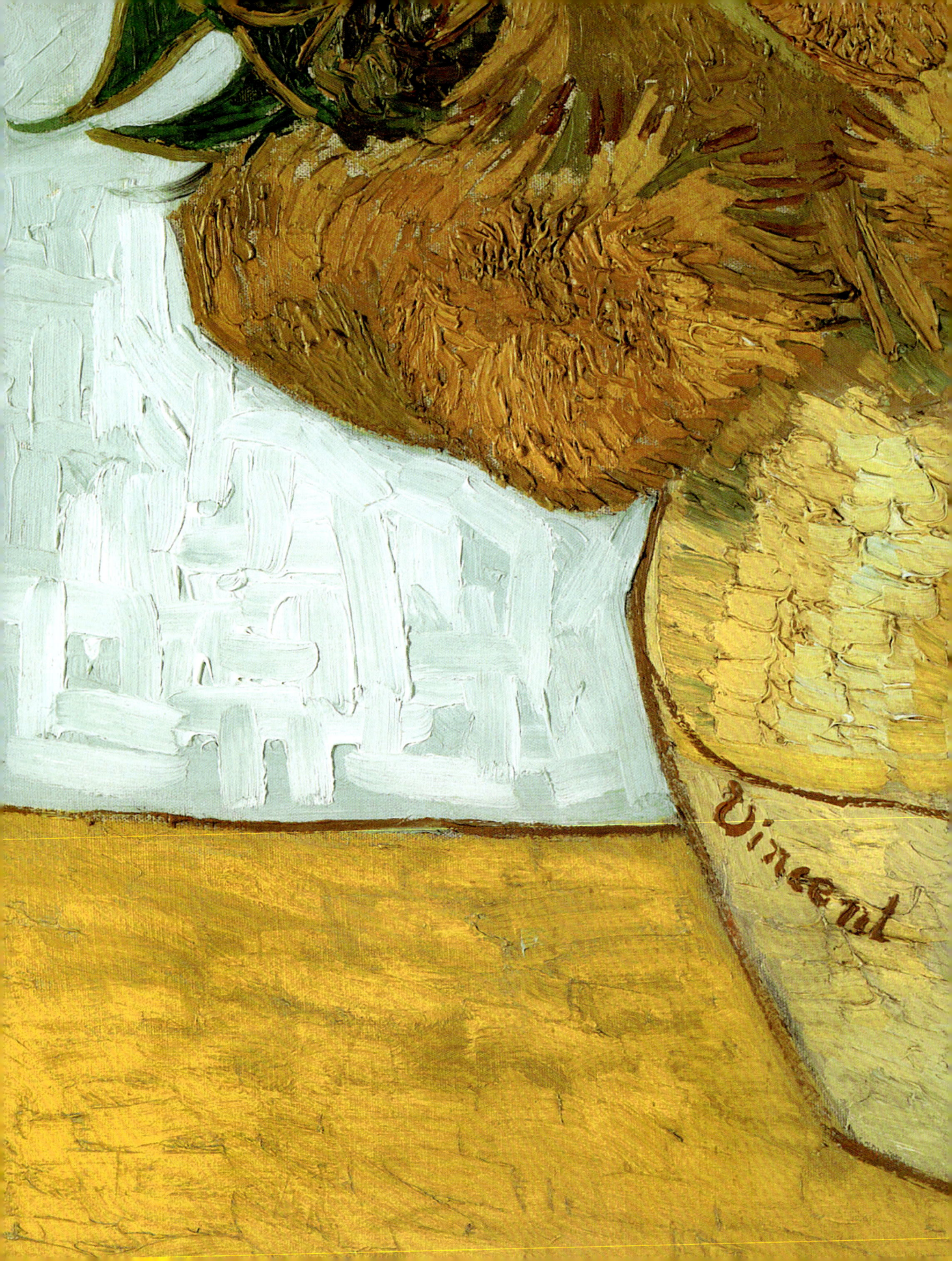

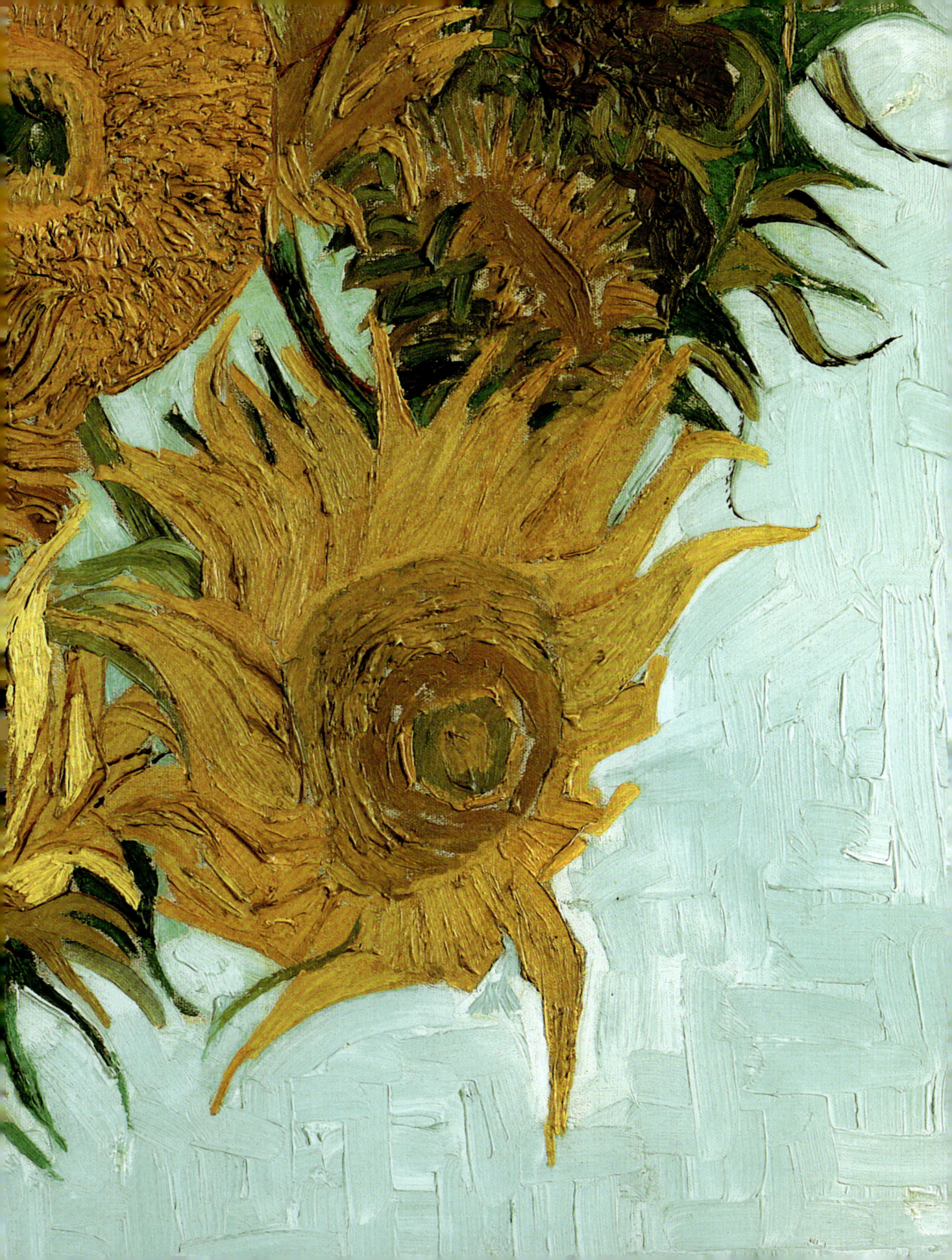

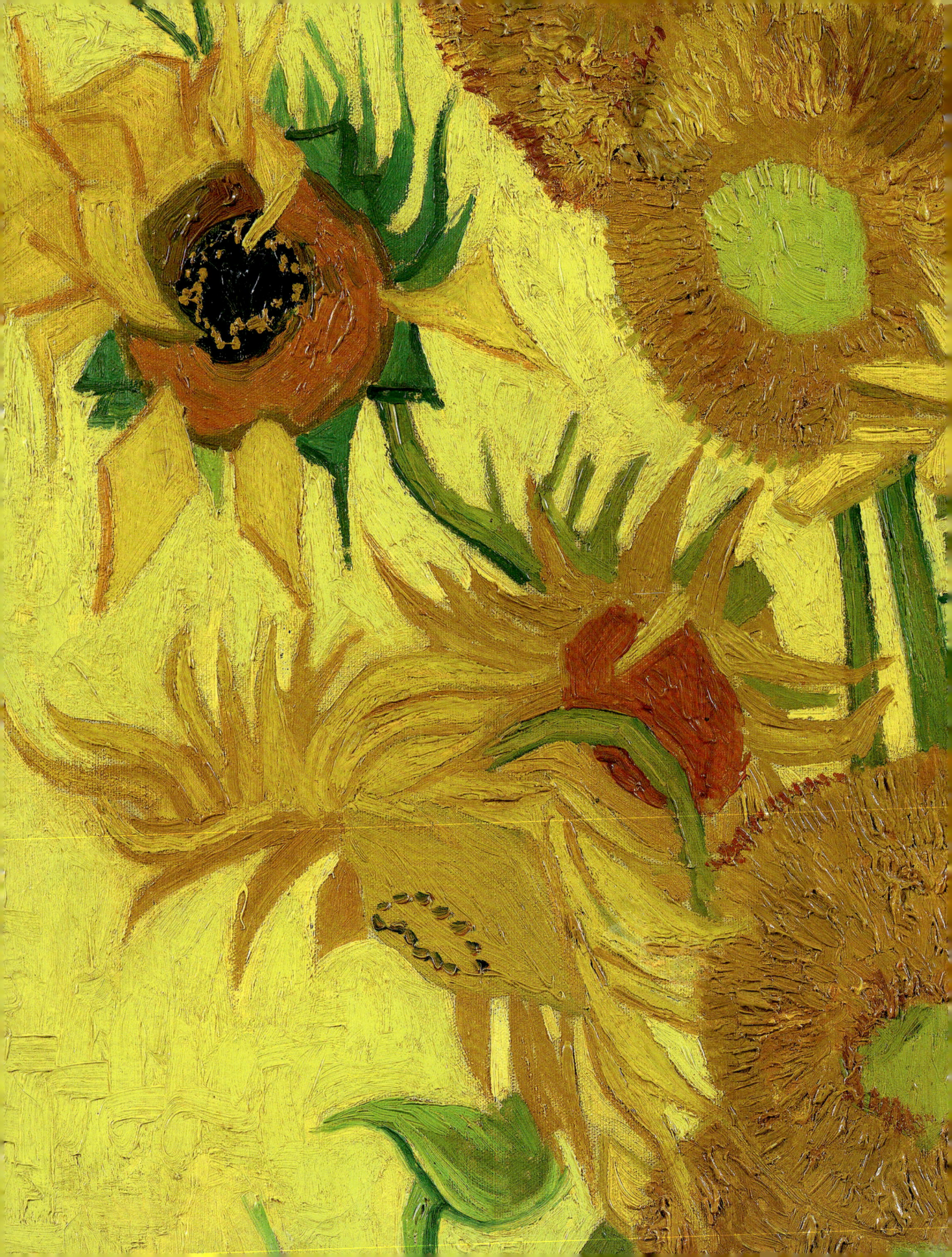

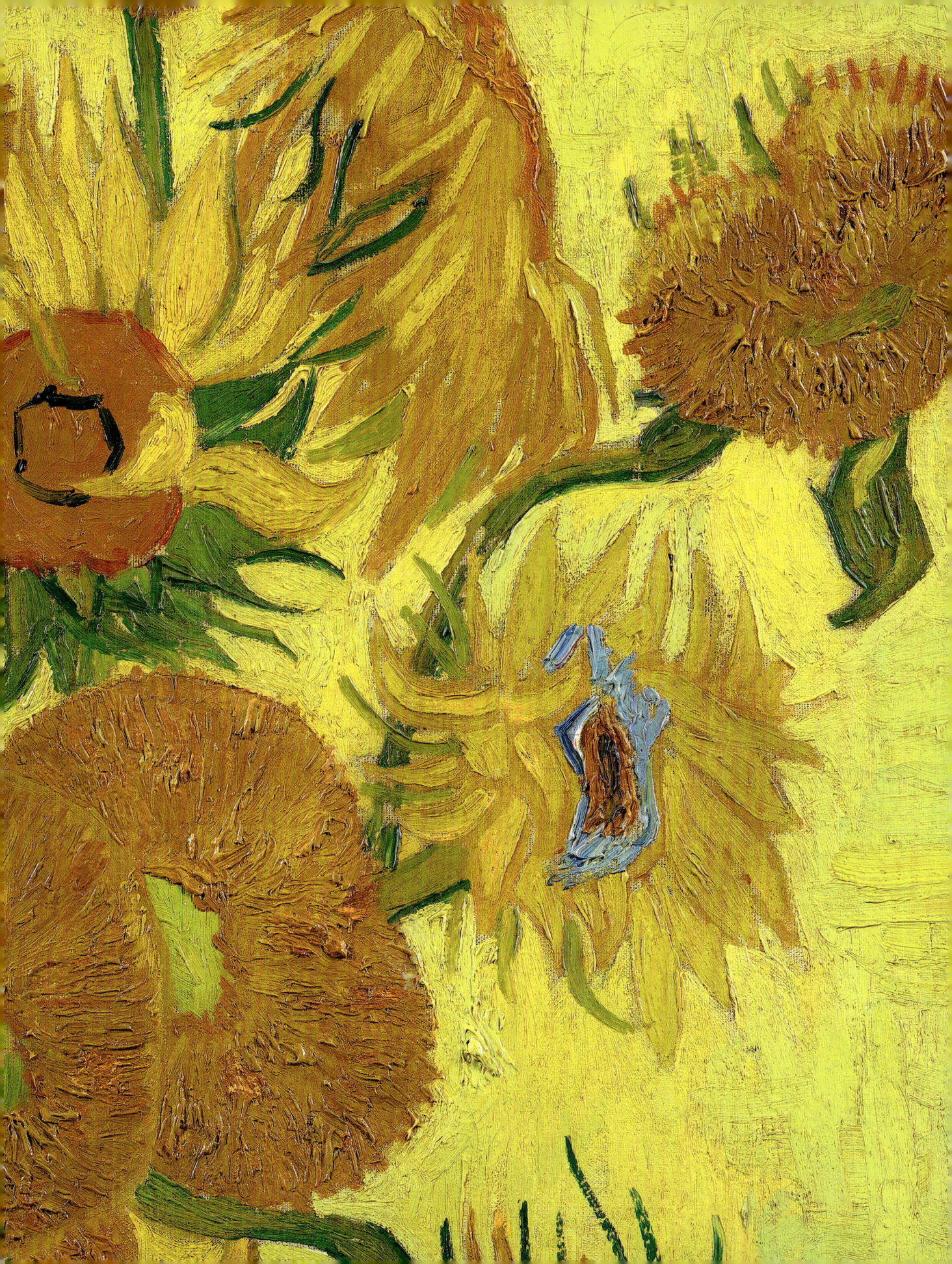

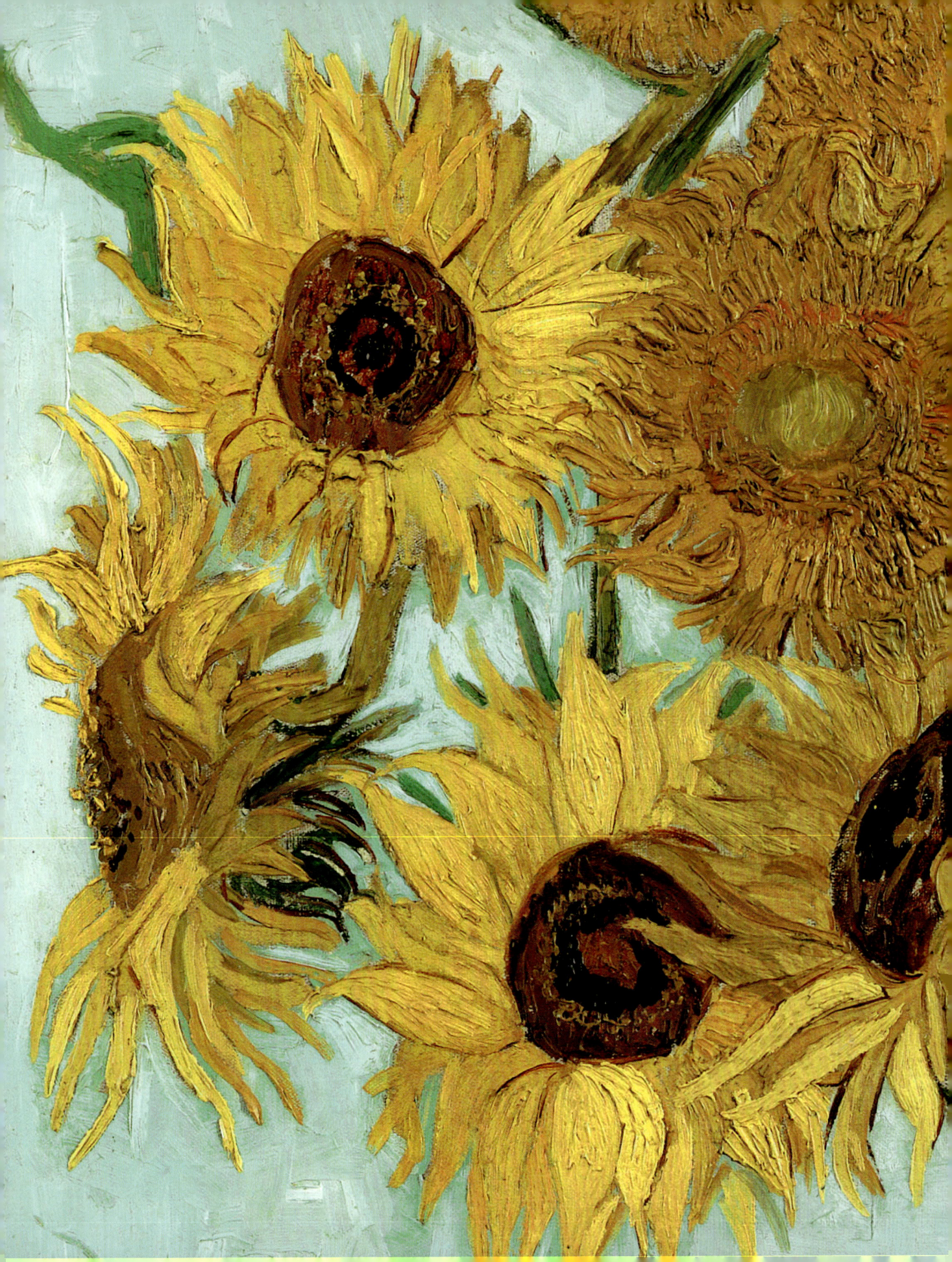

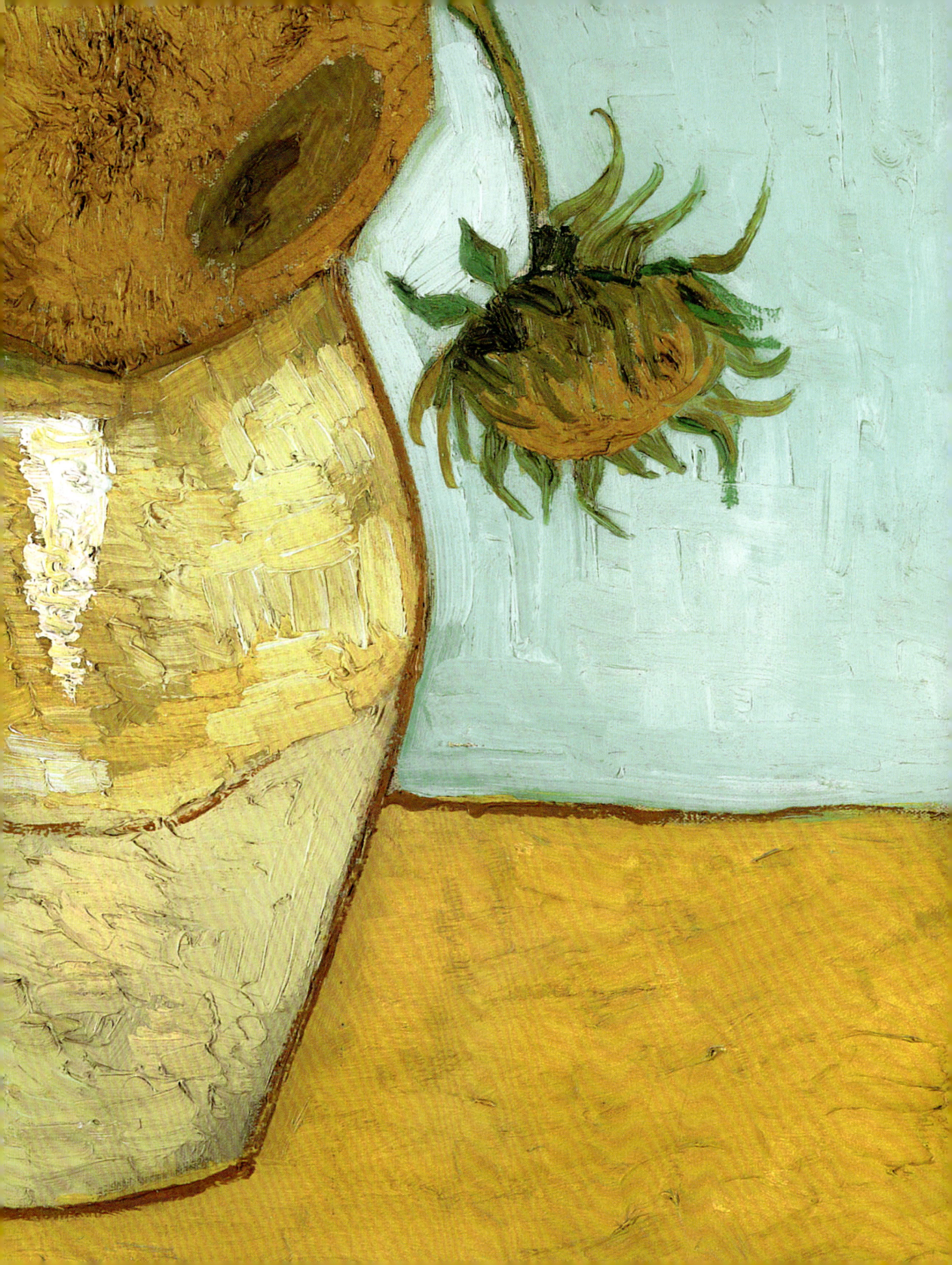

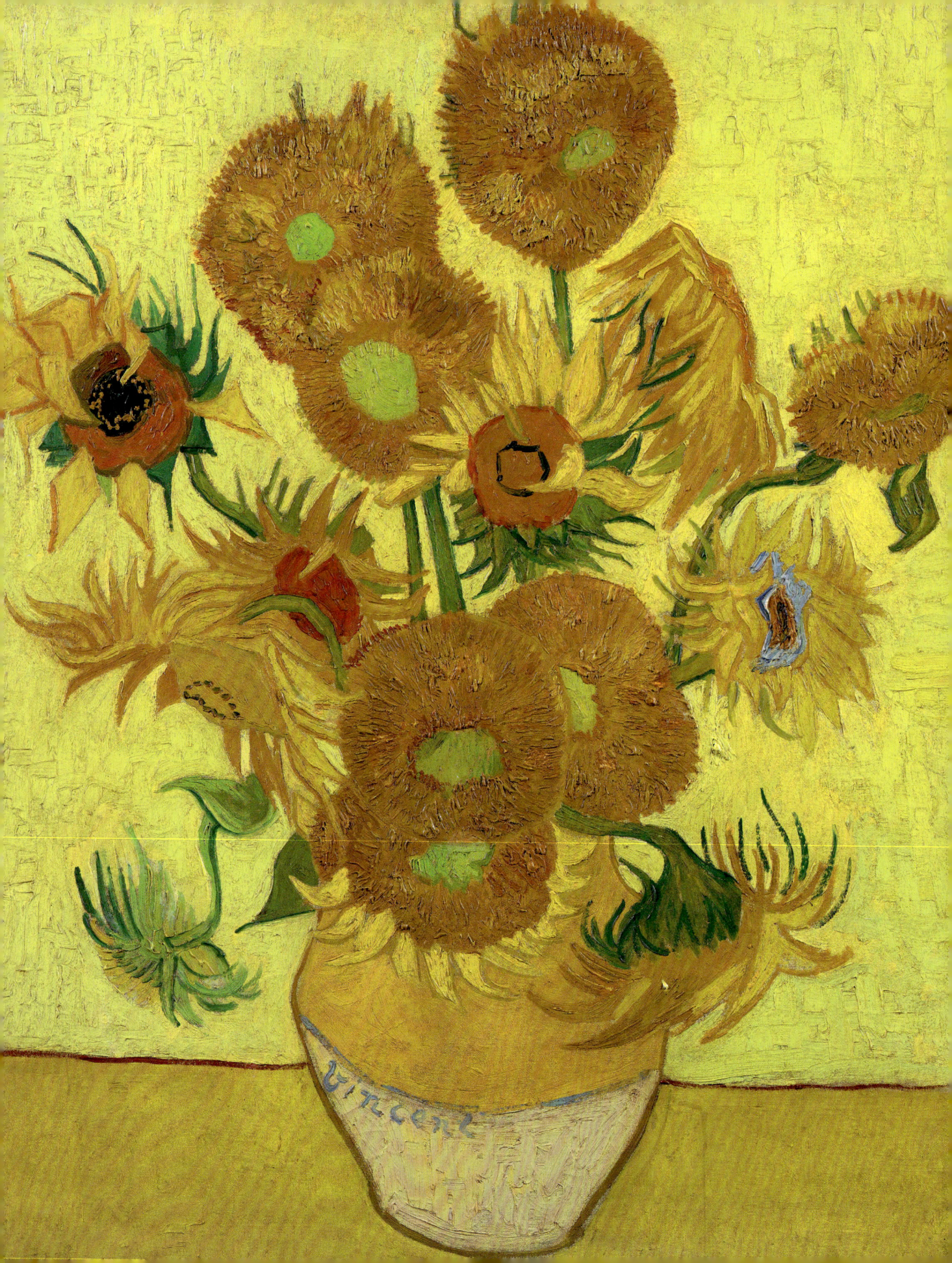

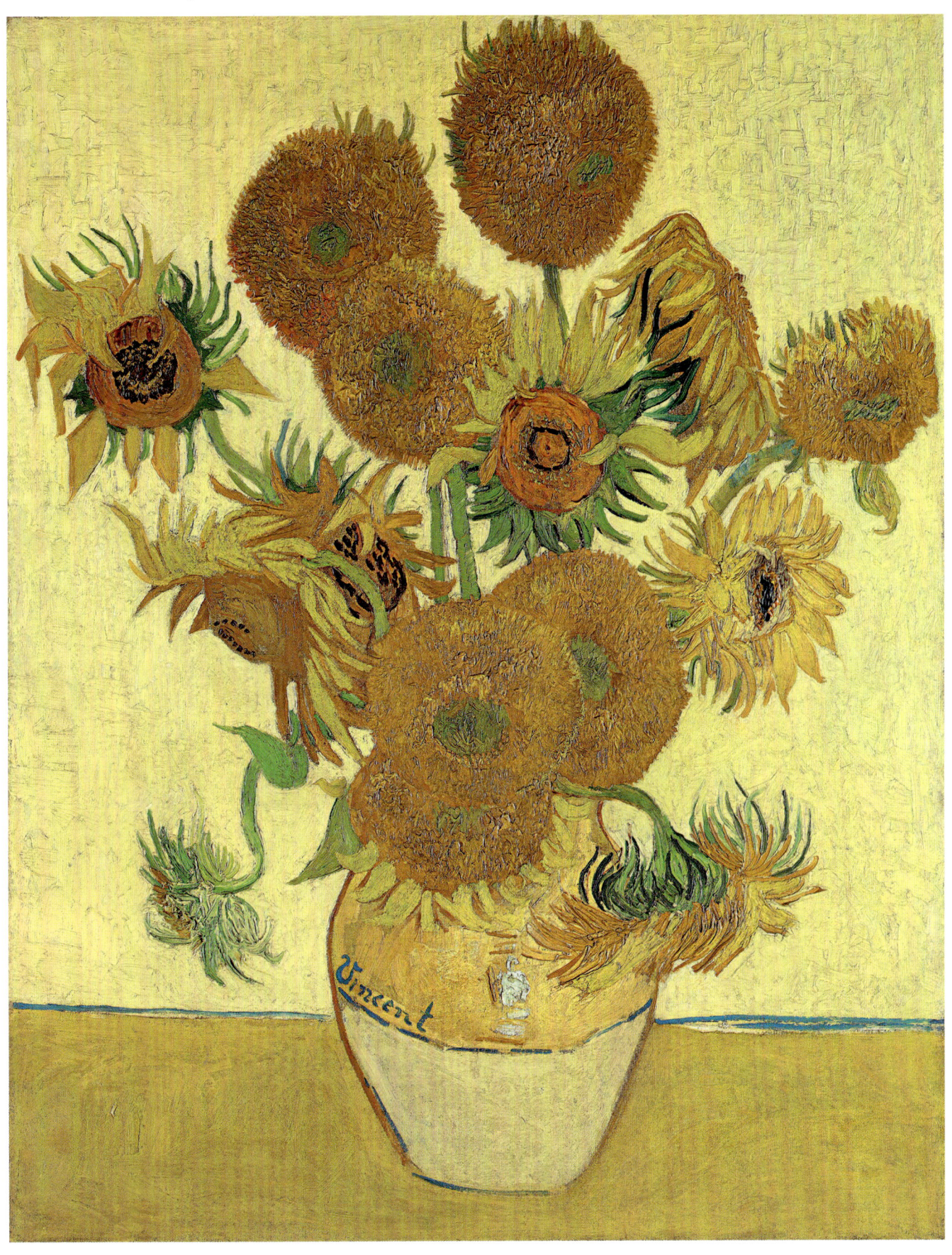

**Sunflowers,** August 1888, oil on canvas, 95 × 73 cm, London, The National Gallery
**Vase with Twelve Sunflowers,** January 1889, oil on canvas, 95 × 73 cm, Amsterdam, Van Gogh Museum (left)

"Now there's a painting of night without black. With nothing but beautiful blue, violet and green, and in these surroundings the lighted square is coloured pale sulphur, lemon green. I enormously enjoy painting on the spot at night."

Vincent Van Gogh
Letter to his sister Willemien,
September 1888

**Café Terrace at Night (detail)**
September 1888
Oil on canvas, 80.7 × 65.3 cm
Otterlo, Kröller-Müller Museum

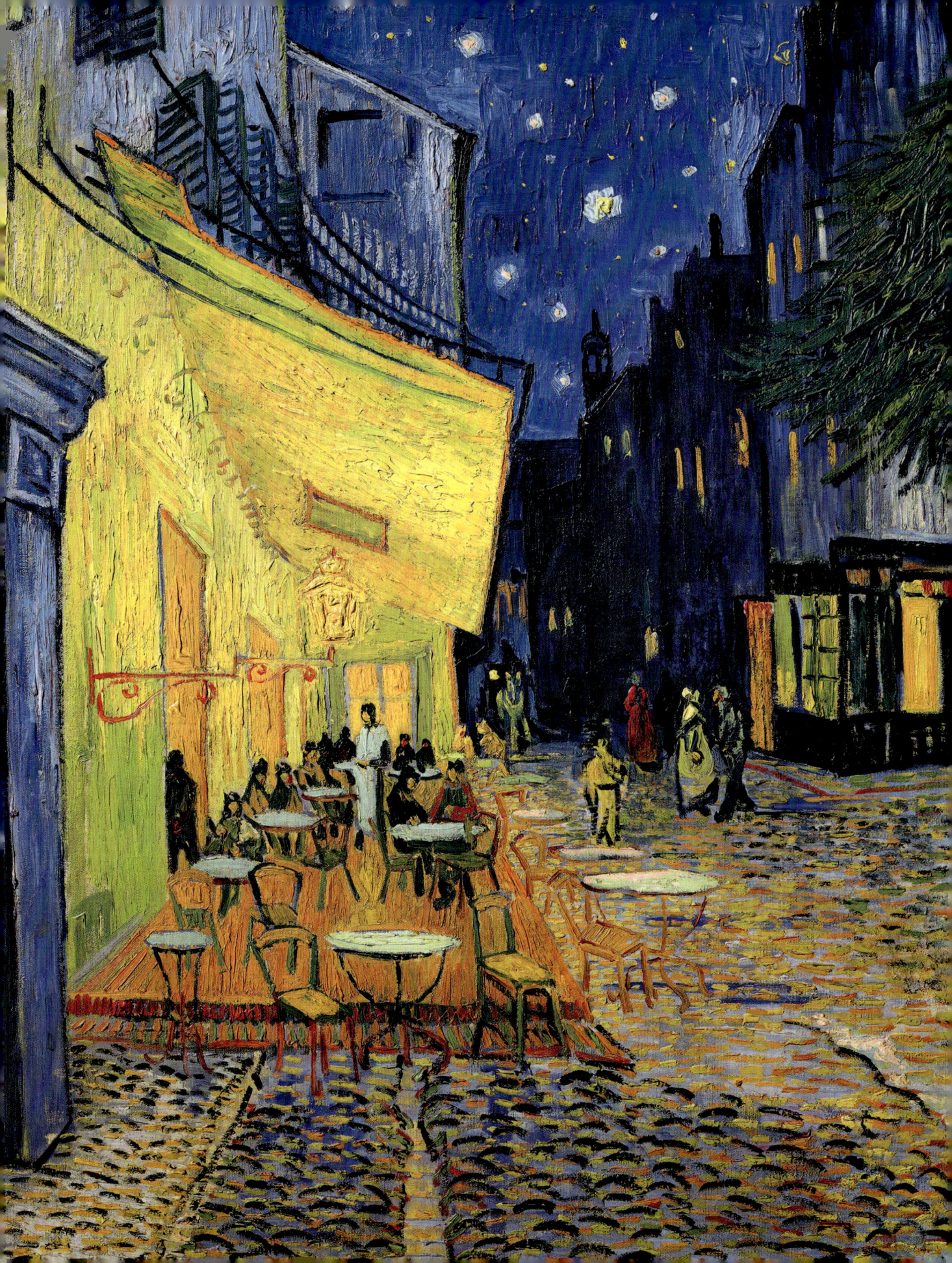

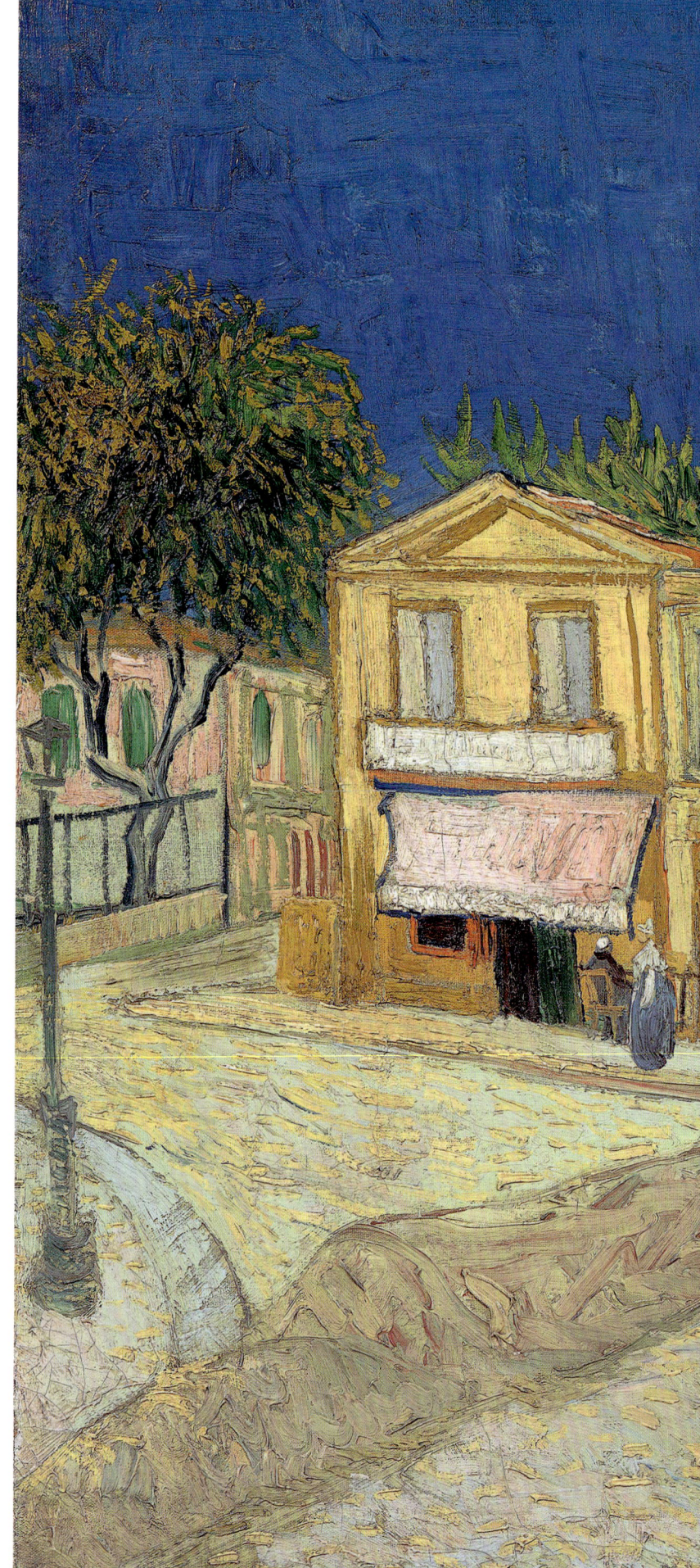

**The Yellow House**

September 1888
Oil on canvas, 72 × 91.5 cm
Amsterdam, Van Gogh Museum

**The Starry Night**

September 1888
Oil on canvas, 72.5 × 92 cm
Paris, Musée d'Orsay
(double page below, detail)

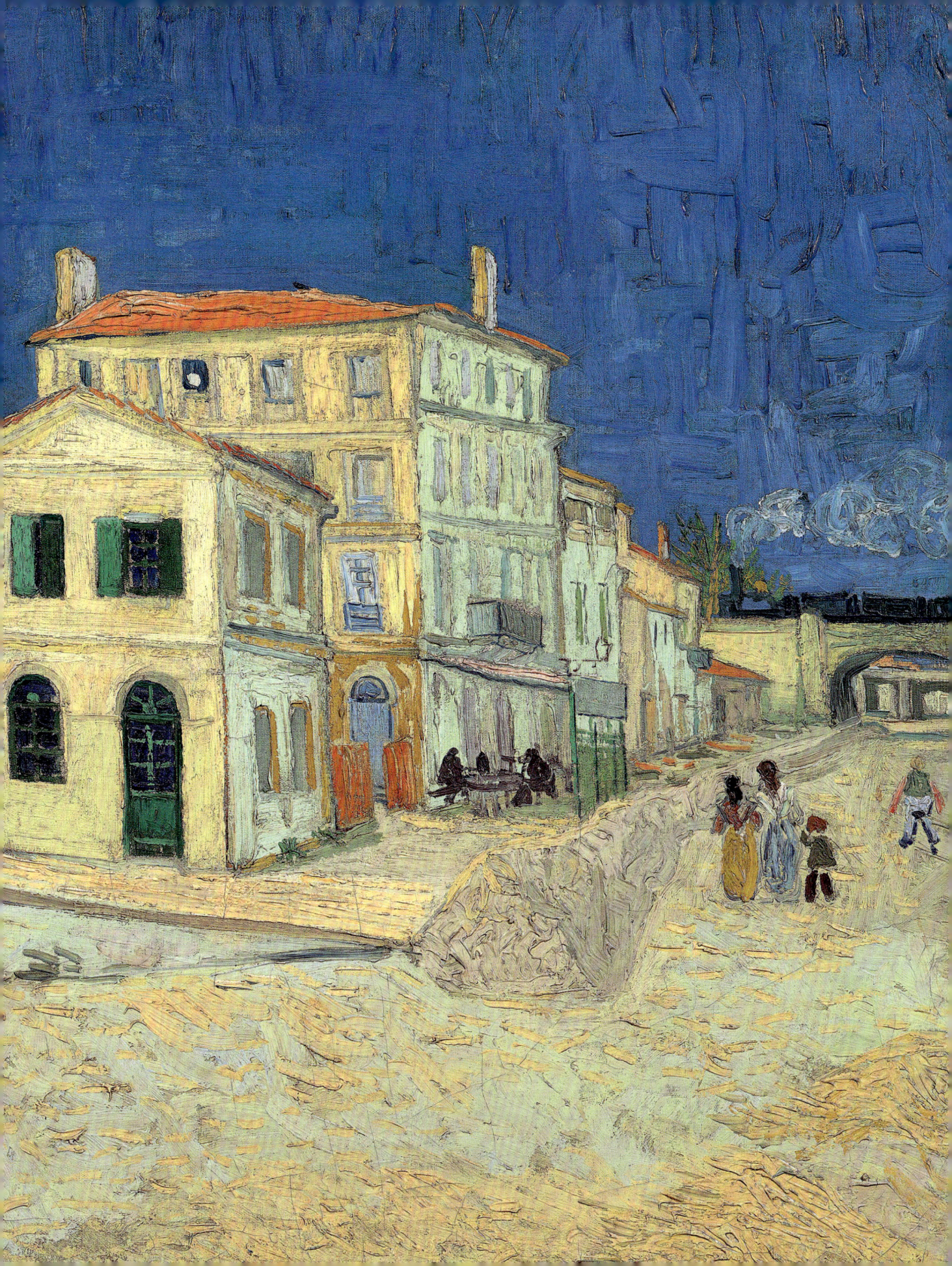

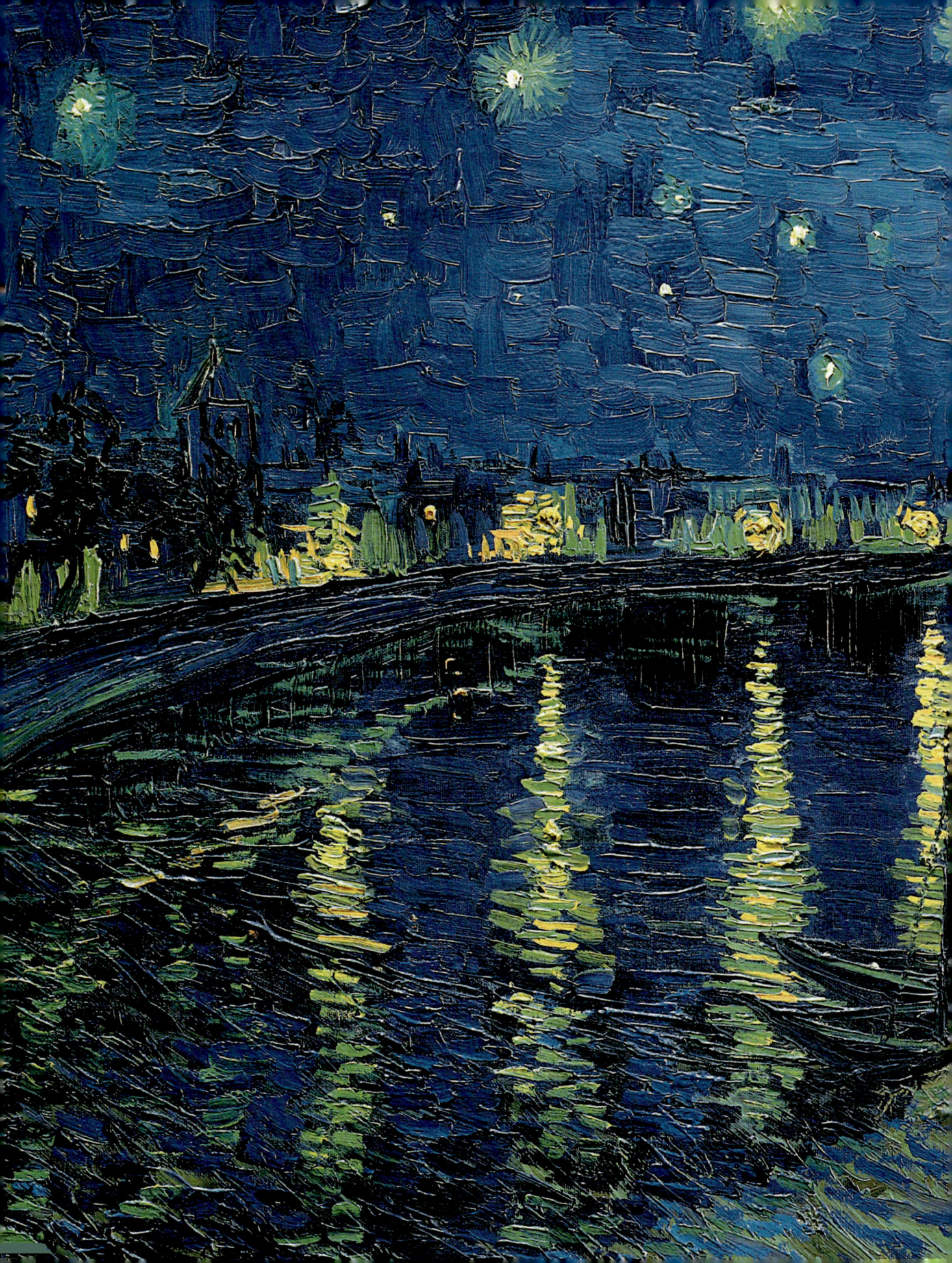

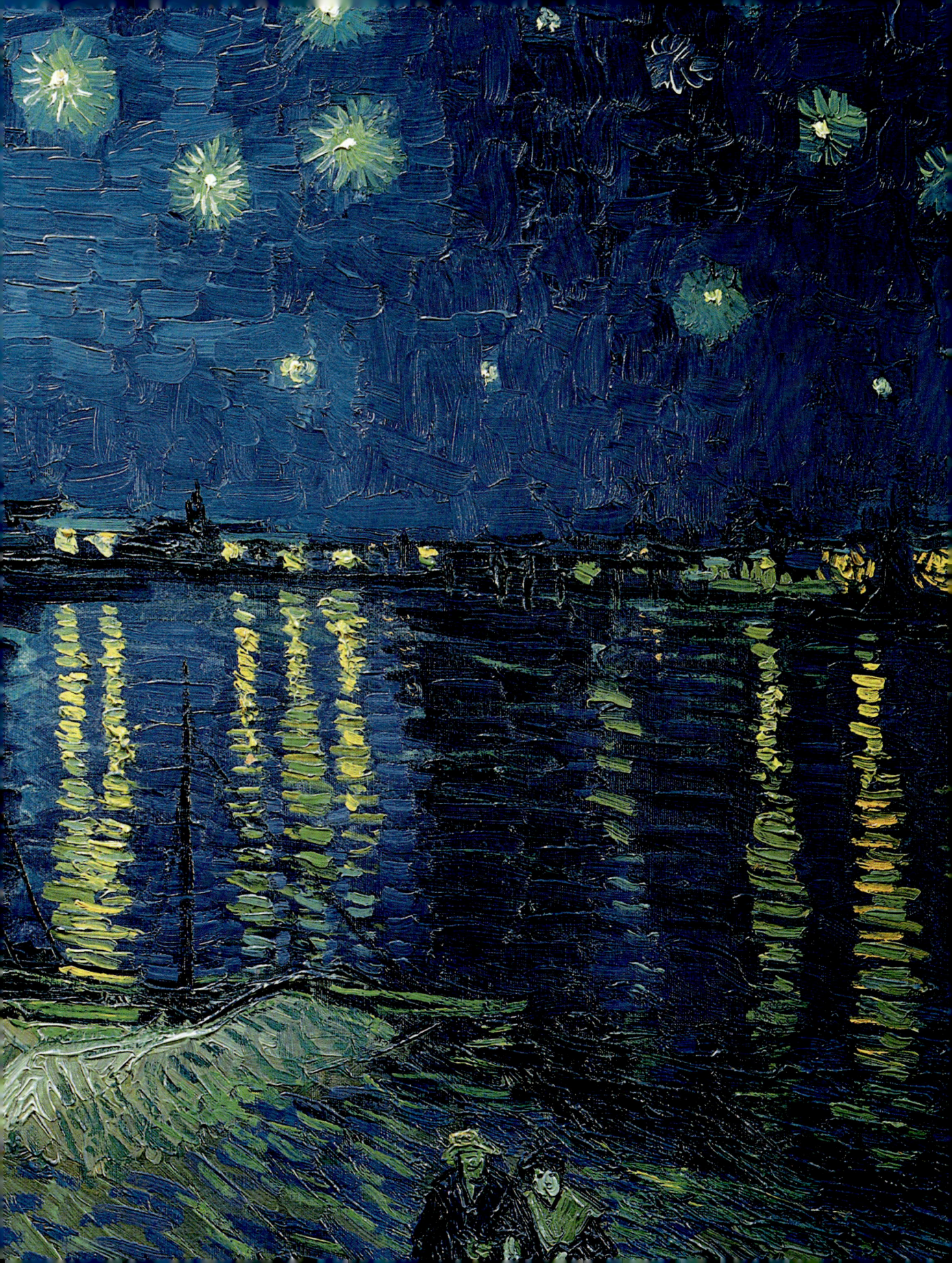

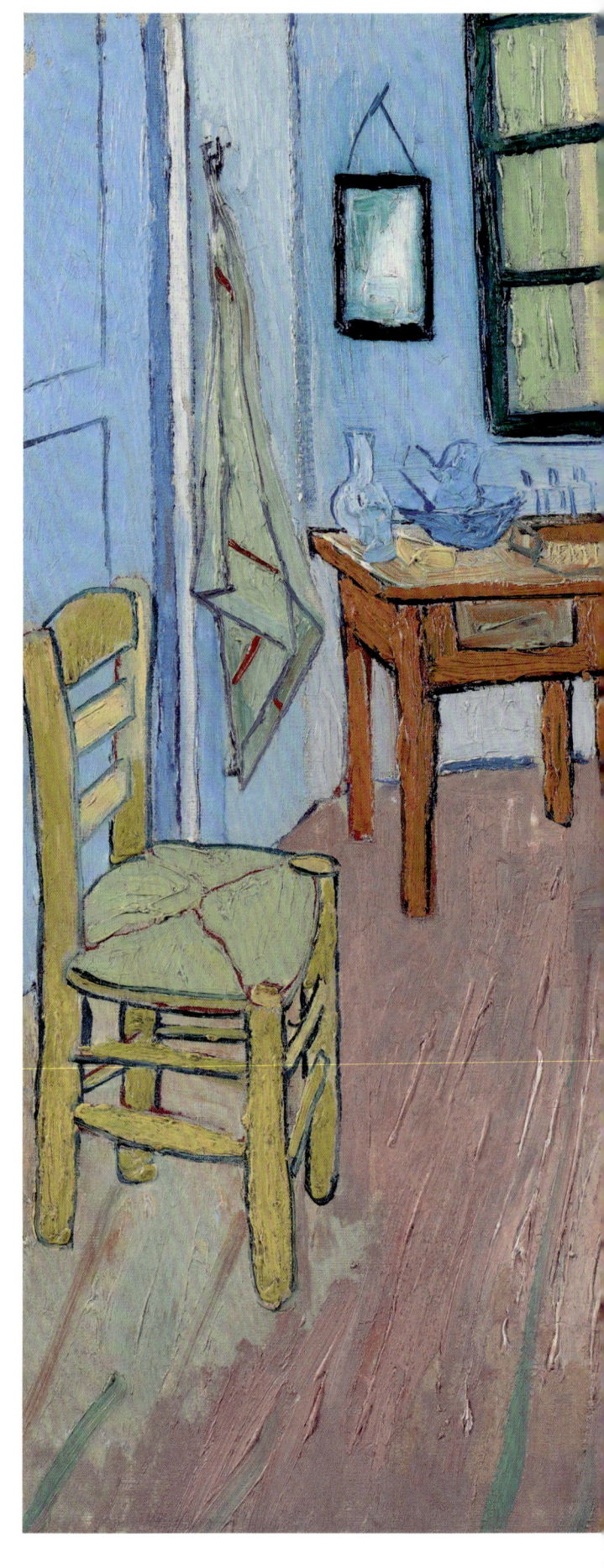

**Bedroom in Arles**

September 1889
(Reprise of the painting of October 1888)
Oil on canvas, 73.6 × 92.3 cm
Chicago, Art Institute of Chicago

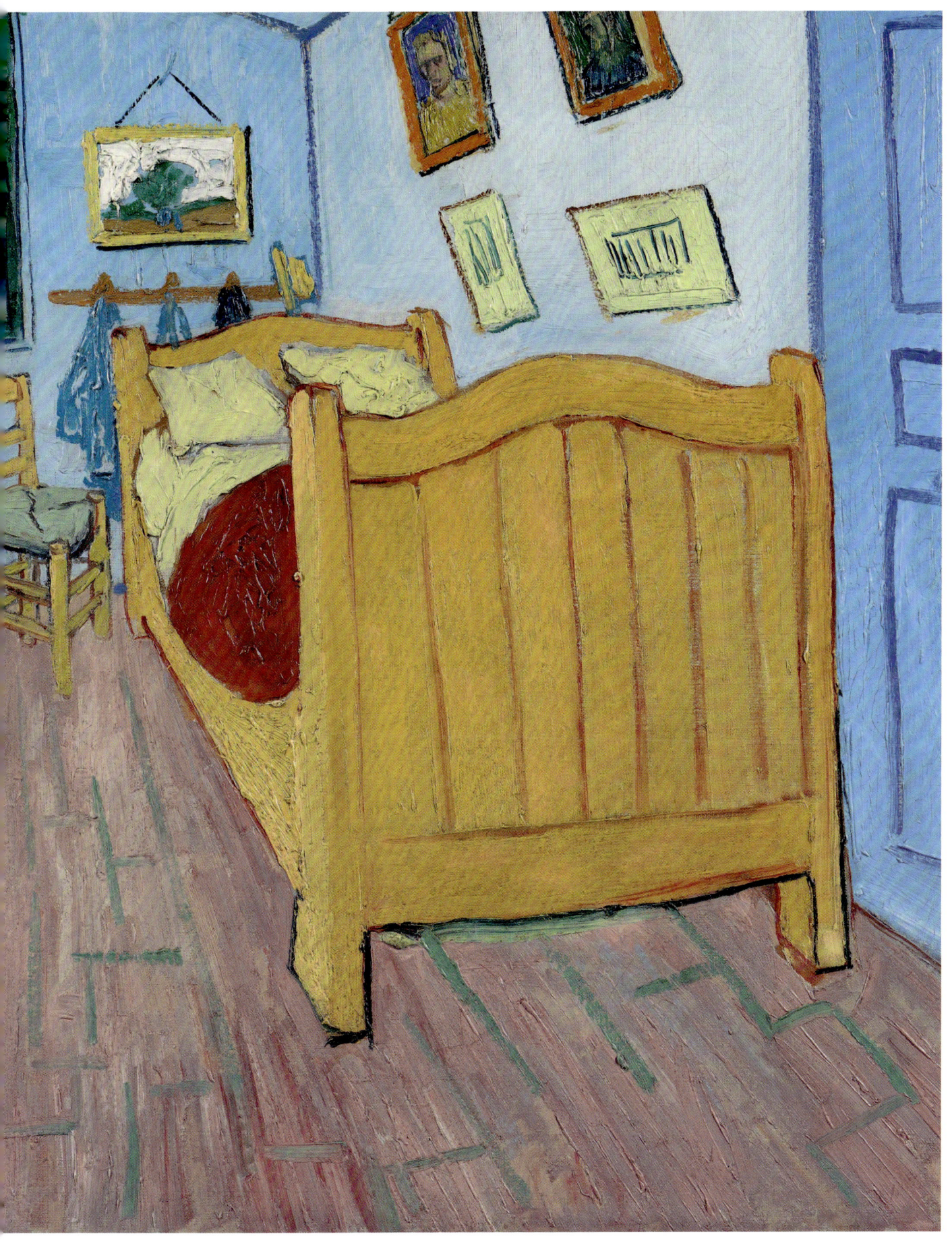

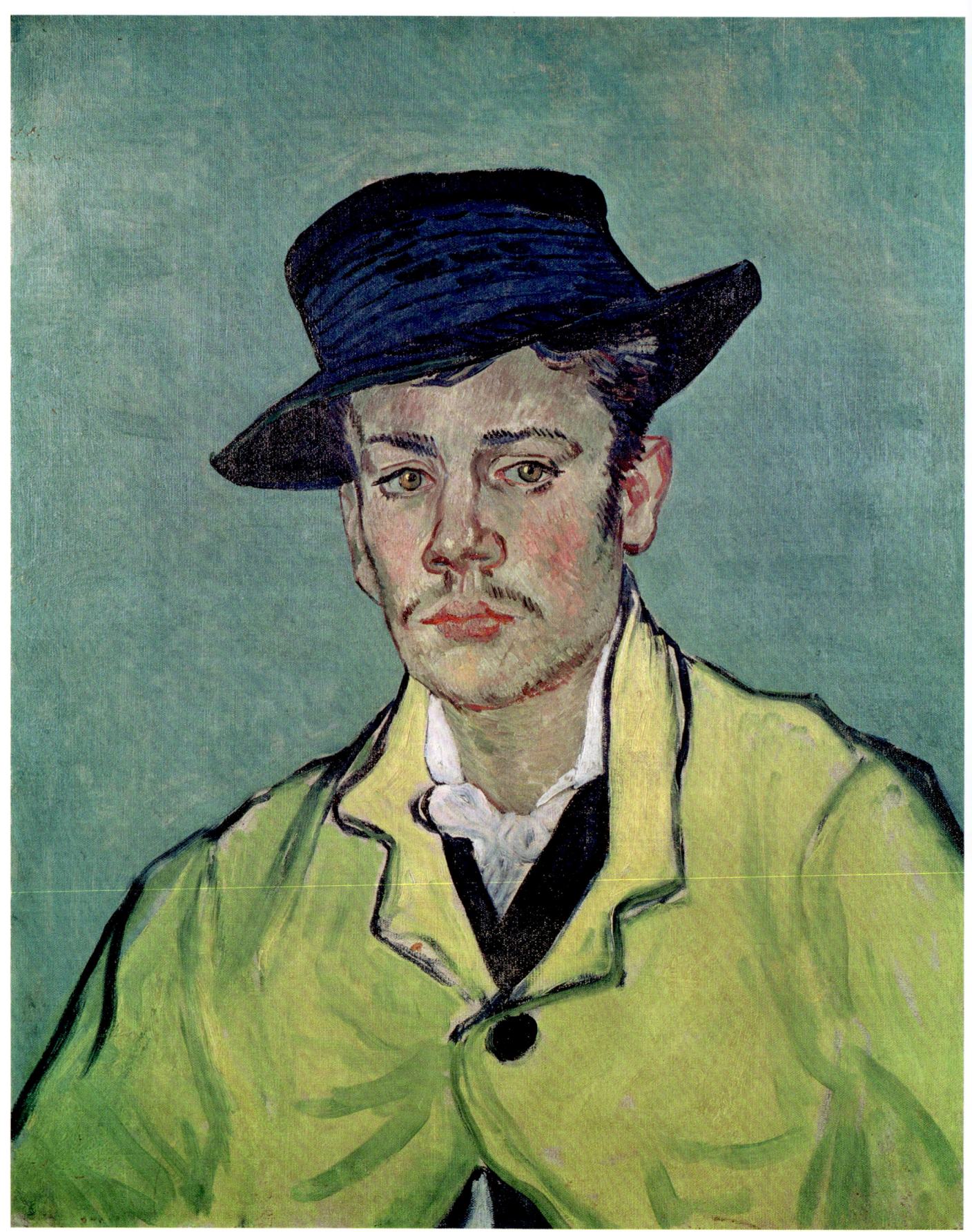

**Portrait of Armand Roulin,** December 1888, oil on canvas, 65 × 54.1 cm, Essen, Folkwang Museum

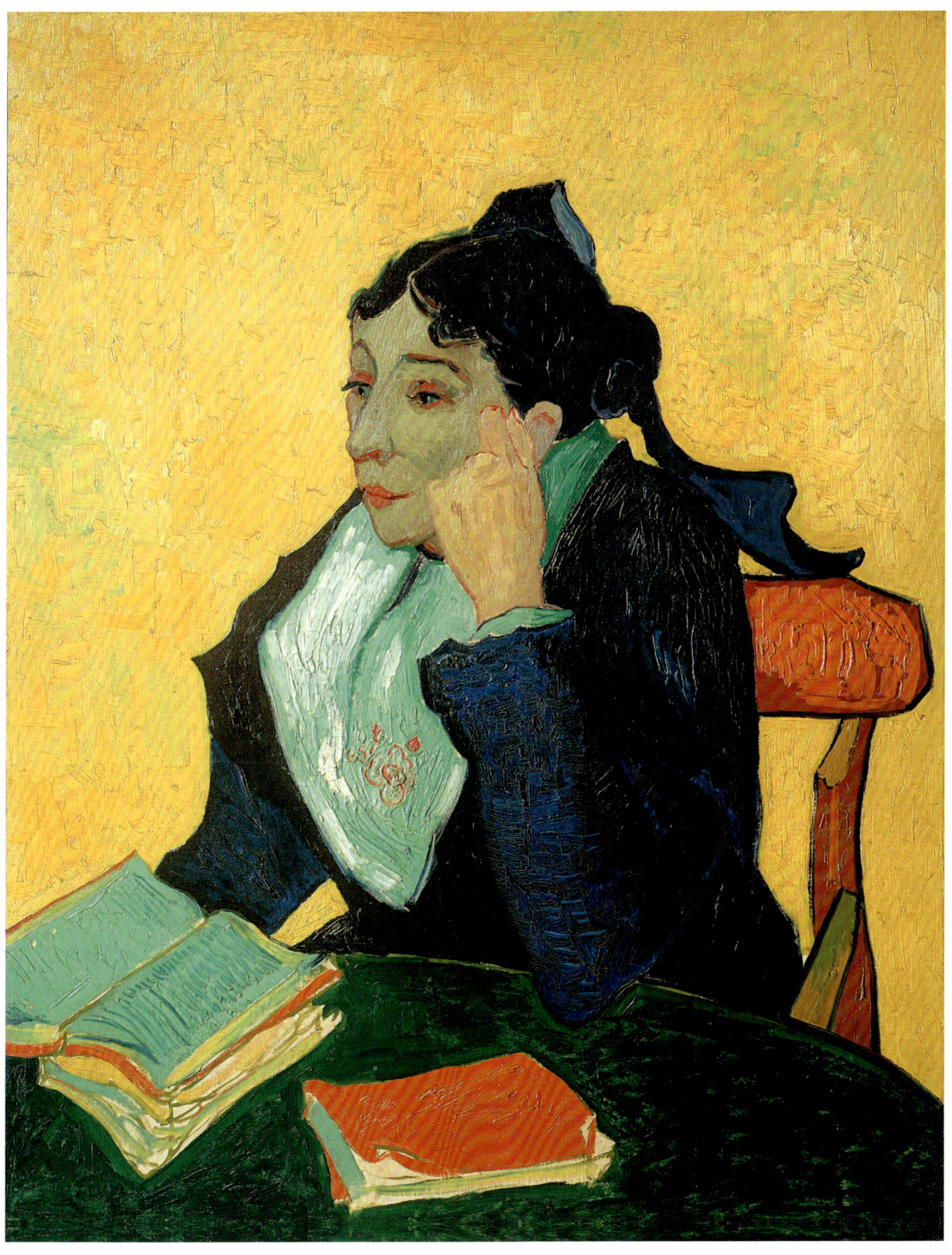

**L'Arlésienne (Madame Ginoux),** November 1888, oil on canvas, 91.4 × 73.7 cm, New York, The Metropolitan Museum of Art

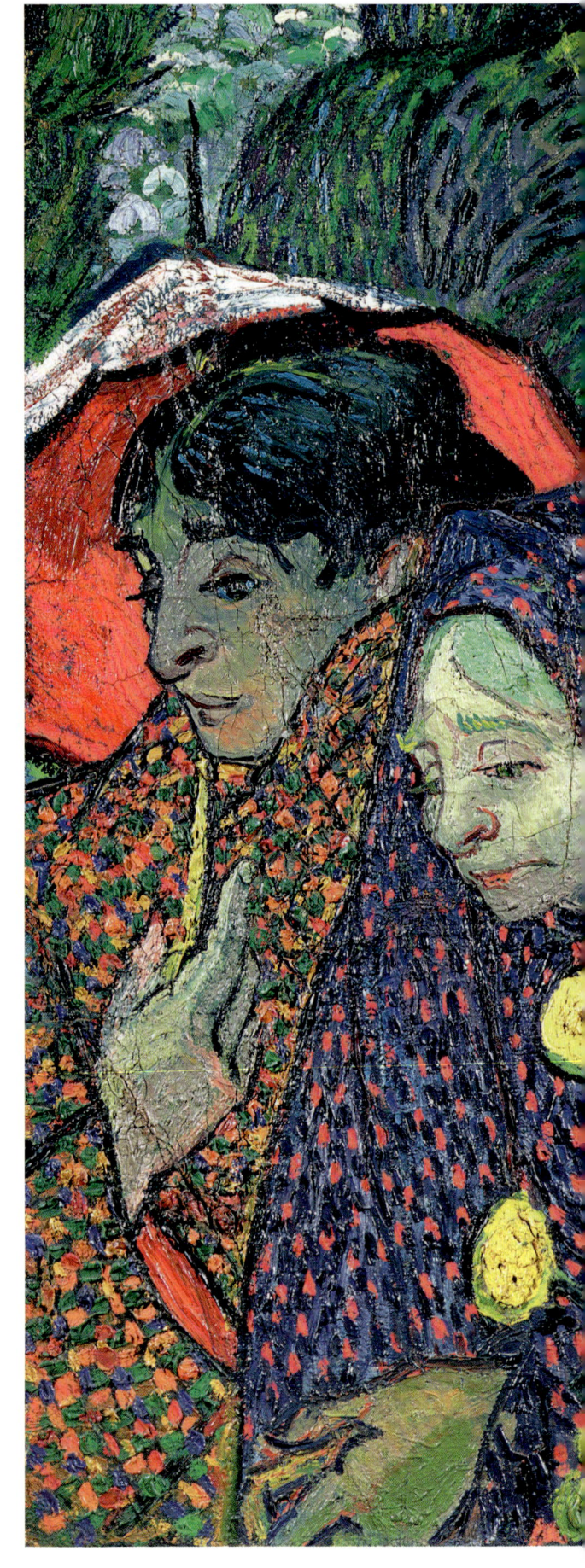

**Memory of the Garden at Etten**

November 1888
Oil on canvas, 73.5 × 92.5 cm
Saint Petersburg, State Hermitage
Museum

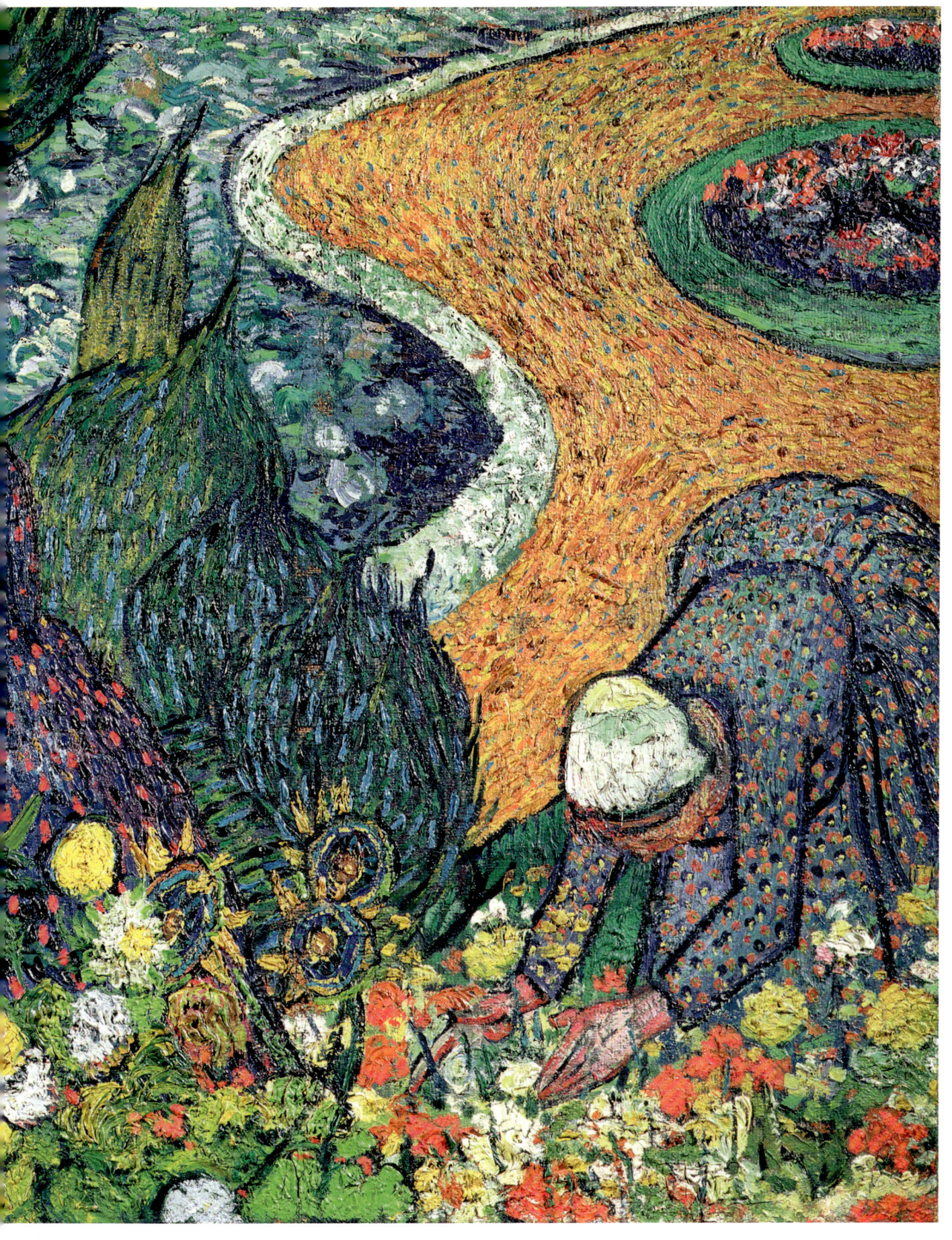

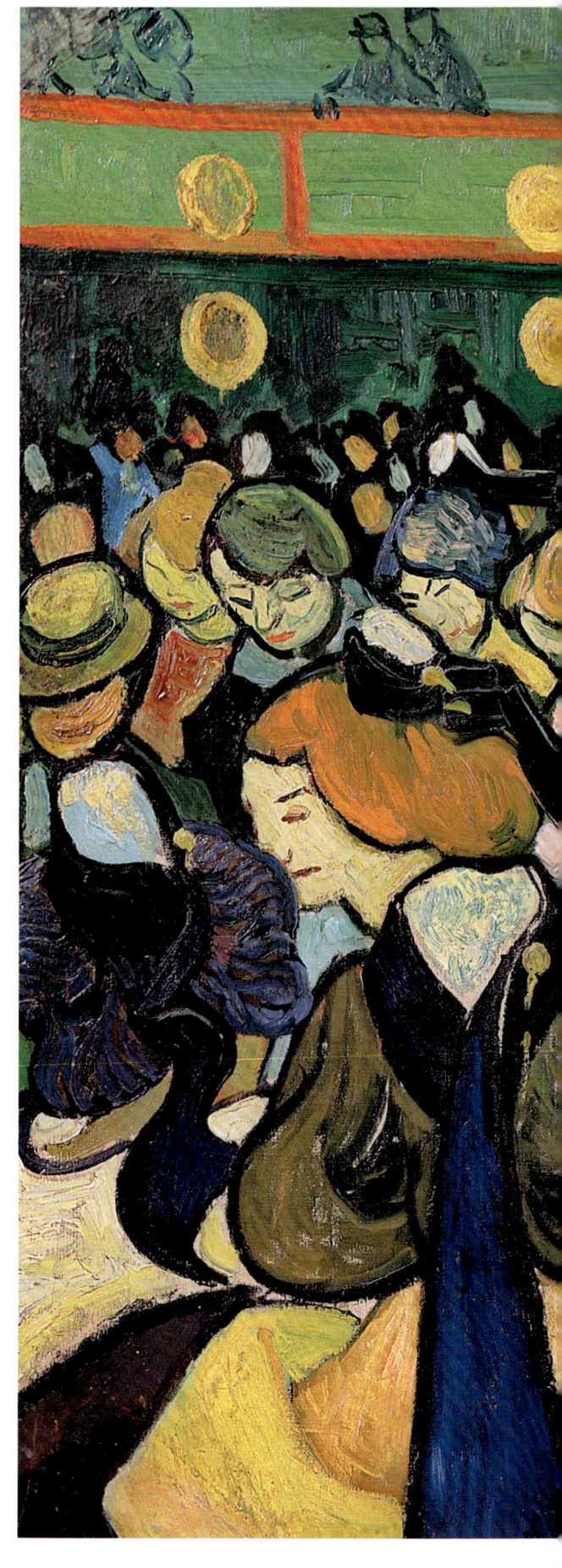

**The Dance Hall in Arles**

December 1888
Oil on canvas, 65 × 81 cm
Paris, Musée d'Orsay

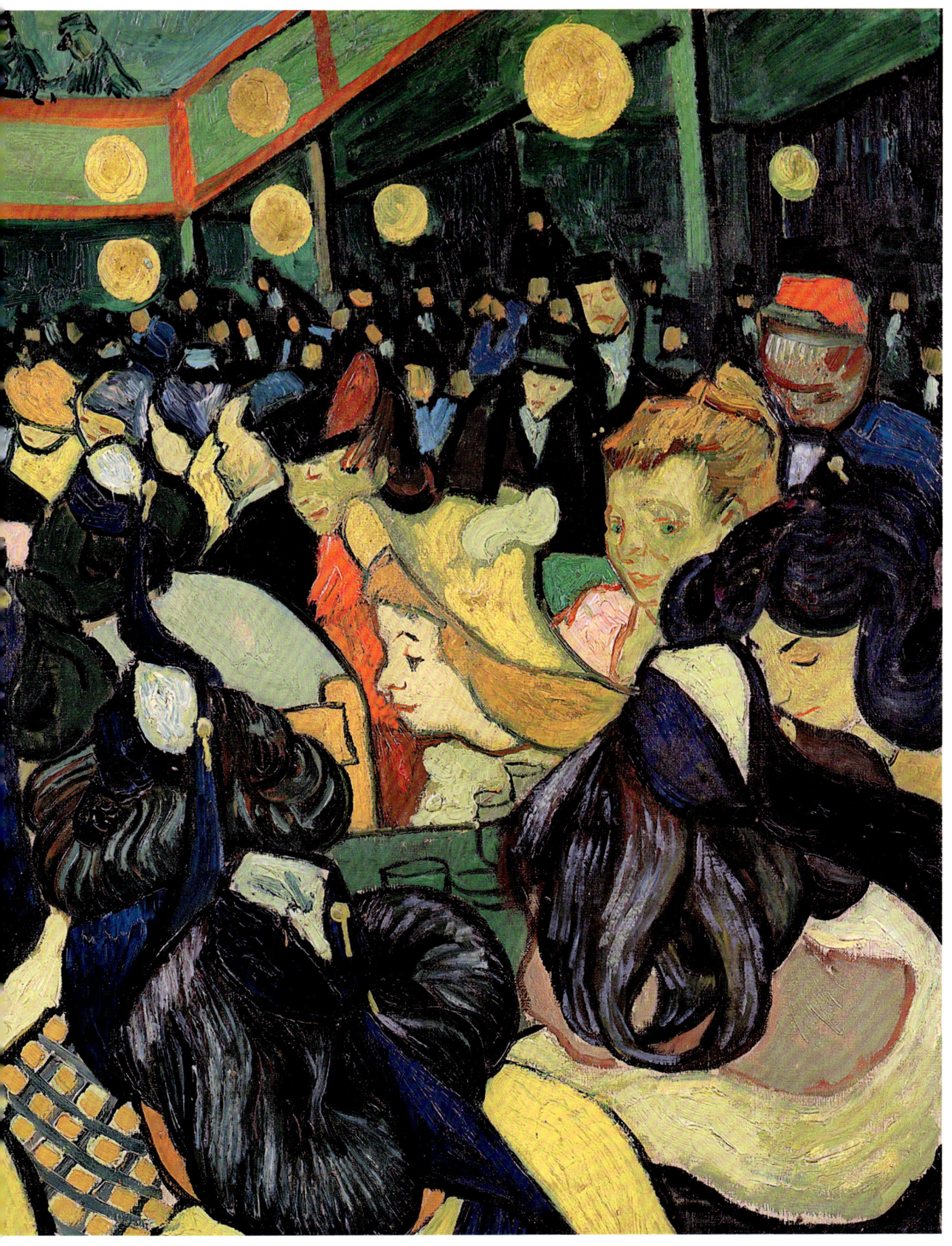

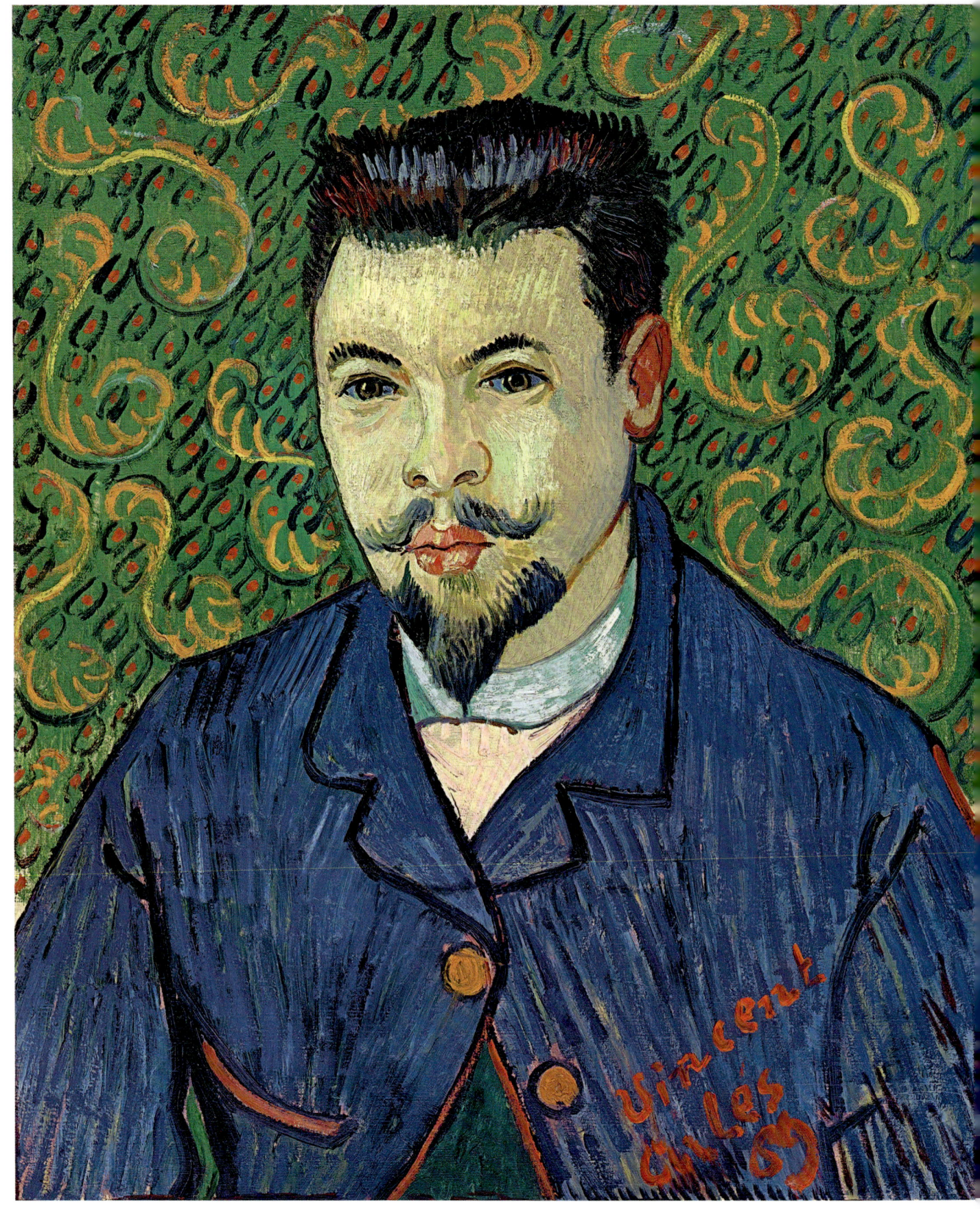

**Portrait of Doctor Félix Rey,** January 1889, oil on canvas, 64 × 53 cm, Moscow, Pushkin Museum

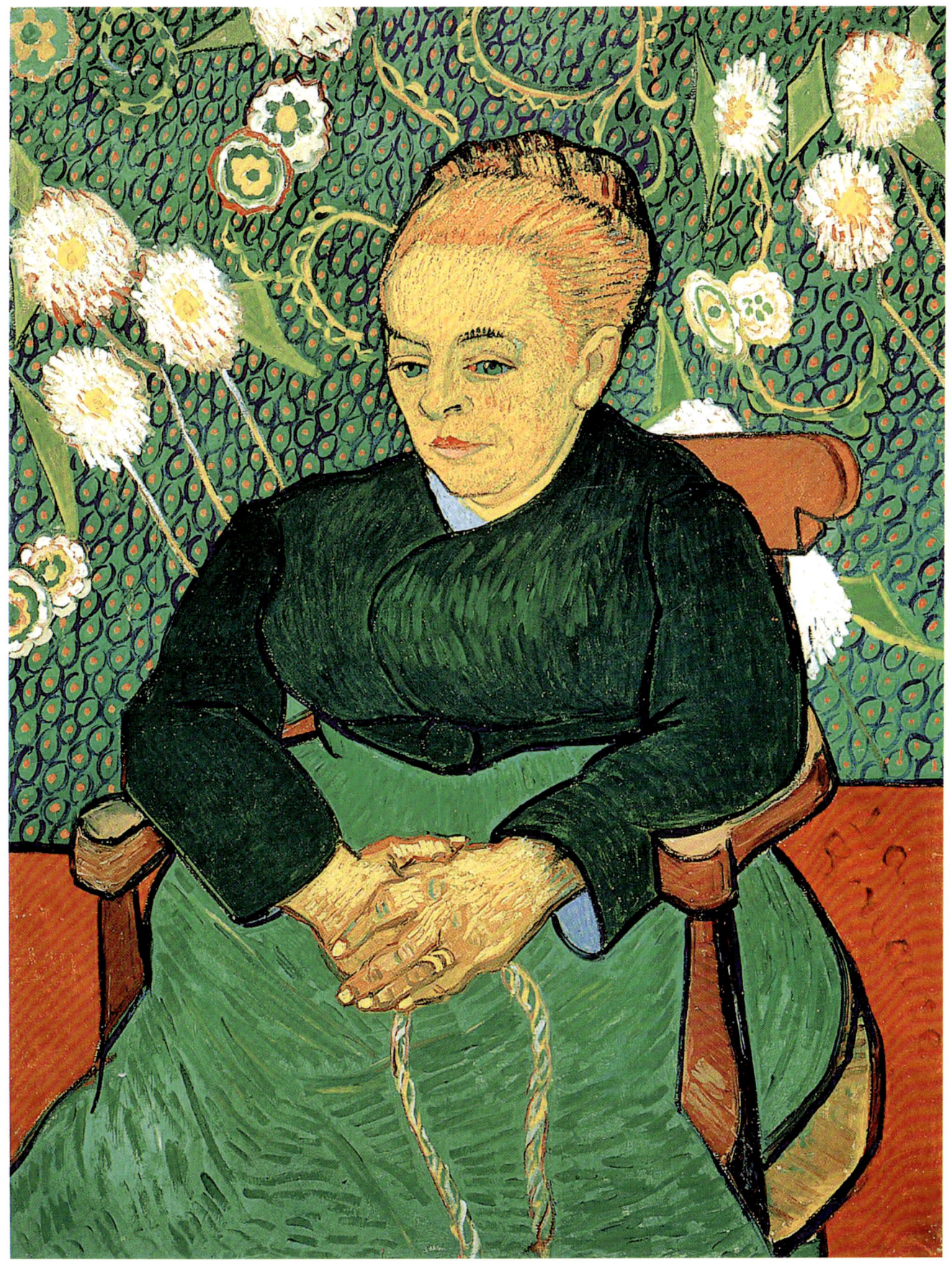

**Madame Augustine Roulin Rocking a Cradle (La Berceuse),** January 1889, oil on canvas, 92 × 73 cm, Boston, Museum of Fine Arts

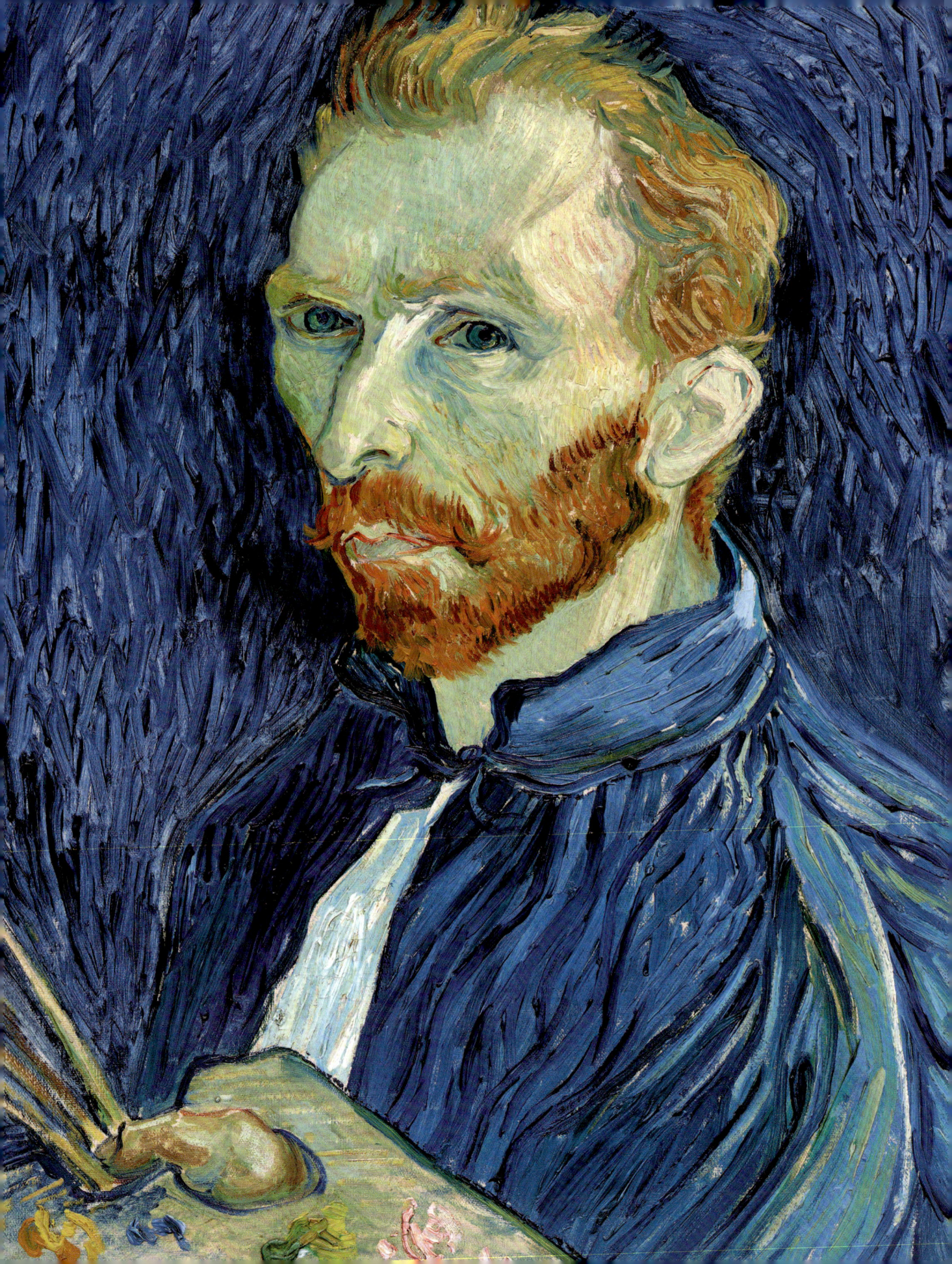

# Saint-Rémy

## To the point of vertigo

Following the tragic episode in Arles, which revealed his illness, Van Gogh spent a year in the Saint-Paul-de-Mausole hospice, in Saint-Rémy-de-Provence, undergoing treatment. During his stay, he was beset by violent crises, during which he fell prey to hallucinations, terrors and prostration; these alternated with periods of calm and lucidity, during which he worked with impressive enthusiasm. He found his first motifs, which he treated in numerous versions, within the asylum itself (p. 104), where he was allowed to convert a room into a studio, and in the surrounding gardens (pp. 94-95), which were unkempt and overgrown with bushes, pines, cypresses (p. 96) and beds of irises (p. 88 and foldout). His bedroom window overlooked a field of wheat, which he painted several times (pp. 92-93).

From June onwards, Vincent was allowed to leave the hospice; he would, however, be accompanied by a guard, as he had already attempted suicide. He roamed the surrounding countryside, painting paths, undergrowth and work in the fields, and soon set his sights on three motifs, in the form of a series: olive trees, cypresses and mountains. "[...] At best, it will form a kind of ensemble, 'Impressions of Provence'," he wrote to Theo.

However, only the series of olive trees would be completed (pp. 90-91); indeed, Van Gogh felt a particular fascination for their changing colour: "They are old silver, sometimes with more blue in them, sometimes greenish, bronzed, fading white above a soil that is yellow, pink, violet-tinted or orange, to dull red ochre." As for the cypress trees, which he described as "beautiful as regards lines and proportions, like an Egyptian obelisk", he loved their tall, black, undulating silhouettes. In his paintings, they stand out like a flame against the turbulent sky (pp. 86-87) or the blondness of a wheat field. The painter also represented the tip of a cypress tree in his famous *Starry Night* (foldout, p. 96), painted in June. Finally, after painting the flat horizons of the Crau, near Arles, Vincent discovered the Alpilles, near Saint-Rémy-de-Provence, in the autumn, where he painted some striking works (p. 89).

He was fascinated by the convulsions of nature, and particularly by stormy clouds, ravines, tumultuous wheat fields, tortured trees; he sought to translate their intense forms using new pictorial techniques reminiscent of the Expressionism of his apprenticeship years. The crosshatching of the Arles period gave way to a violent touch, a dramatisation of lines that Van Gogh imbued with a powerful rhythm, to the point that Theo was struck by it:

"You endangered yourself to the extreme point, where vertigo is inevitable." In July, another crisis forced Van Gogh to be confined to a hospice; however, he considered painting to be his "best lightning rod for [his] illness", soon recovered enough energy to work. Deprived of exterior motifs, he produced replicas of some of his paintings, such as his room in Arles (pp. 72-73), before embarking on a small series of self-portraits (p. 82). These emaciated faces, with their intense gazes, reflect all the suffering contained within him, which he felt was never-ending. Searching for other models, he obtained consent from the hospice's chief supervisor, Charles-Elzéard Trabuc (p. 97), as well as his wife. And to alleviate his boredom, Van Gogh copied engravings by masters he admired: Rembrandt Van Rijn, Eugène Delacroix, and always Jean-François Millet (pp. 102-103). "[...] And then I improvise colour on it but, being me, not completely, of course, but seeking memories of their paintings [...] I find that it teaches and, above all, sometimes consoles.

So then my brush goes between my fingers as a bow would on the violin, absolutely to my pleasure."

In October, the painter was finally allowed to leave the asylum two or three times a week, always under supervision. He returned to depicting landscapes, cypresses and mountains, painted workers picking olives and peasant women digging, and also made a few forays into the city (*The Large Plane Trees (Road Menders at Saint-Rémy)*, pp. 98-99). Winter soon set in, and Van Gogh felt bored to death in this gloomy hospice, where the sick depressed him; however, he consoled himself by copying the works of Jean-François Millet, Honoré Daumier and Gustave Doré (p. 105). In the meantime, Theo worked hard to arrange for him to move closer, aided by Camille Pissarro, who suggested that he meet Docteur Gachet, a friend of artists and a painter himself, who lived in Auvers-sur-Oise. On February 1st, Theo told him that his wife had just given birth to a son, named Vincent. The painter immediately set to work, celebrating the event with a painting of an almond blossom (foldout, p. 112). Around the same time, his brother sent him an article published in the literary magazine *Mercure de France* by the art critic Albert Aurier, who praised his "strange, intensive and feverish" works and his "profound, almost childlike sincerity". That same year, in 1890, ten of Van Gogh's paintings were exhibited at the Salon des Indépendants in Paris, and in Brussels, the Cercle des XX, a group of avant-garde artists, presented six of his paintings at its annual exhibition.

Reviews were very divided, and sometimes violently hostile; one of his works, however, *The Red Vineyard,* was acquired by Anna Boch, a member of the group. A step forward had been taken, and Van Gogh no longer was completely unknown amidst artistic circles.

In late February, however, while he was visiting the Ginoux family in Arles, he was beset by a terrible crisis that lasted for two long months, during which he twice attempted to poison himself. At the end of this cruel ordeal, he felt the urgent need to leave the Midi. The painter had regained his lucidity and, refusing to be accompanied by anyone, took the train to Paris alone on 16 May 1890. A few days later, he would arrive in Auvers-sur-Oise.

**Self-portrait** (detail, p. 82)
1889, oil on canvas, 57.8 × 44.5 cm, Washington, National Gallery of Art

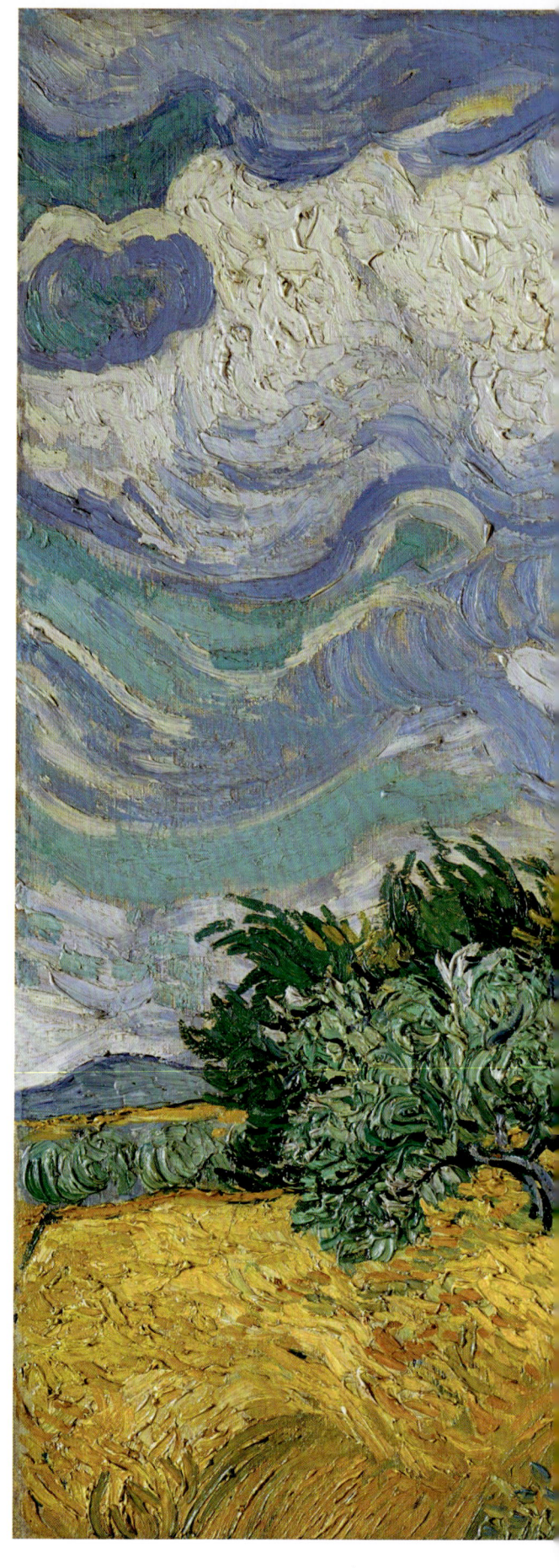

**Wheat Field with Cypresses**

Late June 1889
Oil on canvas, 73.2 × 93.4 cm
New York, The Metropolitan Museum of Art

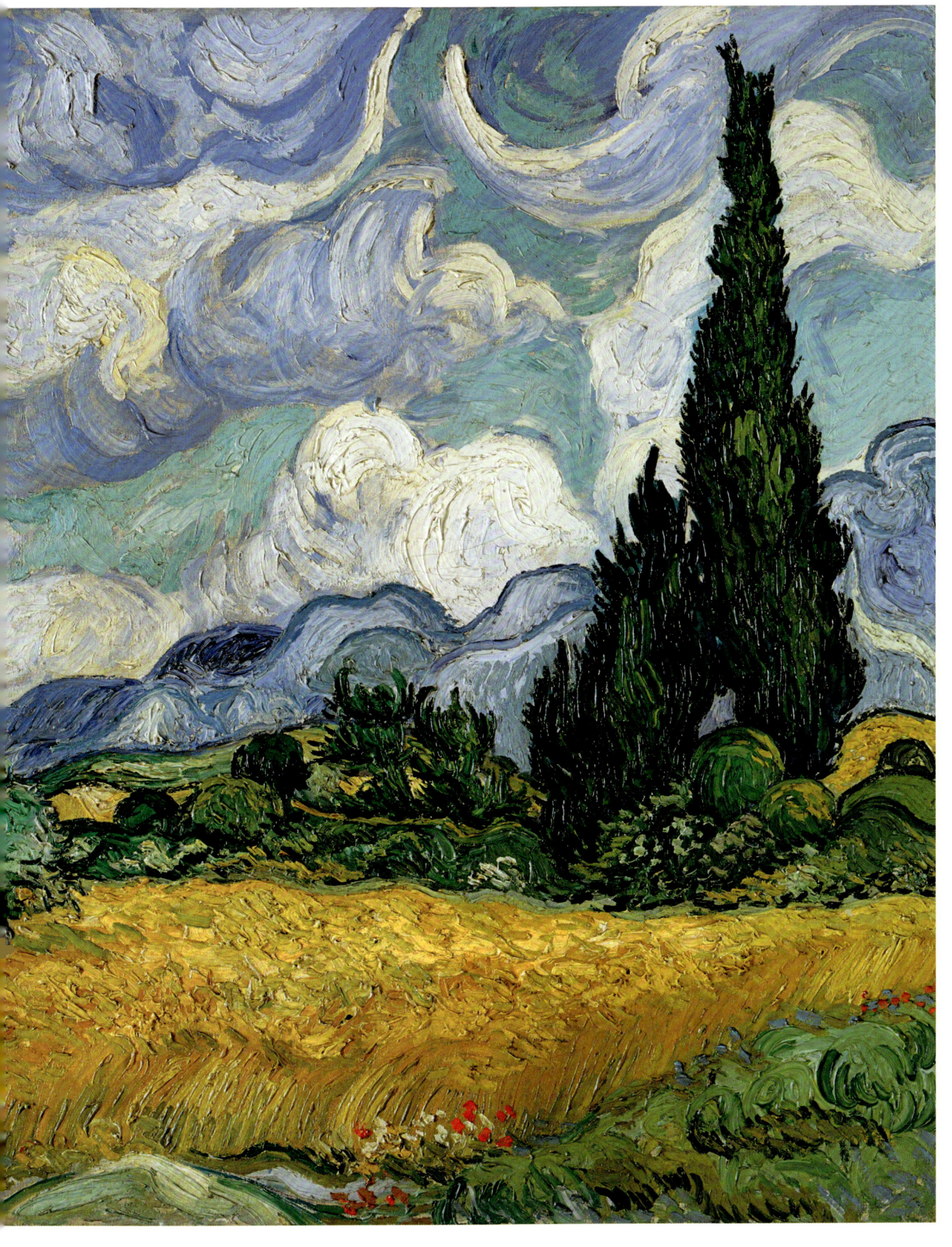

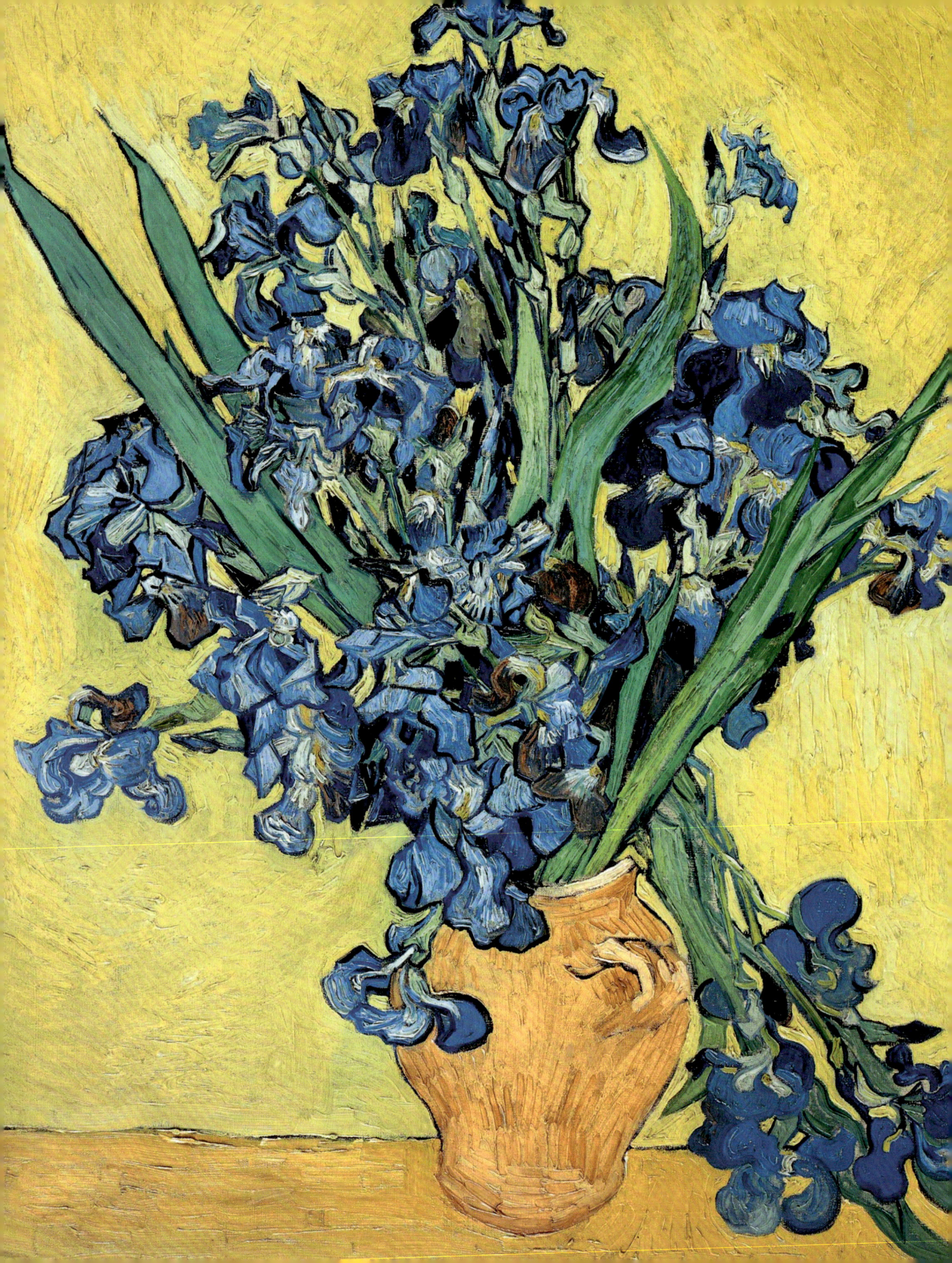

## Iris

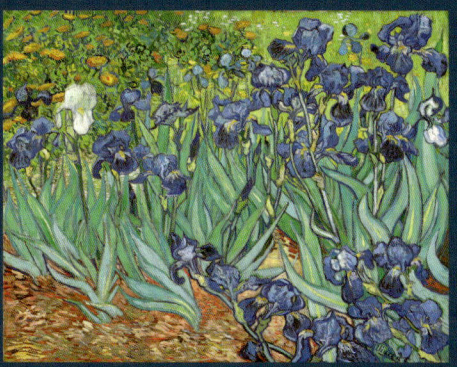

Interned at his request in Saint-Rémy-de Provence in 1889, Van Gogh was forbidden from leaving the hospital for the first few weeks. His subjects were therefore limited to the hospice and the vast gardens that surrounded it. The irises blooming in May provided the motif for this splendid painting, which depicts a tangle of leaves from which the violet flowers emerge, punctuated by the small yellow spot of the pistil. This was an opportunity for the artist to play on the harmony of complementary colours, thus accentuating the luminosity of the entire work.

To the left stands a single, majestic white iris. In the background, orange marigolds echo the ochre earth of the flowerbed. Although the artist considered this painting to be a mere study, his brother Theo immediately acknowledged its importance, and sent it to the annual art exhibition called the *Salon des indépendants* in September, along with *Starry Night Over the Rhône*. The first owner of this painting of irises was the writer and art critic Octave Mirbeau, who also acquired one of the *Sunflowers* at the same time.

*Iris*, 1889, oil on canvas, 71 × 93 cm, Los Angeles, J. Paul Getty Museum
*Irises*, May 1890, oil on canvas, 92.7 × 73.9 cm, Amsterdam, Van Gogh Museum (left, detail)

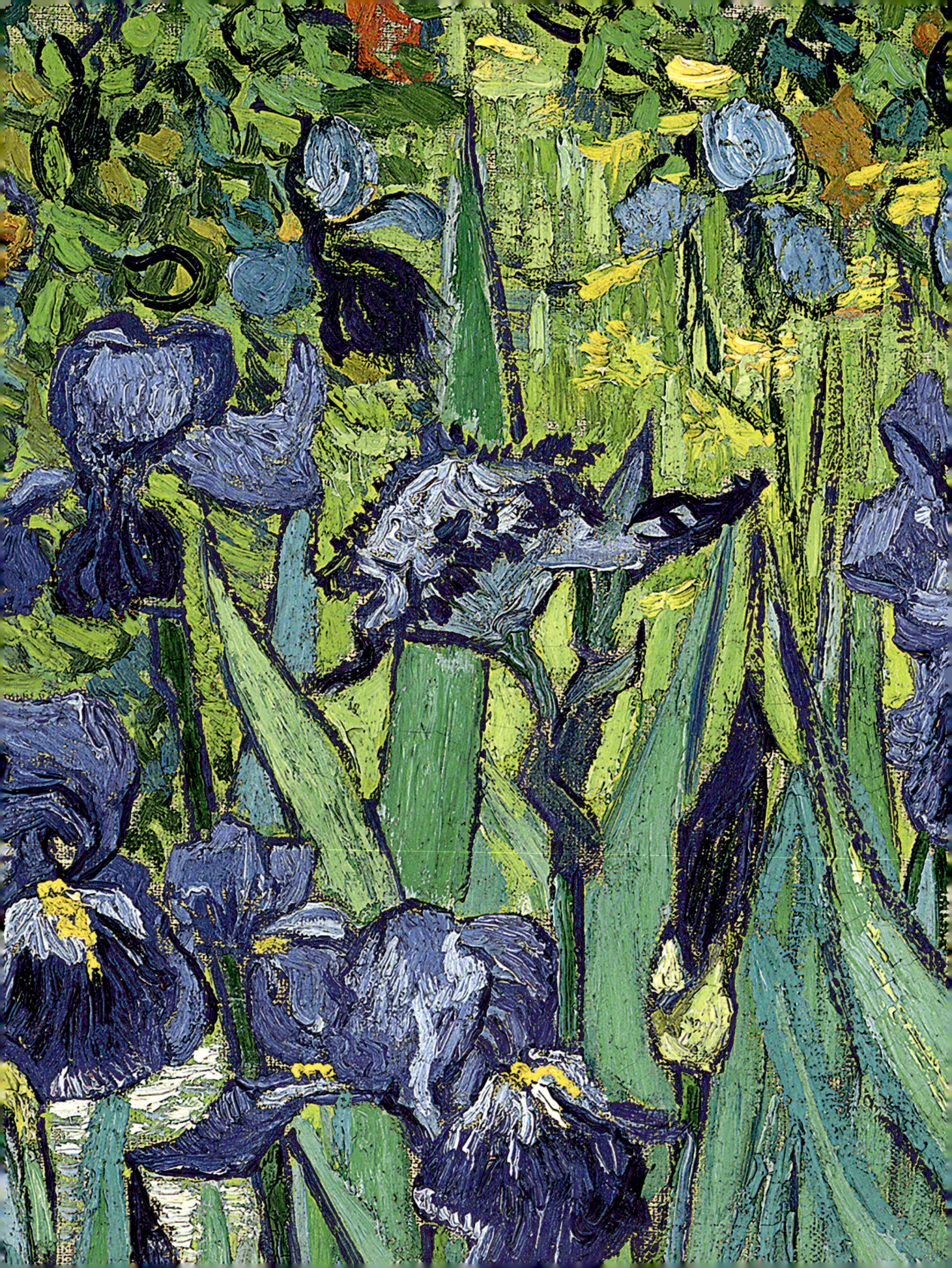

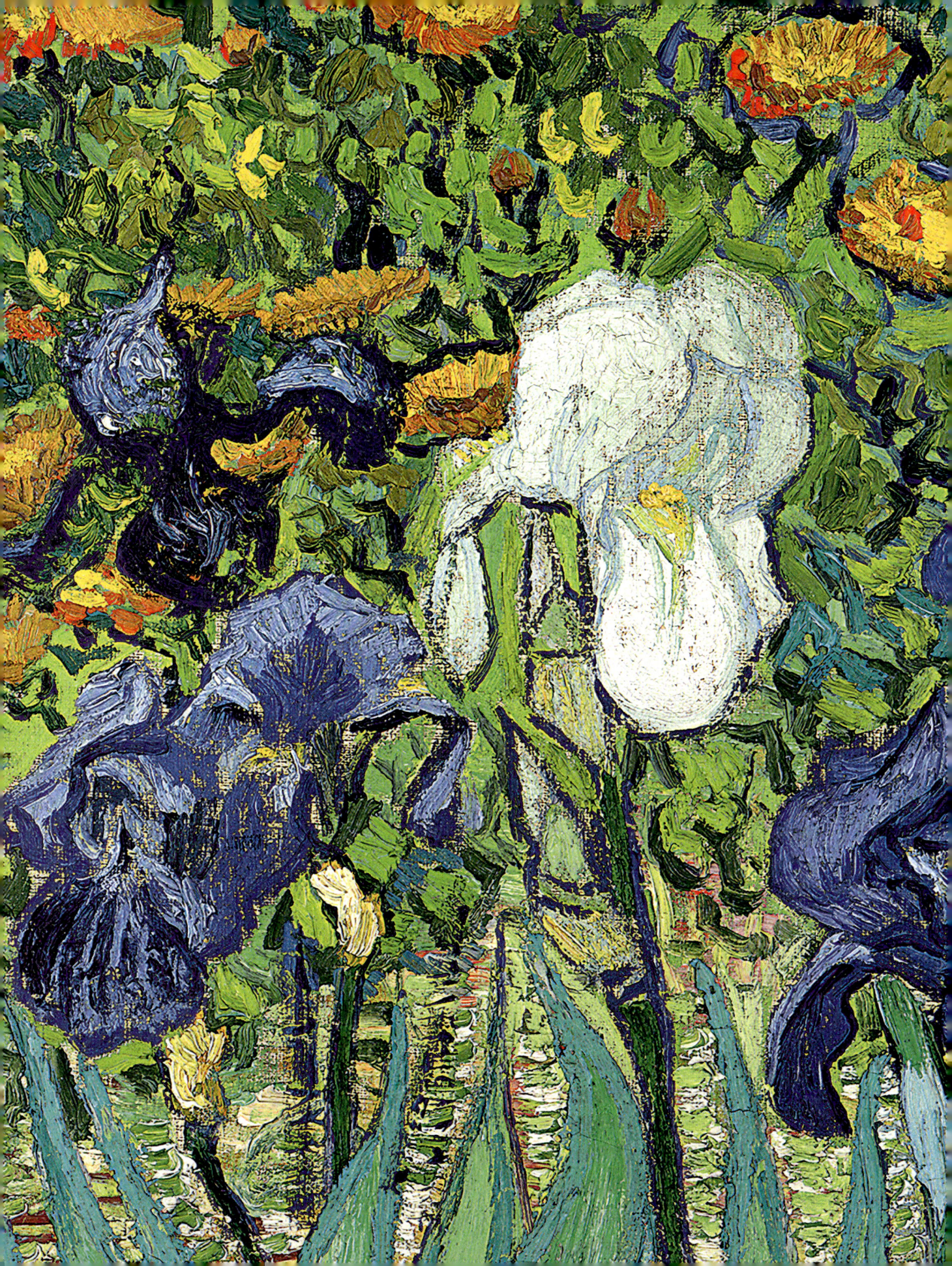

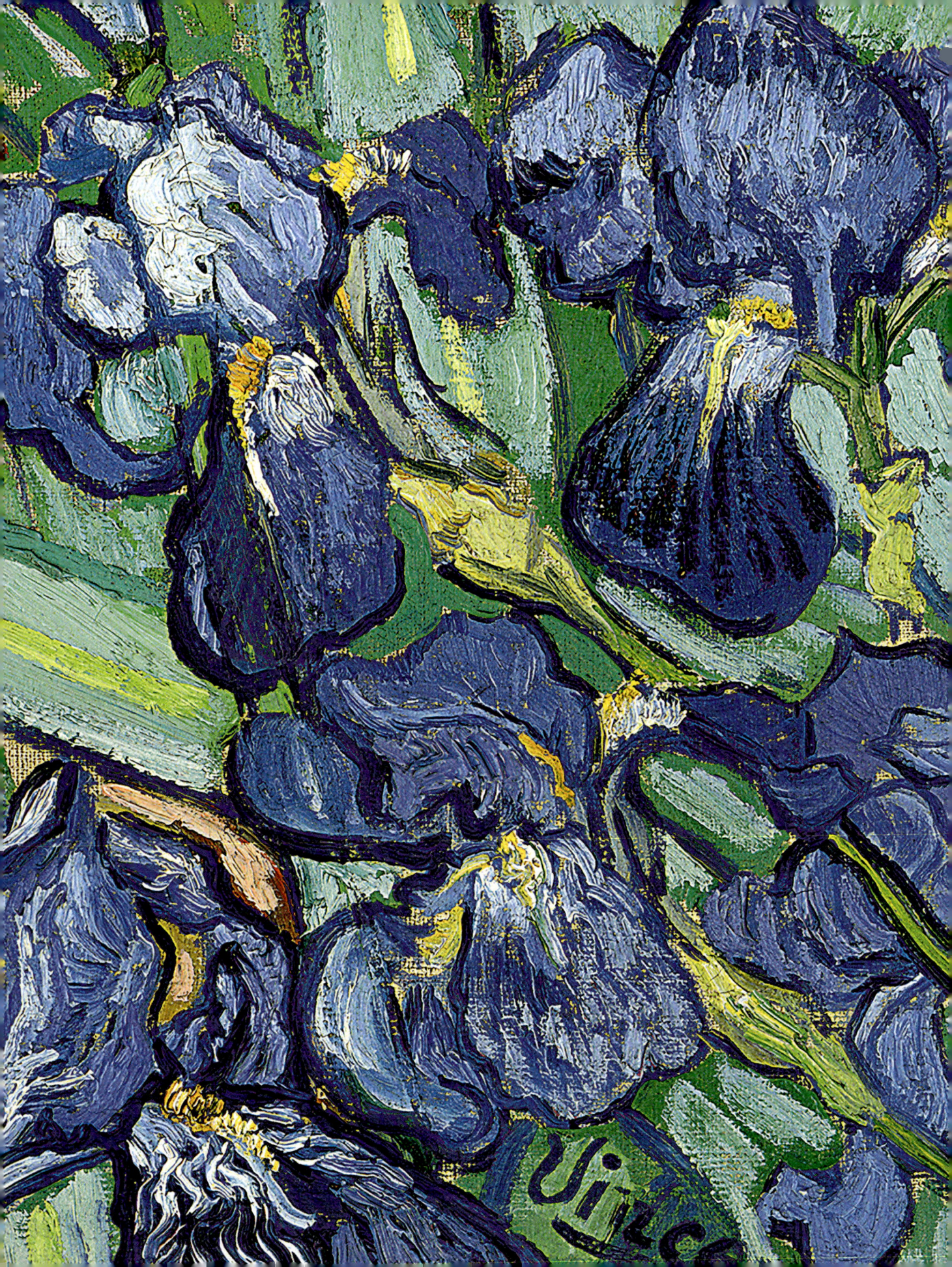

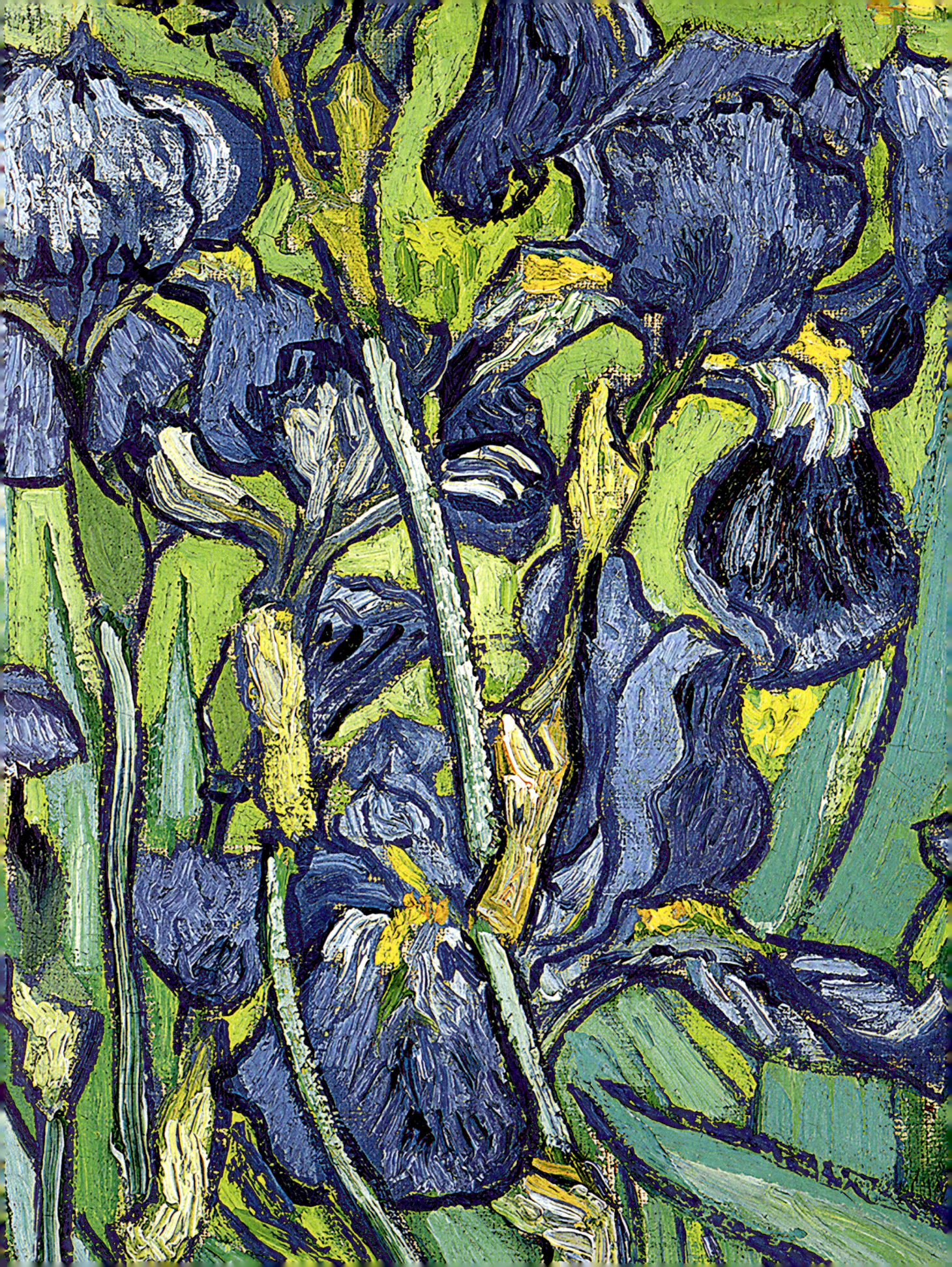

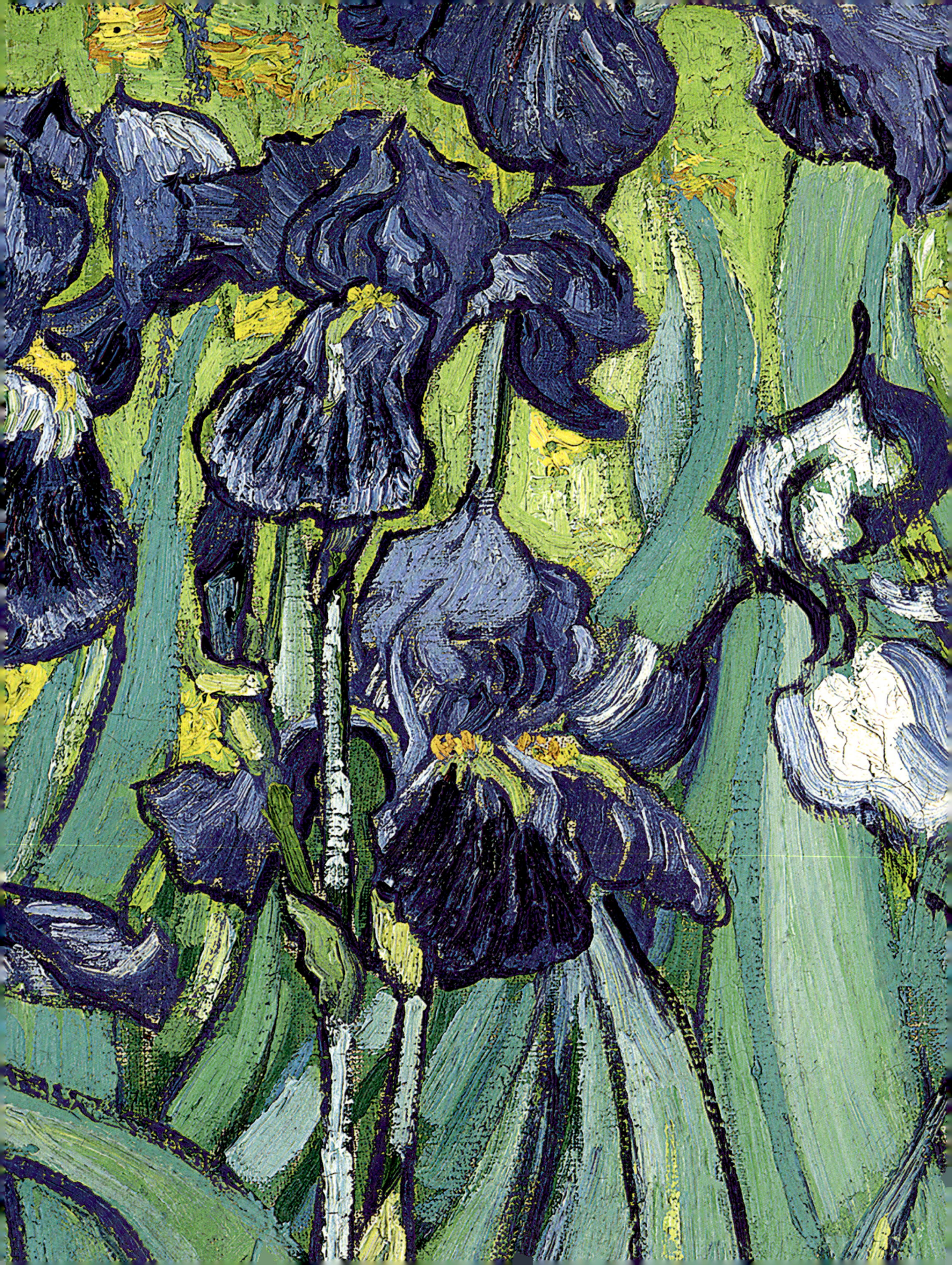

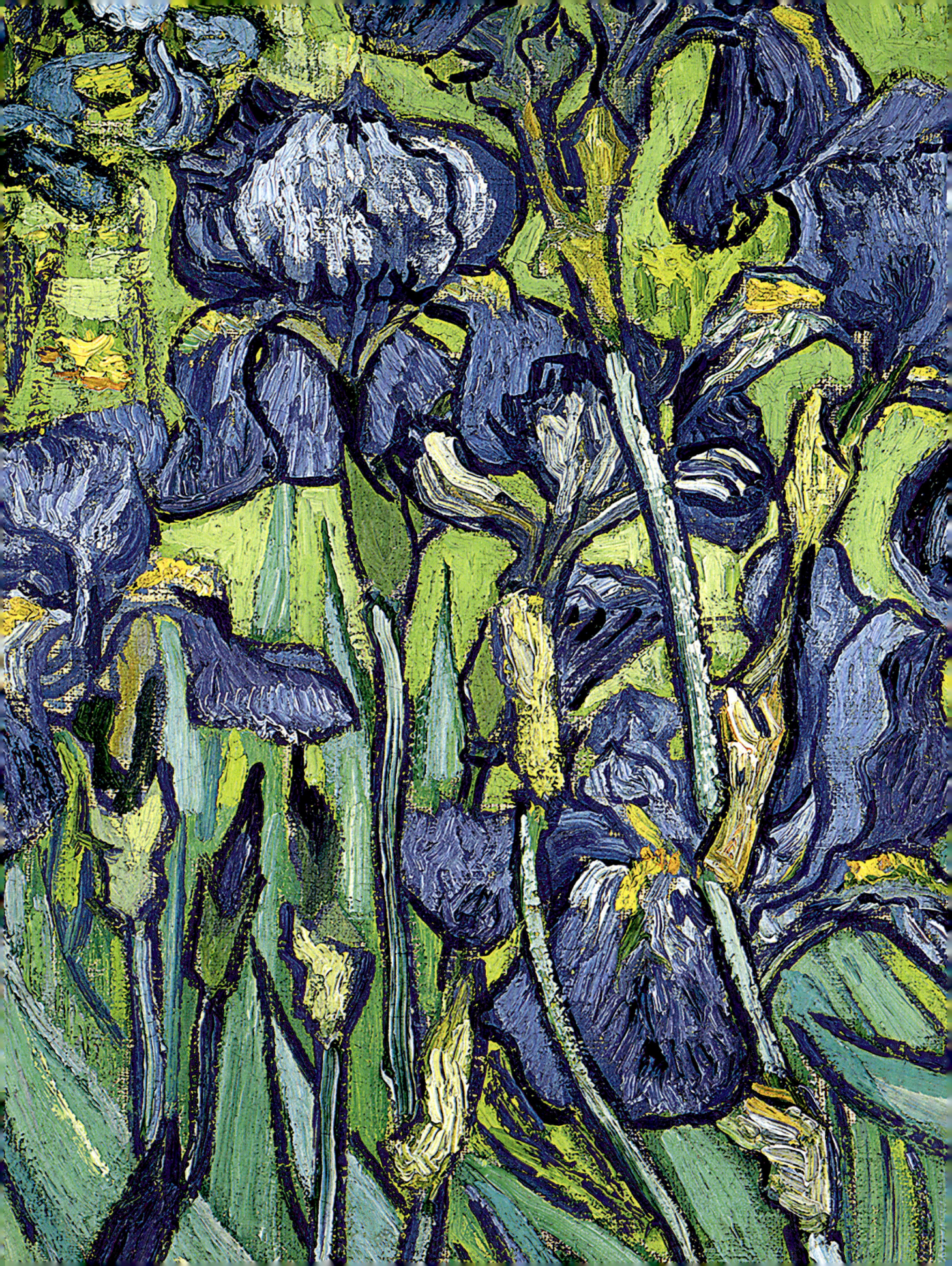

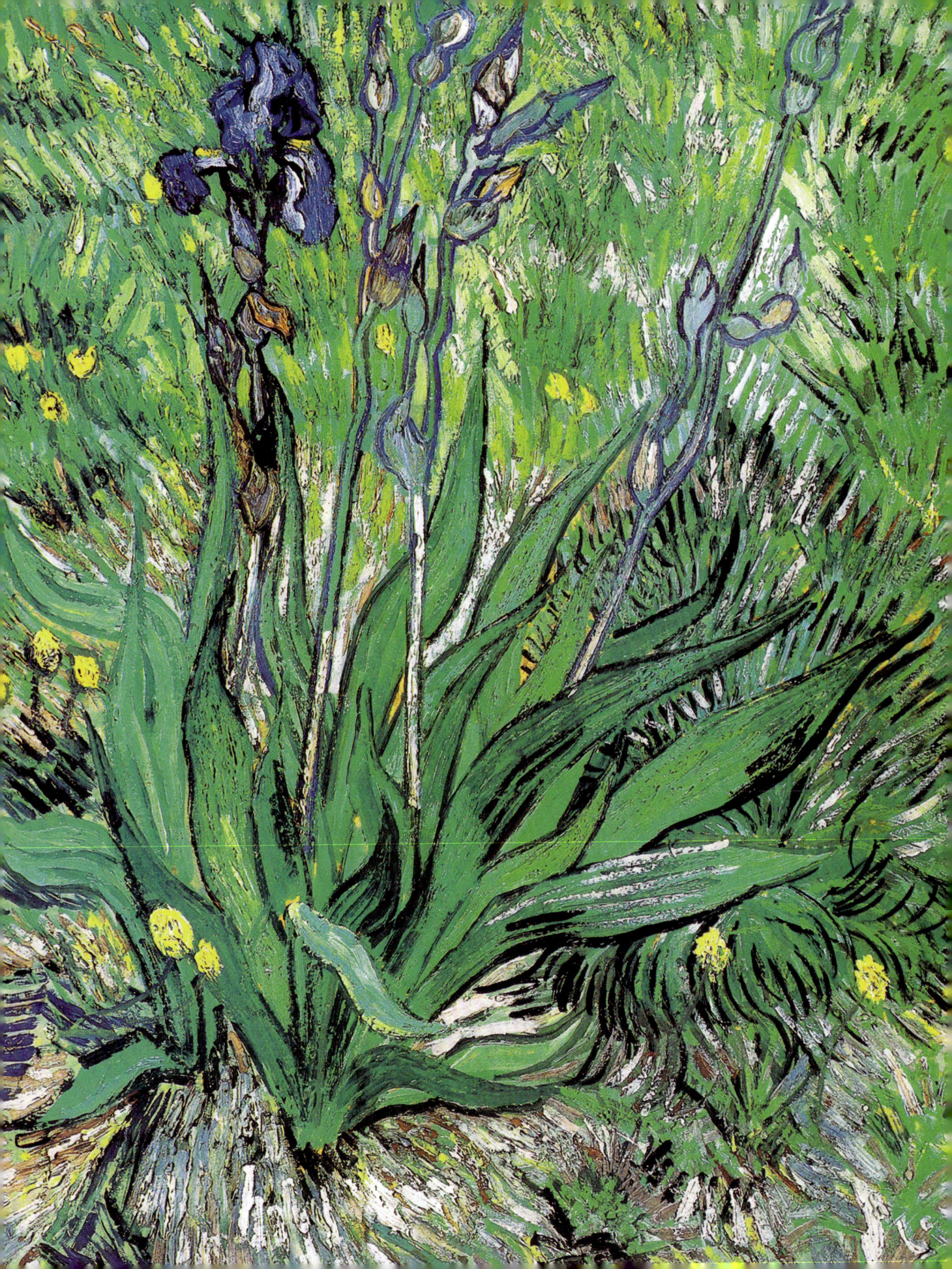

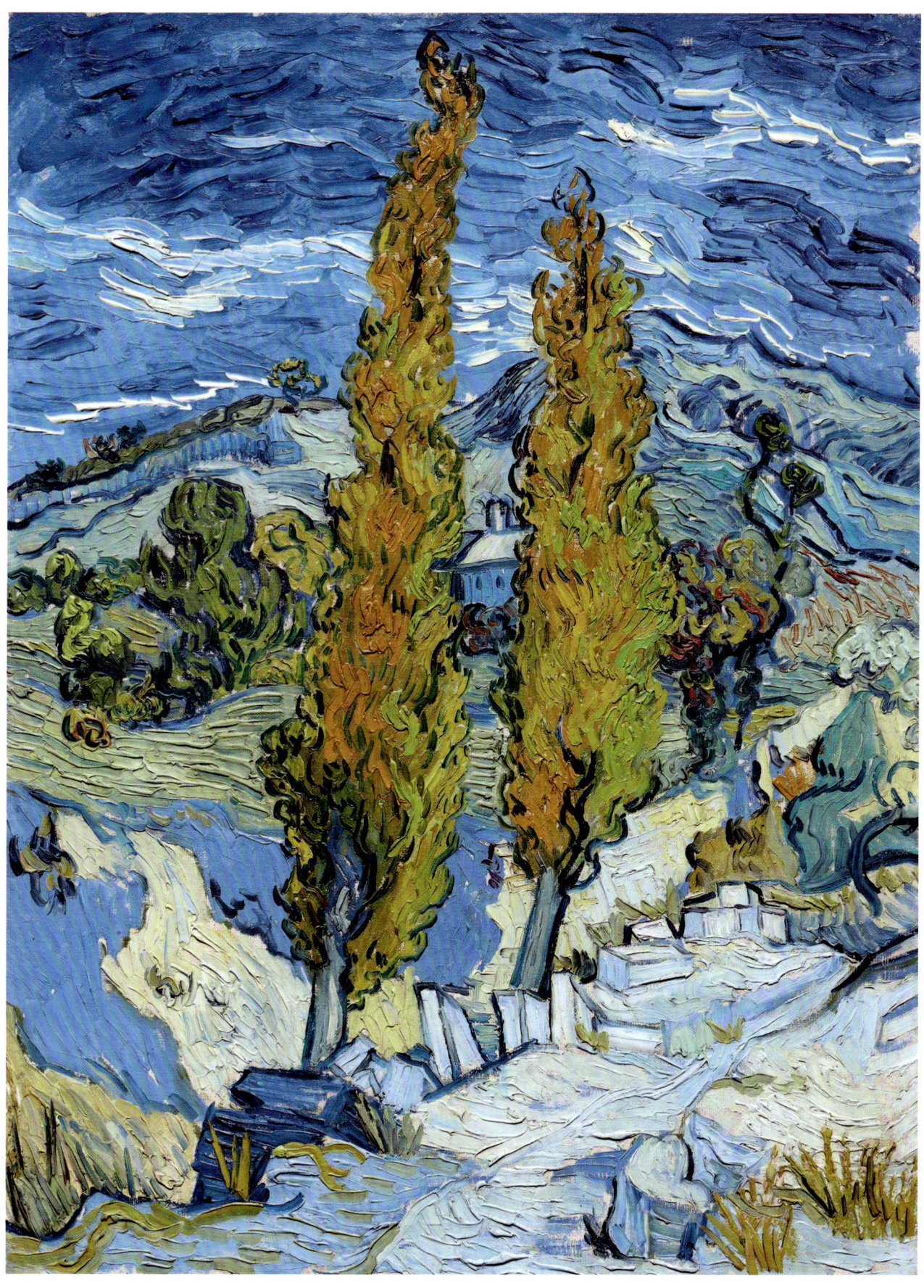

**Two Poplars in the Alpilles near Saint-Rémy,** October 1889, oil on canvas, 61.6 × 45.7 cm, The Cleveland Museum of Art
**Vase with Irises Against a Yellow Background,** May 1889, oil on board pasted on canvas, 62.2 × 48.3 cm, Ottawa, National Gallery of Canada (left)

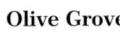

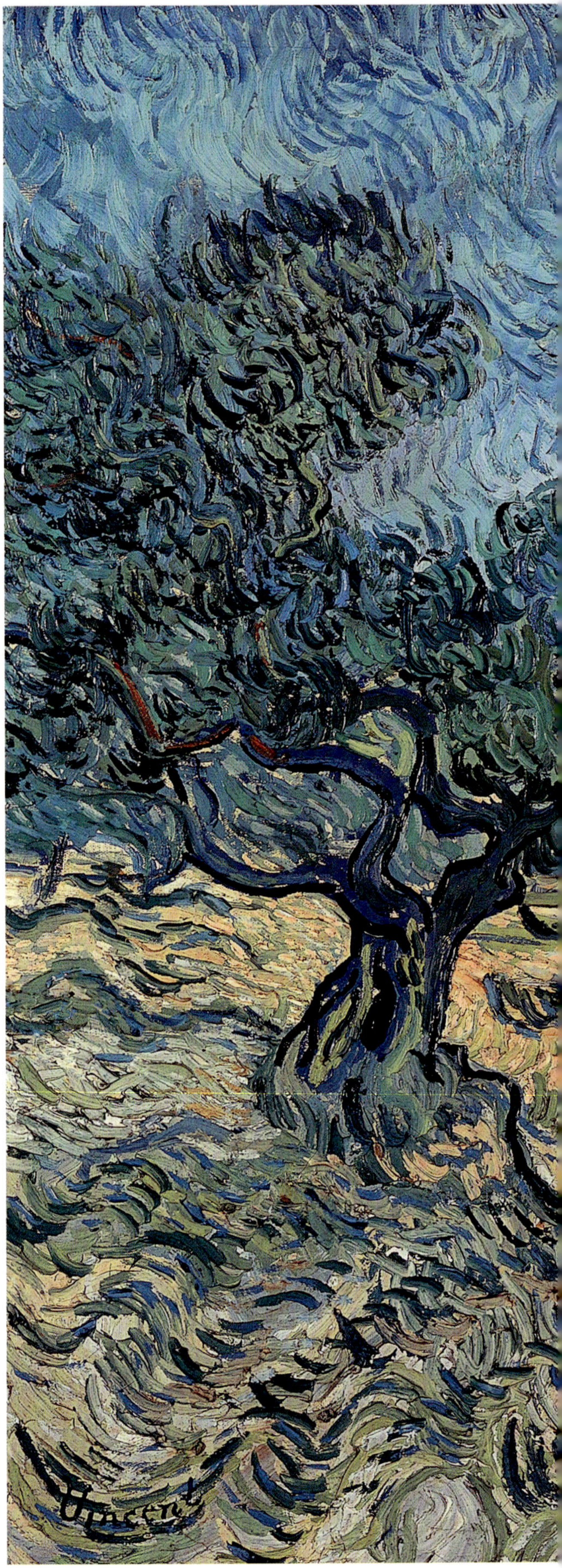

**Olive Grove**

June 1889
Oil on canvas, 72 × 92 cm
Otterlo, Kröller-Müller Museum

**Wheat Field with Reaper
(Harvest in Provence)**

September 1889
Oil on canvas, 73.2 × 92.7 cm
Amsterdam, Van Gogh Museum
(double page below, detail)

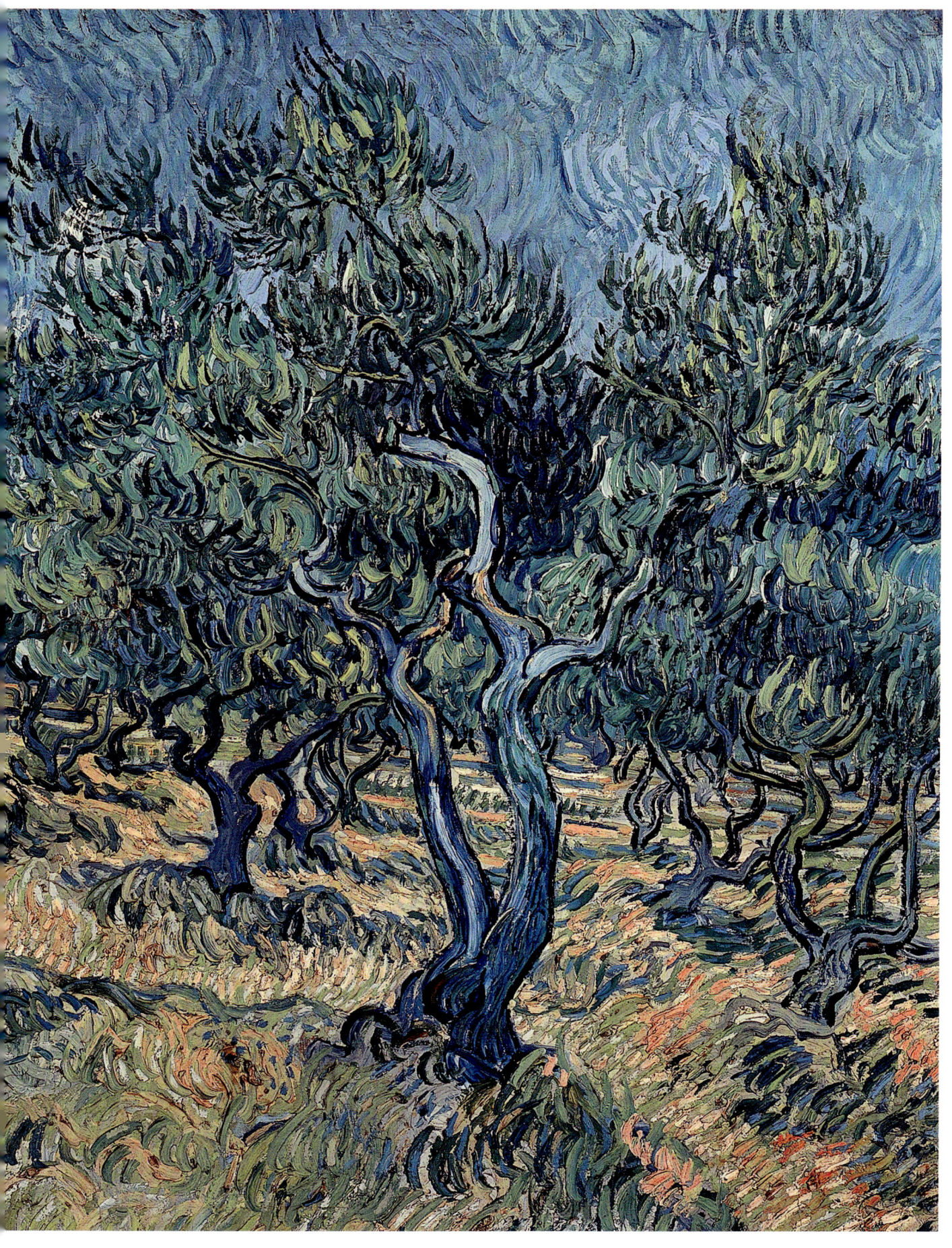

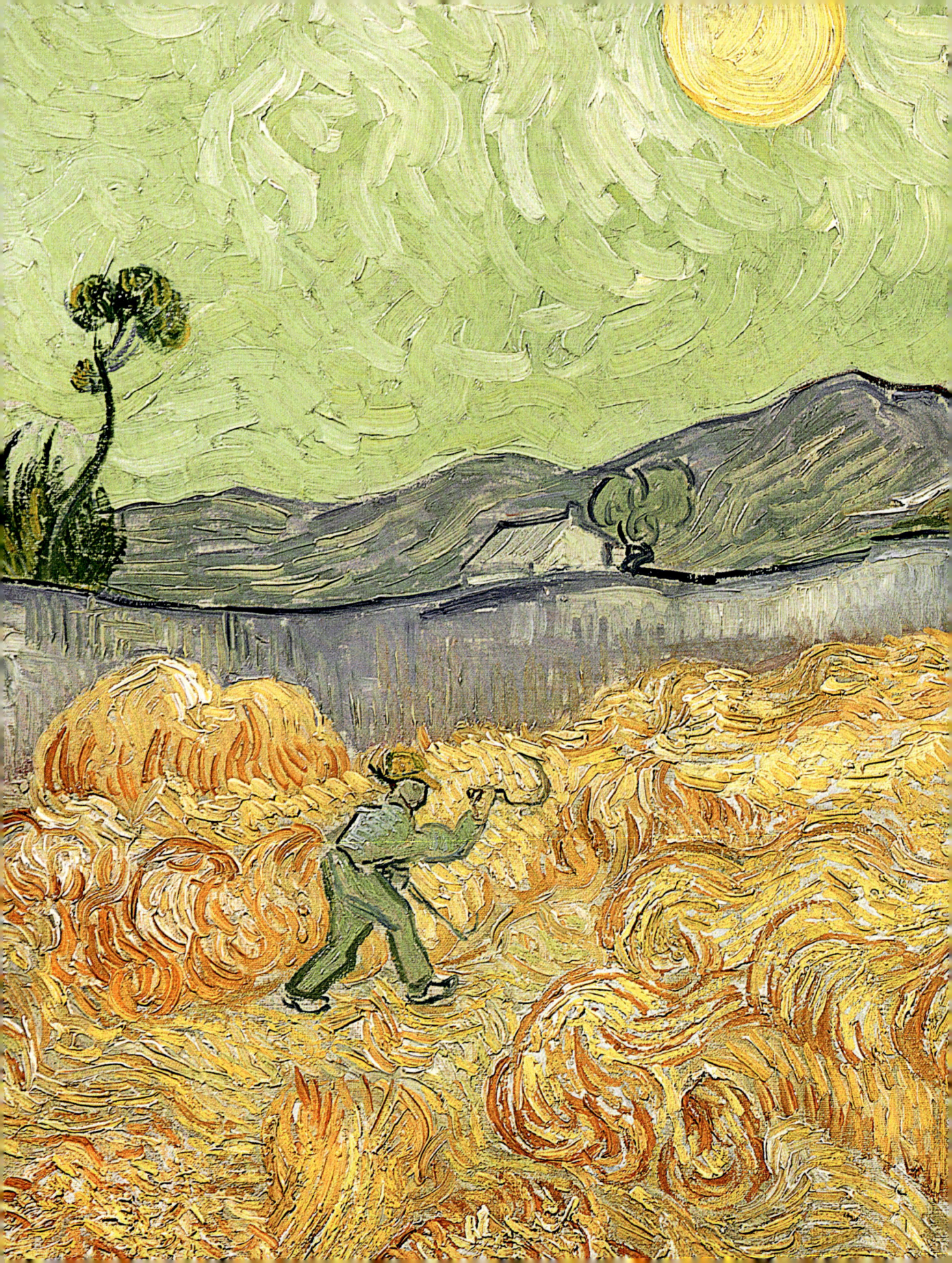

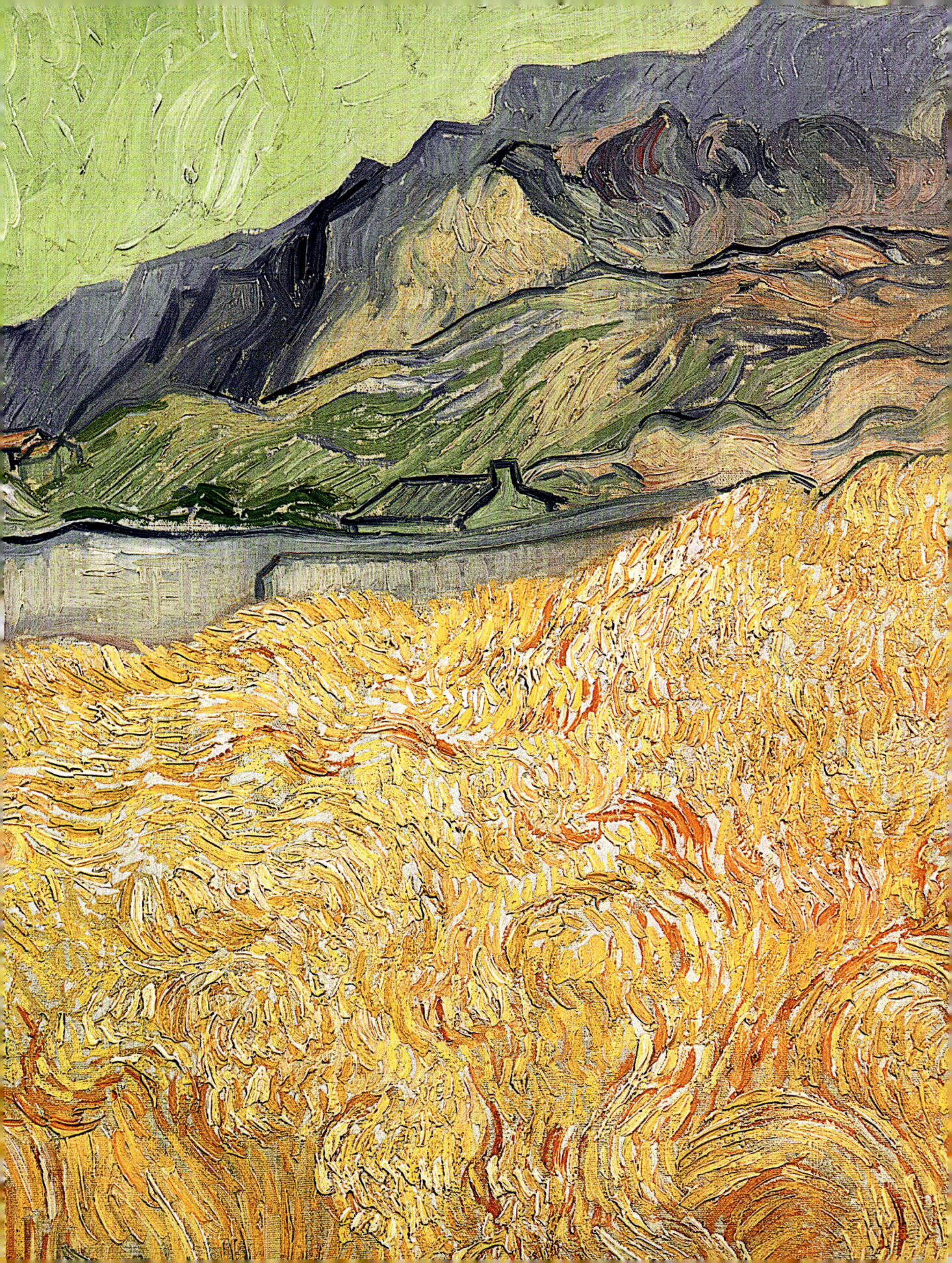

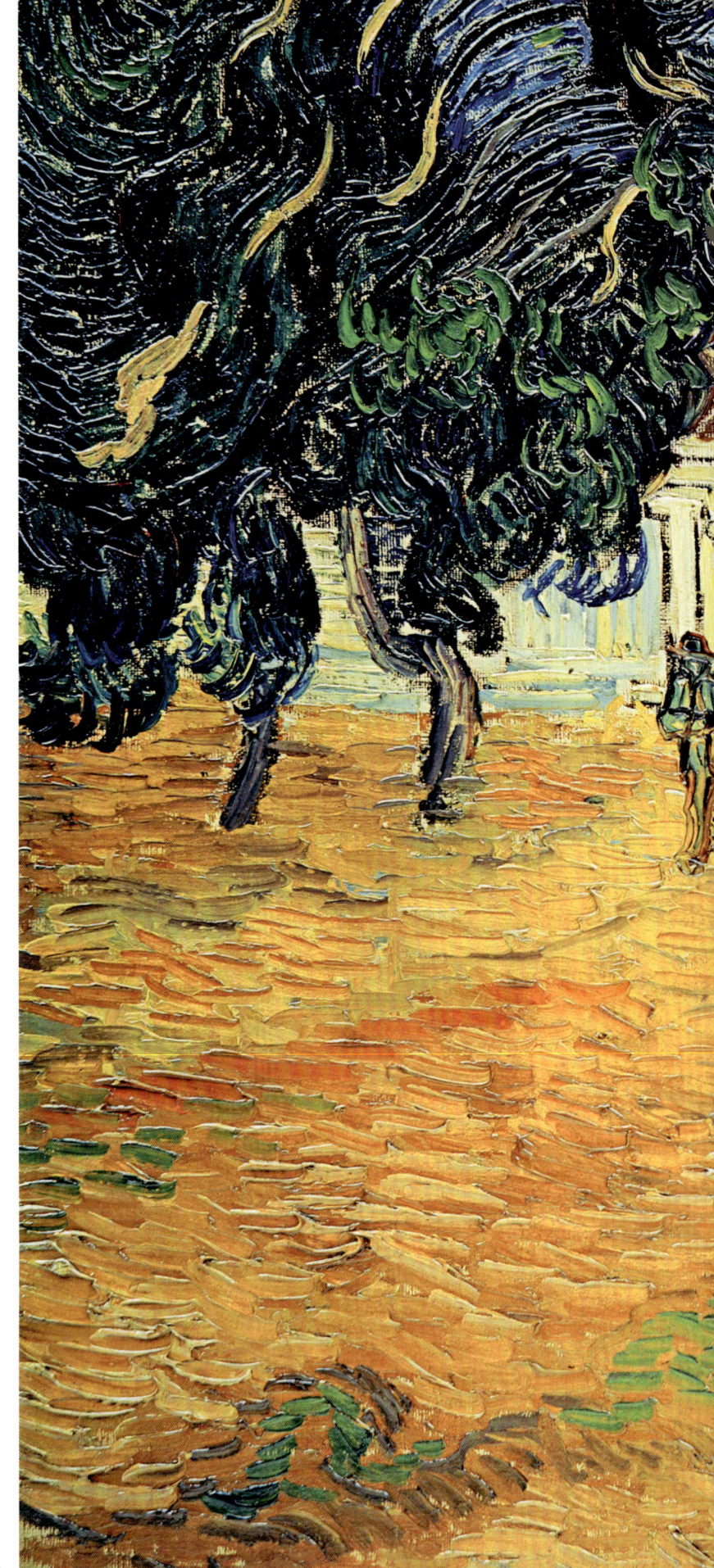

**The Garden of the Hospital
Saint-Paul**

October 1889
Oil on canvas, 50 × 63 cm
Private collection

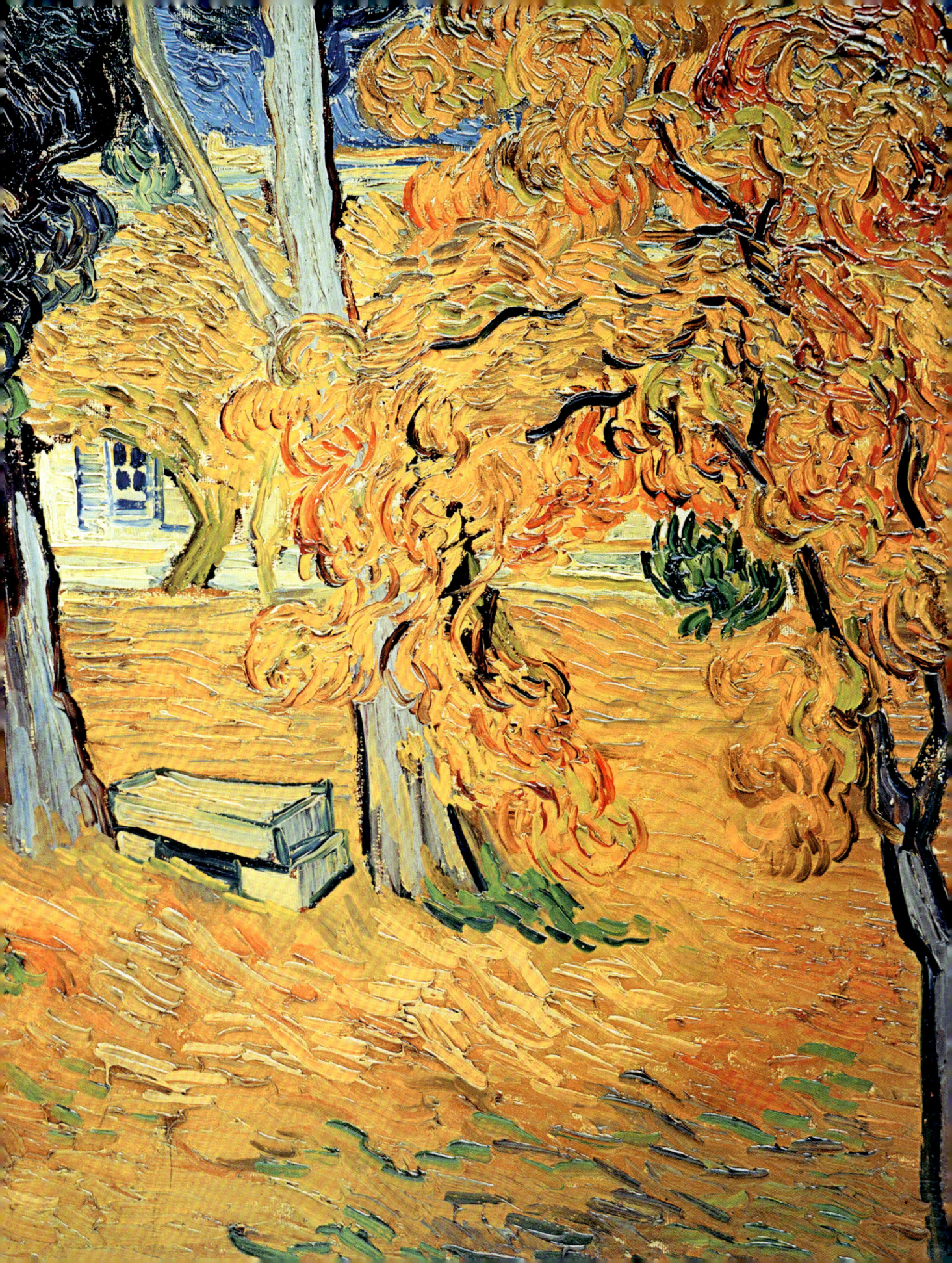

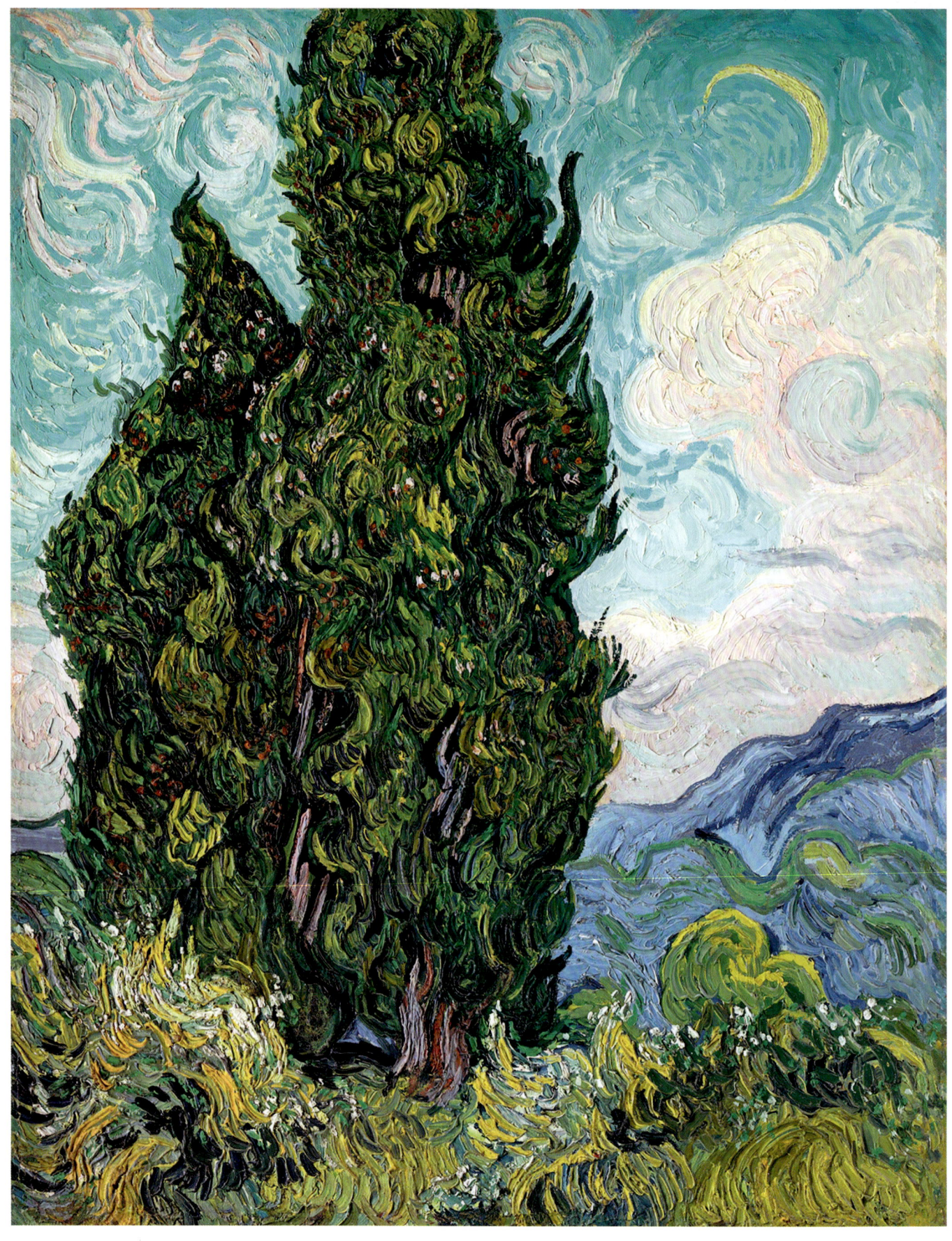

**Cypresses,** 1889, oil on canvas, 93.4 × 74 cm, New York, The Metropolitan Museum of Art

# The Starry Night

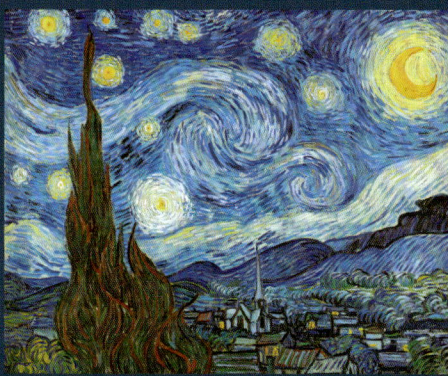

Ever since his arrival in Arles in February 1888, Van Gogh had sought to capture the night and its light effects. He finally completed his project in September, painting a night sky on the banks of the Rhône, a vast *Starry Night* imbued with a serene atmosphere (Paris, Musée d'Orsay). In June of the following year, while the artist was confined to the hospice in Saint-Rémy-de-Provence following a bout of dementia, the patch of sky that he could see from his bedroom prompted him to return to the subject. For this *Starry Night,* he would try his hand at the motif several times, placing the moon and the constellations in the sky with perfect exactness. A rather less realistic feature is the contorted representation of all forms, from the clouds to the cypresses; all are treated as volutes, arabesques and swirls that draw the eye towards the back of the canvas. "When I have a terrible need of – shall I say the word – religion, then I go out and paint the stars," he wrote. The church's very pointed steeple is in no way typical of the Midi; this is the church of Nuenen, in the distant Netherlands, which Van Gogh would never see again.

*The Starry Night,* June 1889, oil on canvas, 73.7 × 92.1 cm, New York, MoMA

the big picture

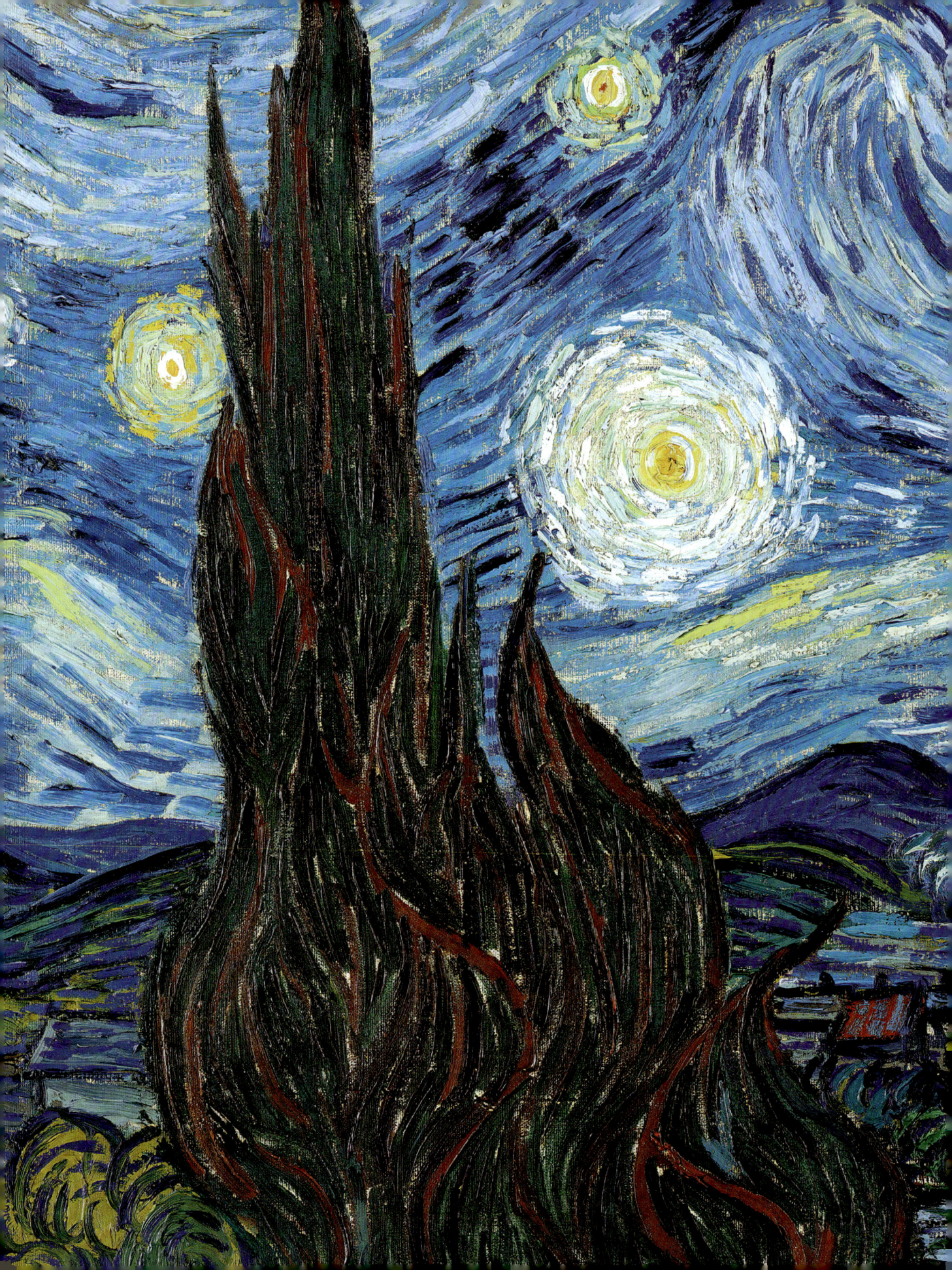

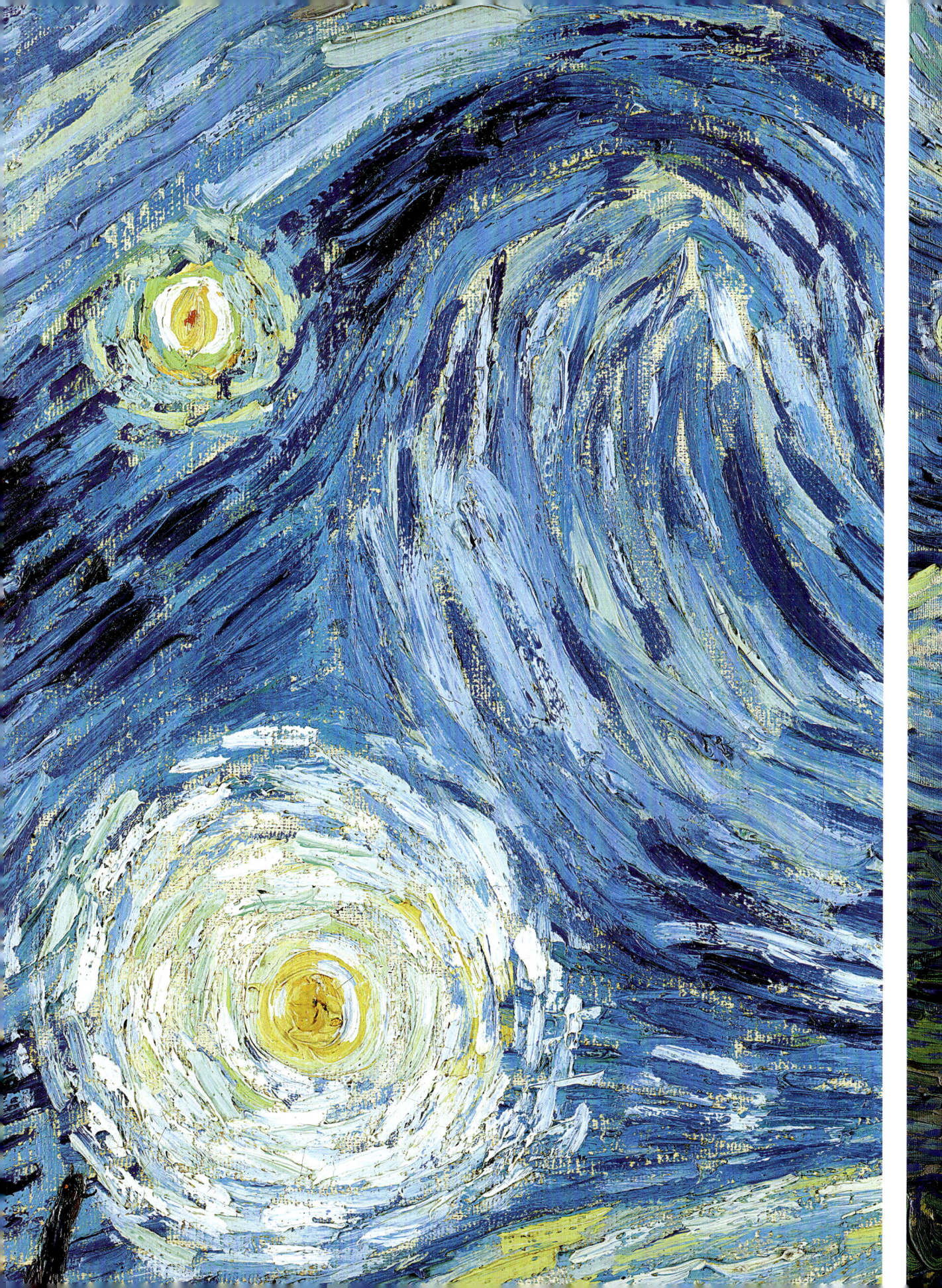

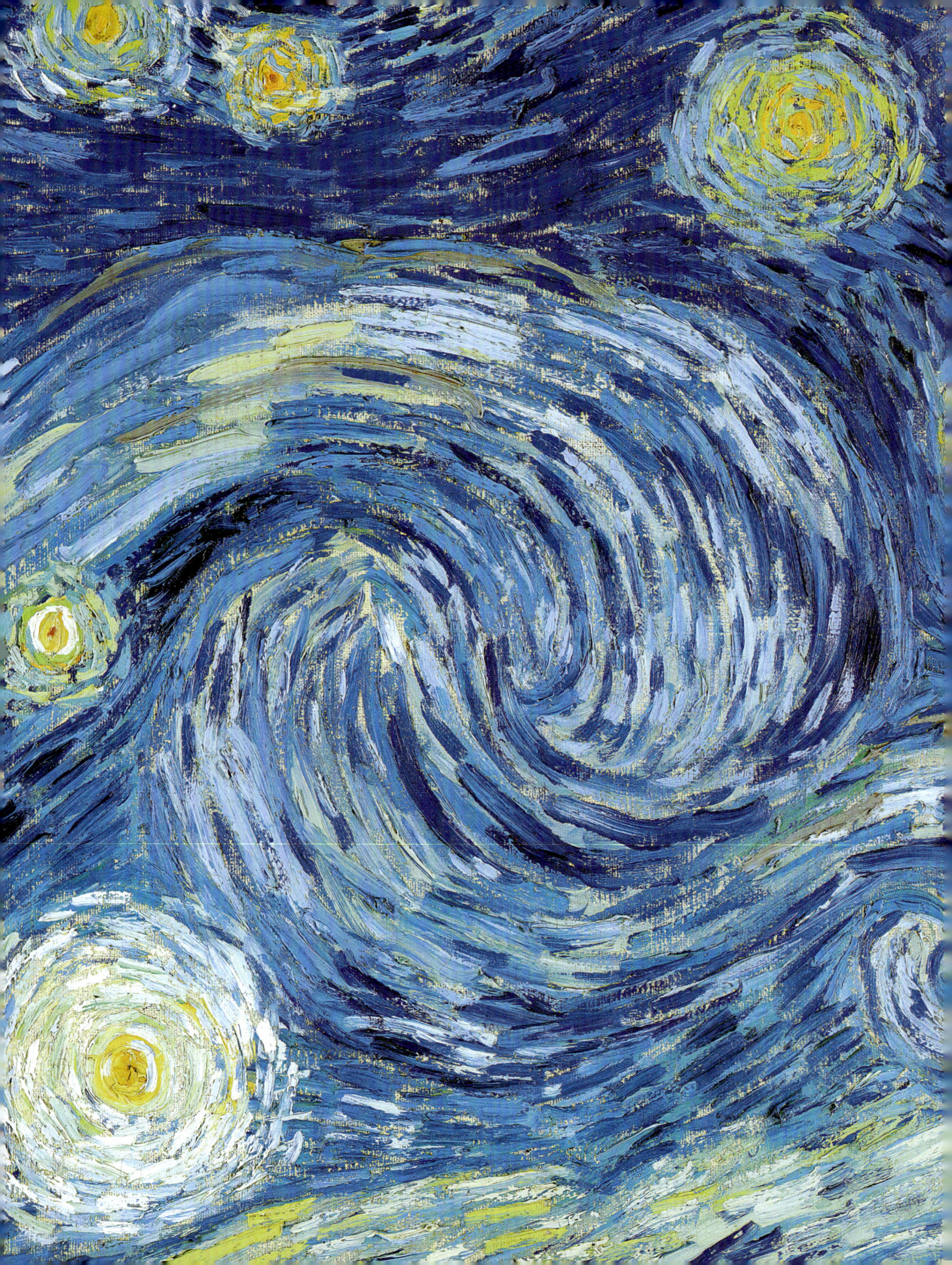

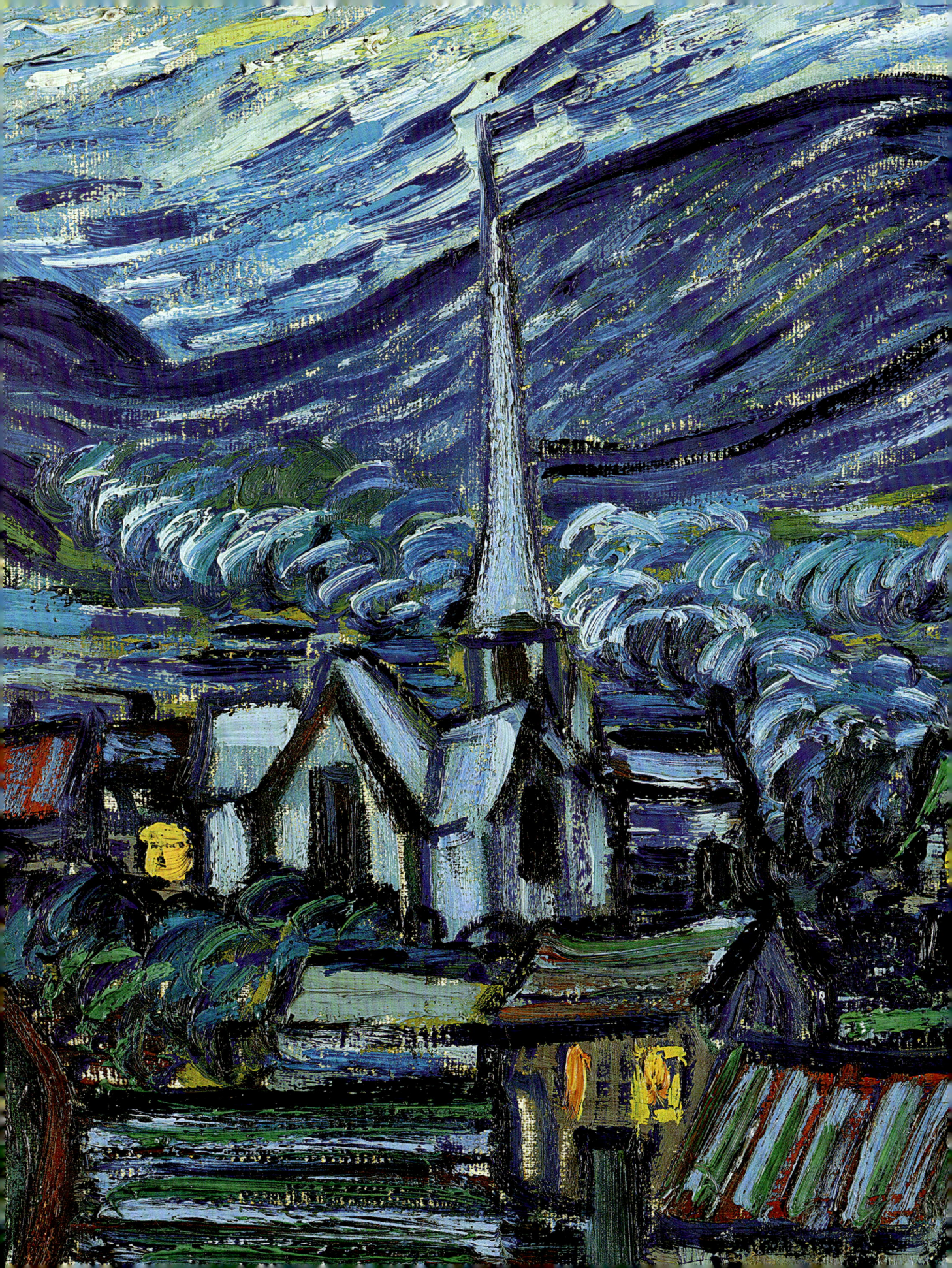

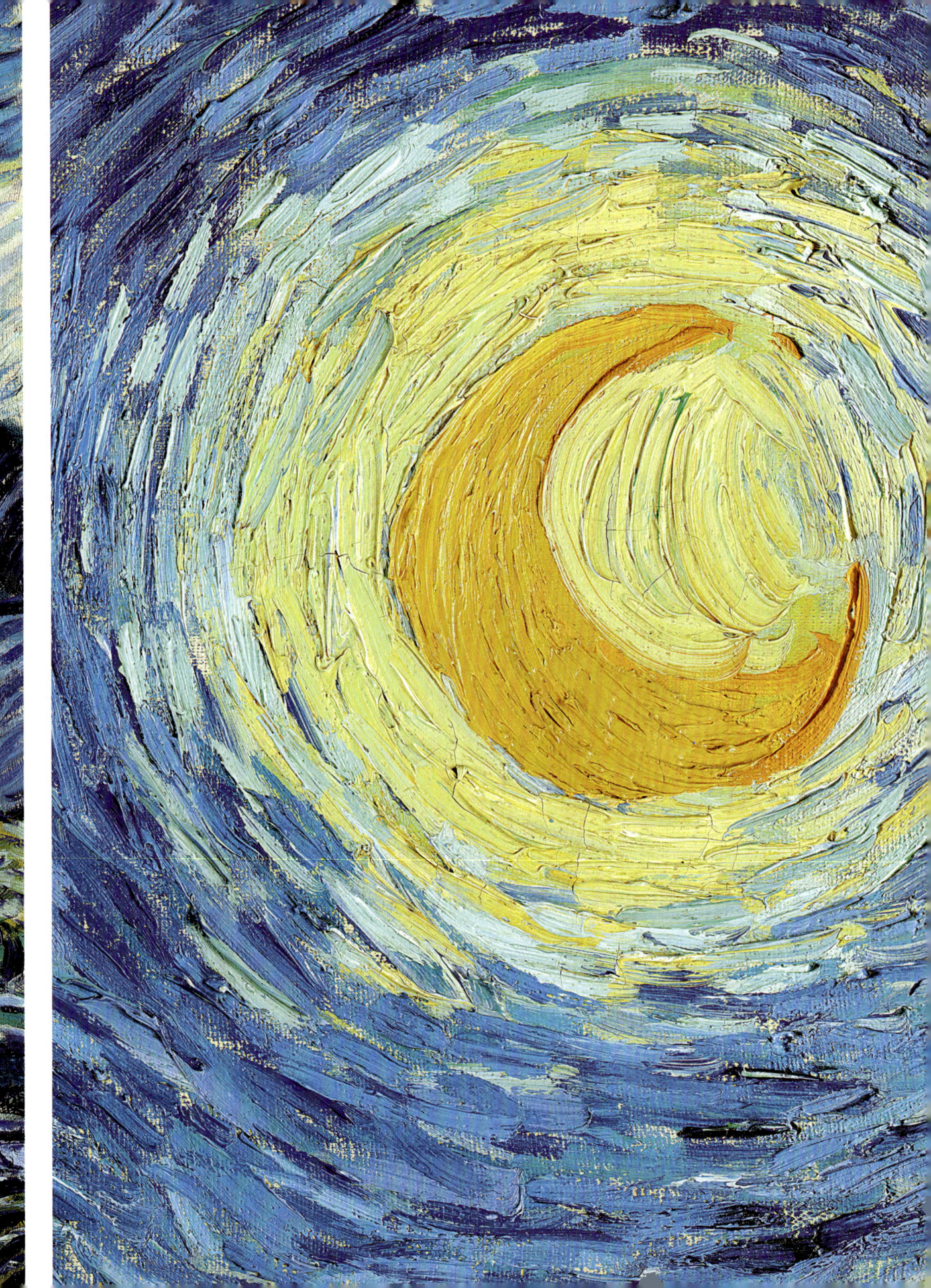

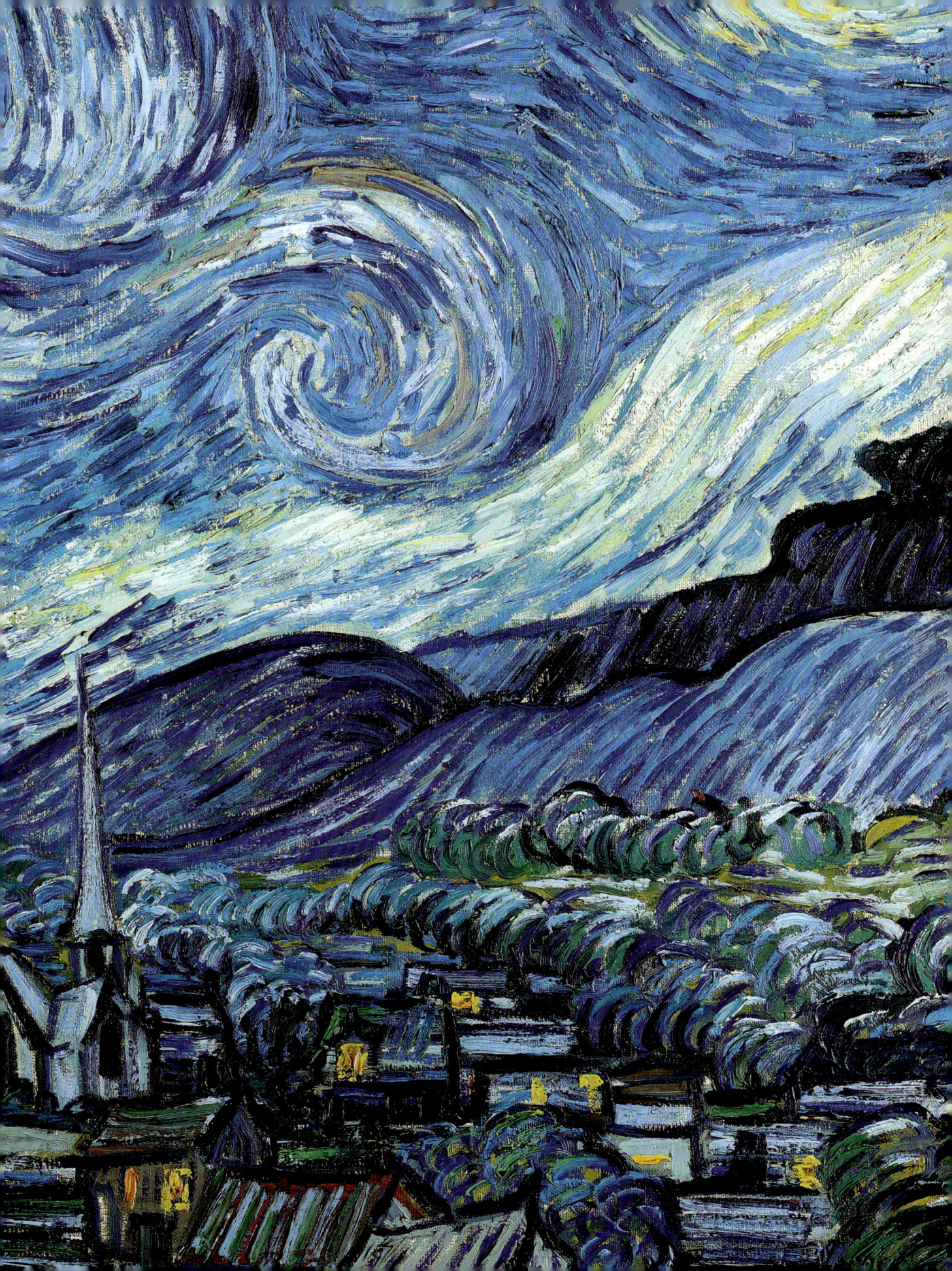

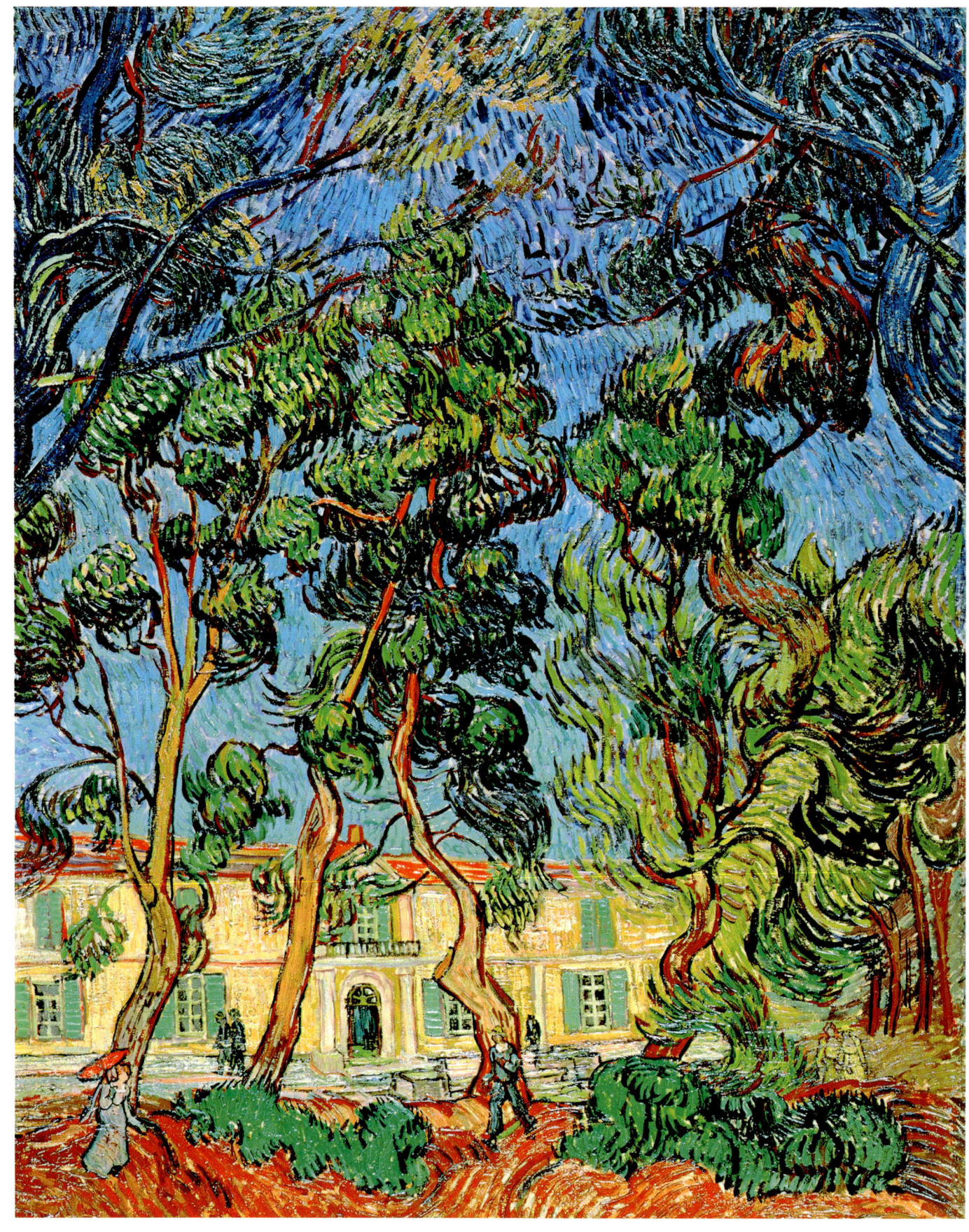

*Hospital at Saint-Rémy*, 1889, oil on canvas, 90.2 × 73.3 cm
The Armand Hammer Collection, Gift of the Armand Hammer Foundation. Los Angeles, Hammer Museum

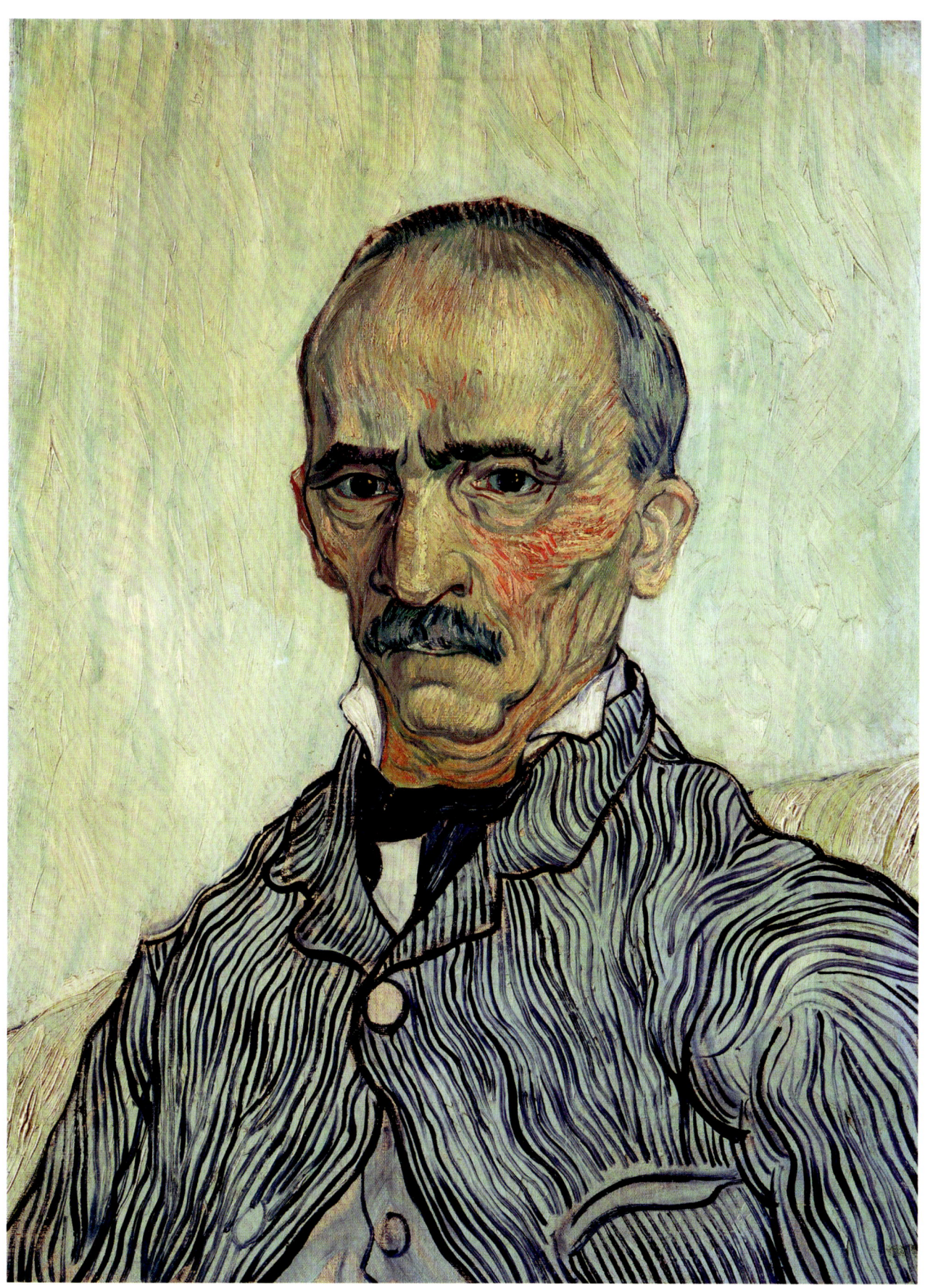

**Portrait of the Superintendent Trabuc in the Hospital Saint-Paul,**
September 1889, oil on canvas, 61 × 46 cm, Solothurn, Kunstmuseum Solothurn

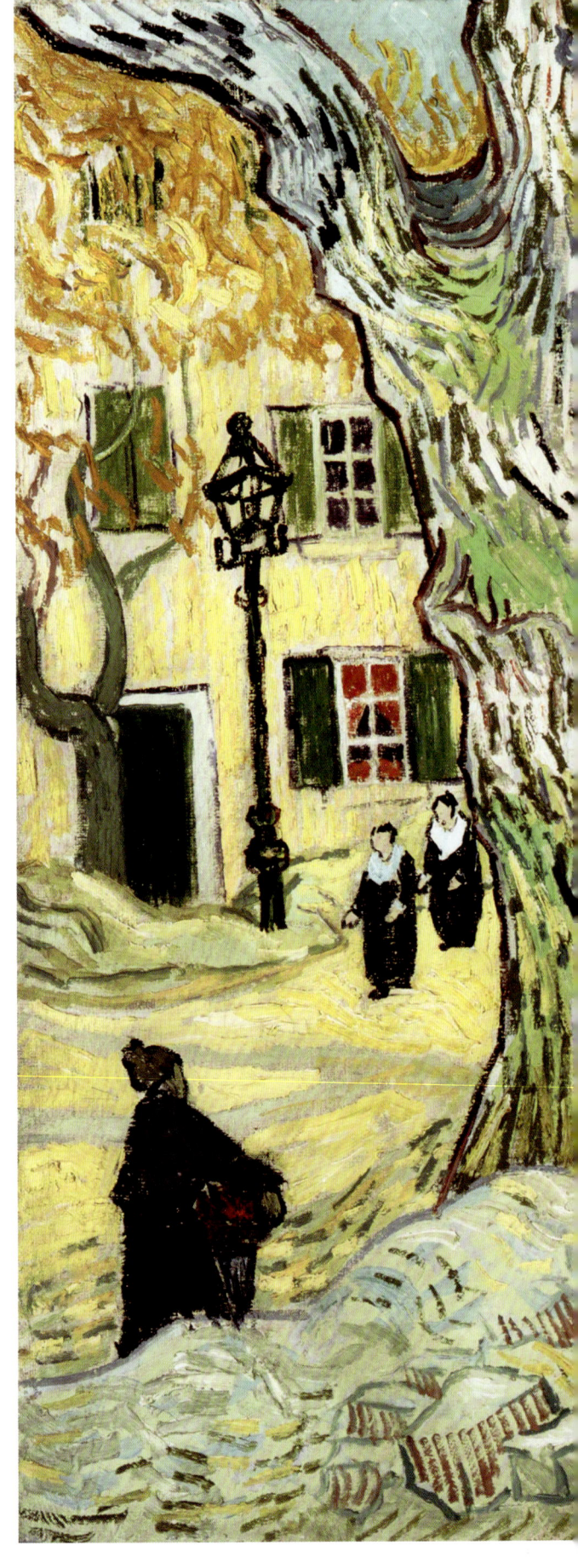

**The Large Plane Trees
(Road Menders at Saint-Rémy)**

November 1889
Oil on canvas, 73.6 × 92.7 cm
Washington, The Phillips Collection

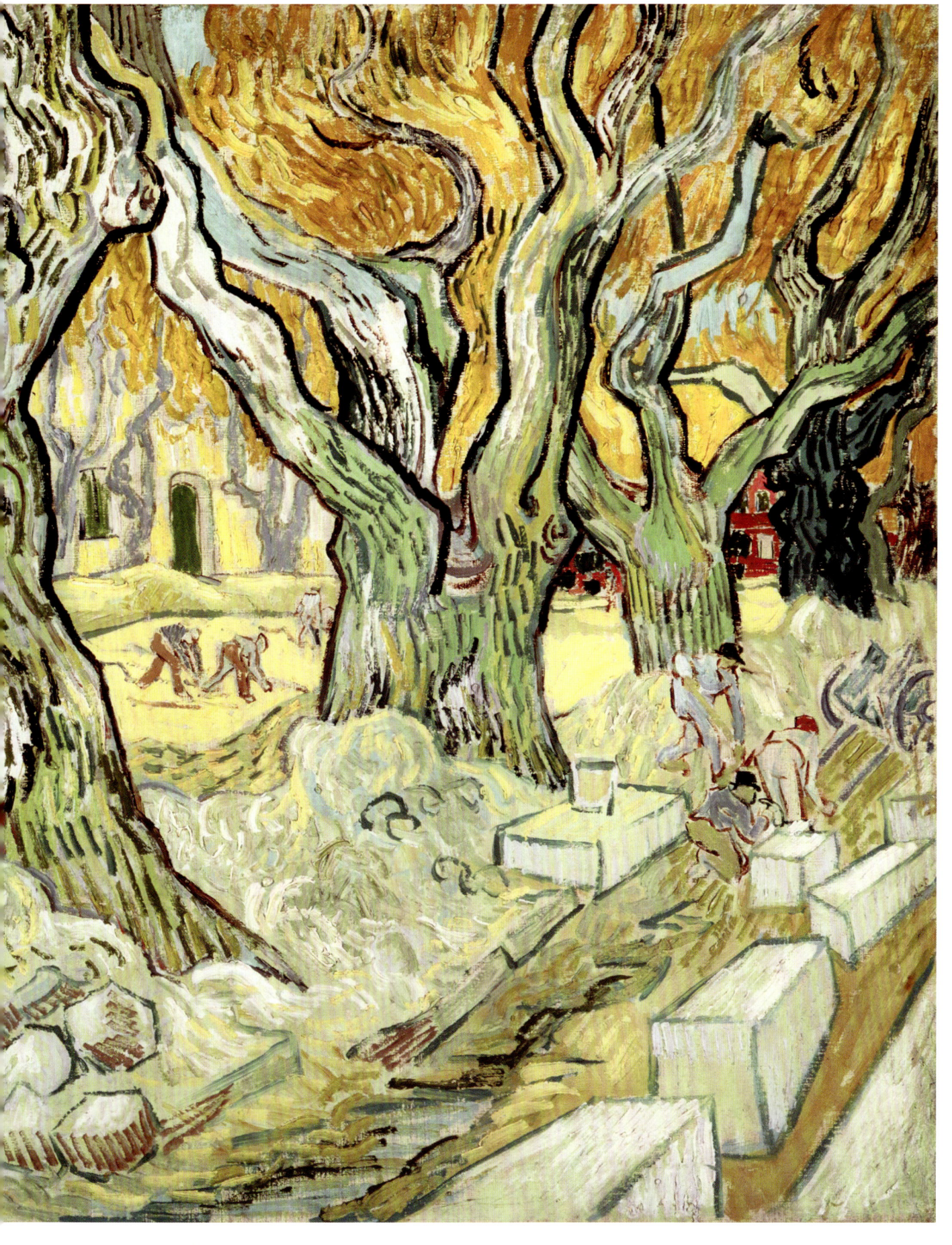

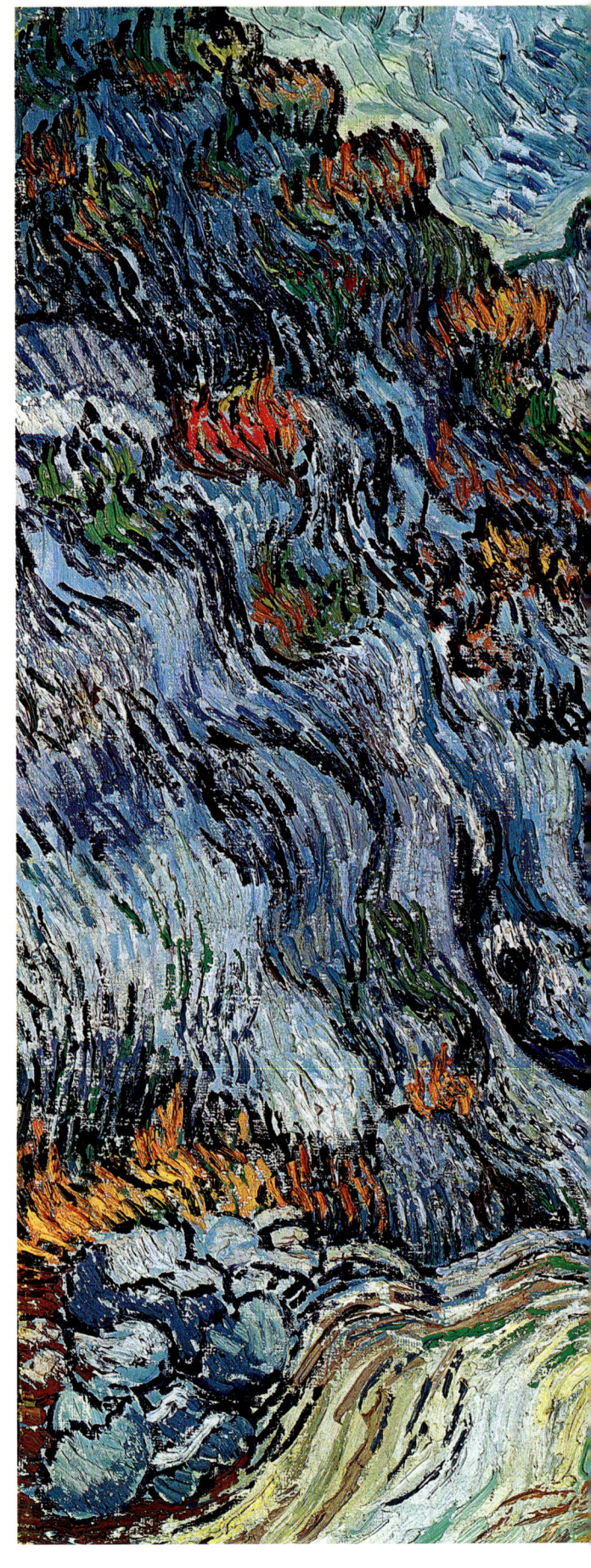

**The Ravine (Les Peiroulets)**

December 1889
Oil on canvas, 72 × 92 cm
Otterlo, Kröller-Müller Museum

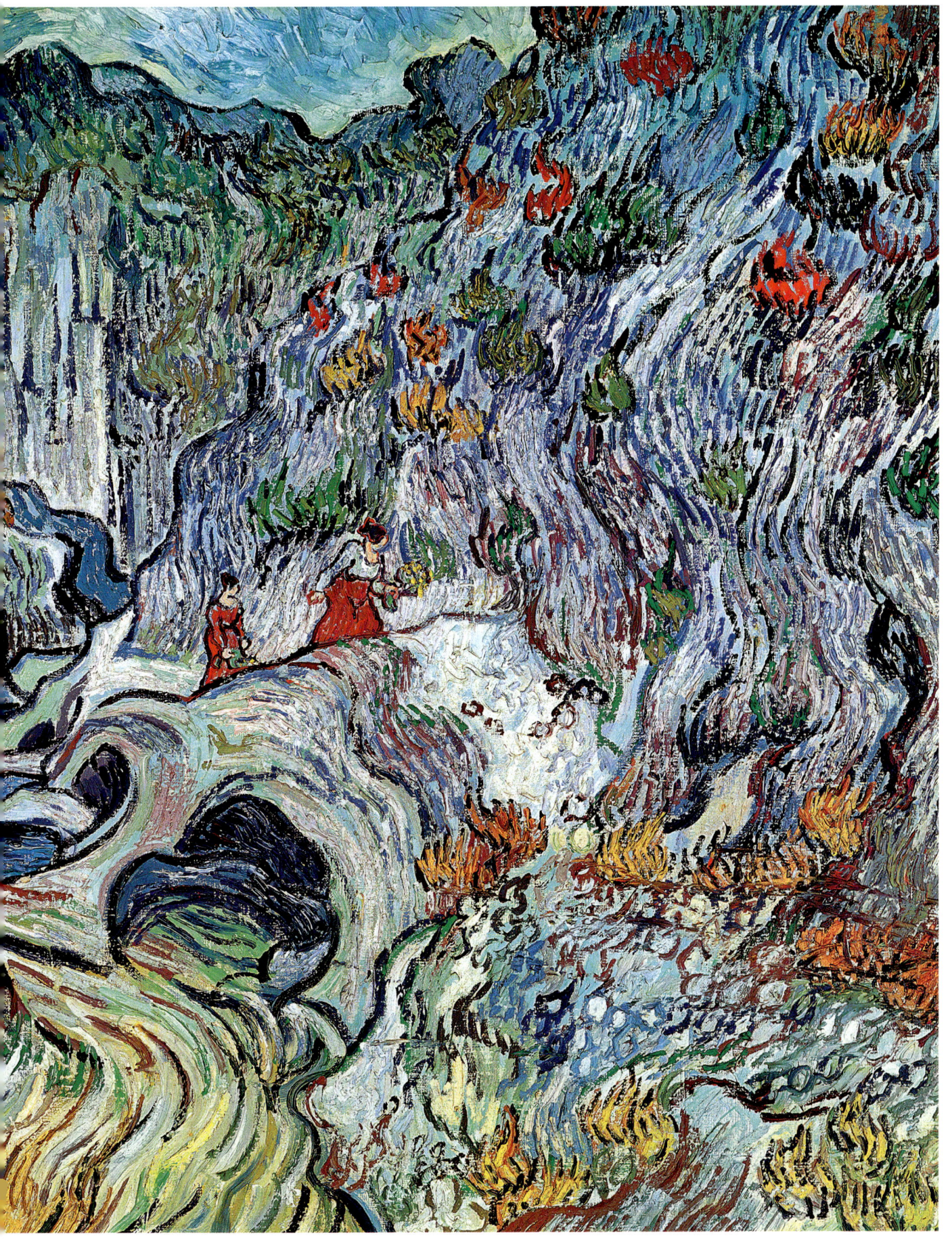

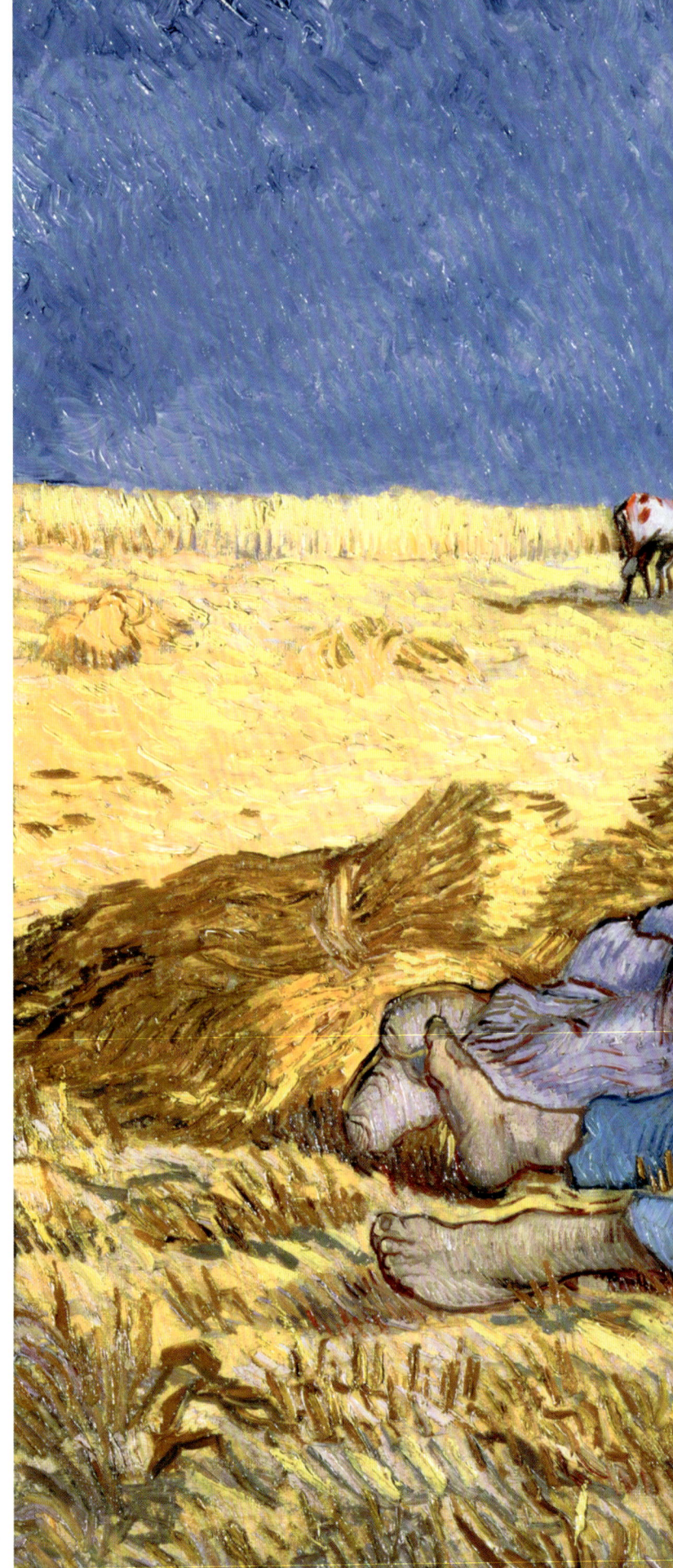

**The Siesta (after Millet)**

January 1890
Oil on canvas, 73 × 91 cm
Paris, Musée d'Orsay

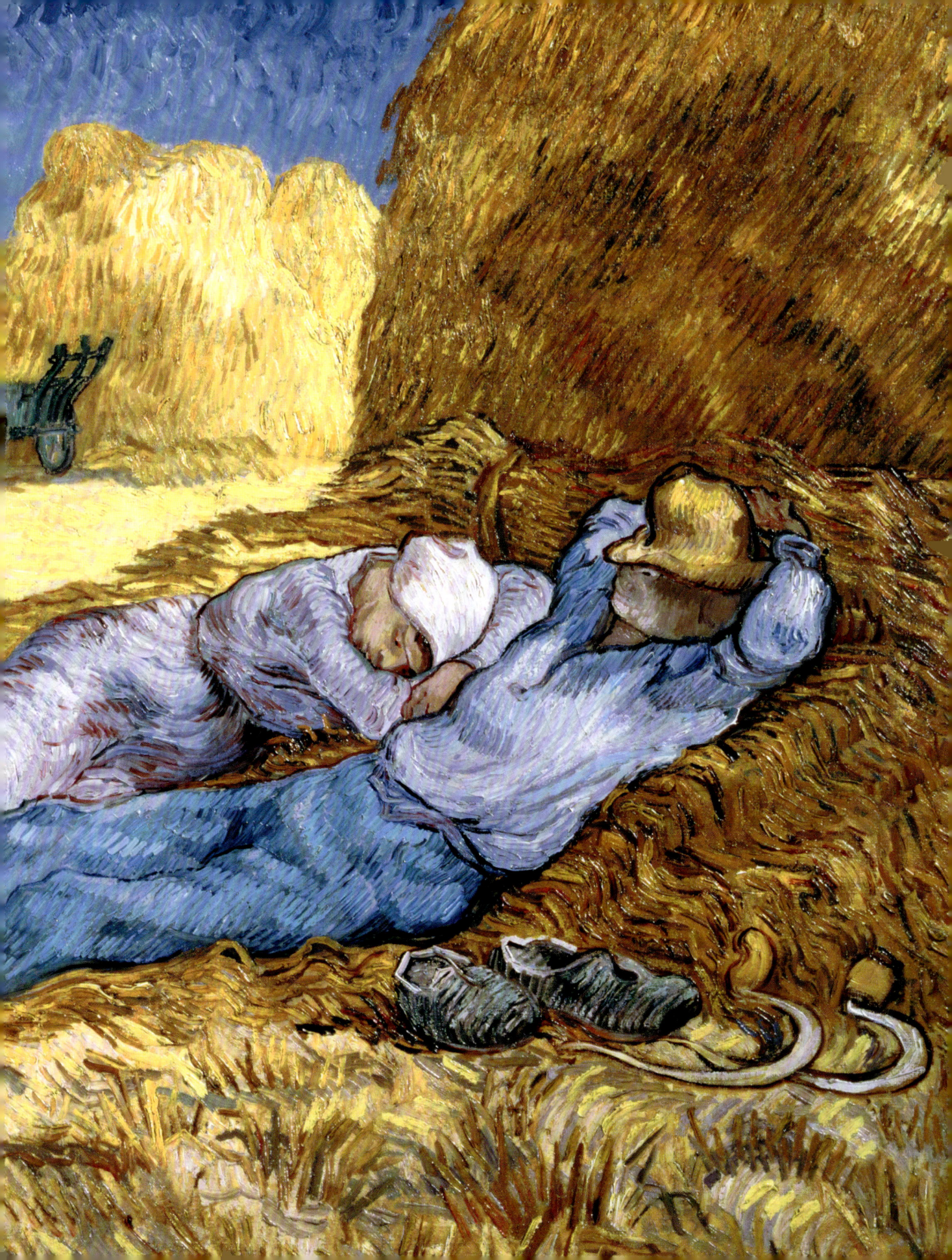

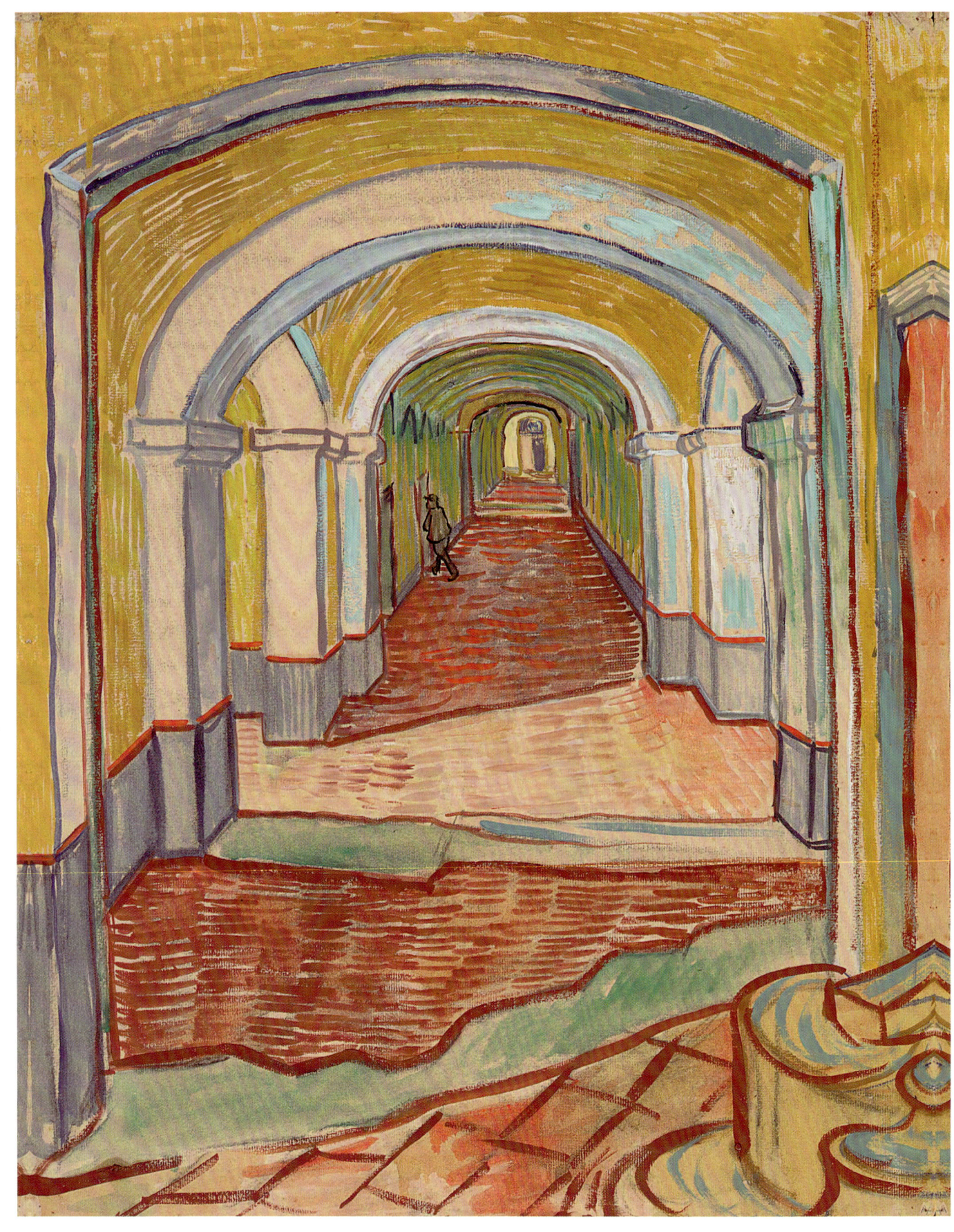

**Corridor in the Asylum,** September 1889, oil and black chalk on paper, 65.1 × 49.1 cm, New York, The Metropolitan Museum of Art

# Self-portrait

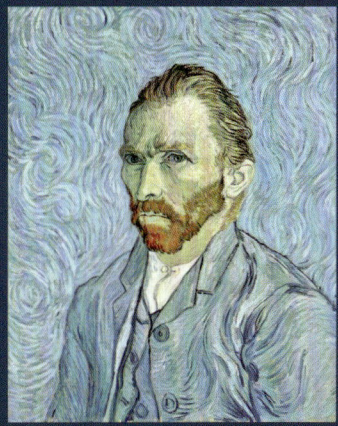

Akin to Rembrandt Van Rijn, Vincent Van Gogh often used himself as a model; in the space of ten years, he painted or drew over forty-three self-portraits. Painting oneself is no trivial matter, and always entails questions about one's own identity. The artist was fully aware of this when he wrote to his brother Theo: "People say, and I'm quite willing to believe it, that it's difficult to know oneself – but it's not easy to paint oneself either. [...] One finds the same thing in, say, portraits by Rembrandt. It is more than nature, something of a revelation."  In this painting, which he produced in Saint-Rémy-de-Provence, in the summer of 1889, whilst confined to the hospice, Van Gogh depicted himself in a jacket, framed in bust form. All attention is drawn to his emaciated face, which is rendered without complacency, and to his gaze, both hard and anxious. The dominant tones, absinth green and light turquoise, offer a counterpoint to their complementary colour, the orange of Van Gogh's beard and hair. The undulating curves of his clothes are echoed in the background's hallucinatory arabesques.

*Self-portrait*, September 1889, oil on canvas, 65 × 54.5 cm, Paris, Musée d'Orsay

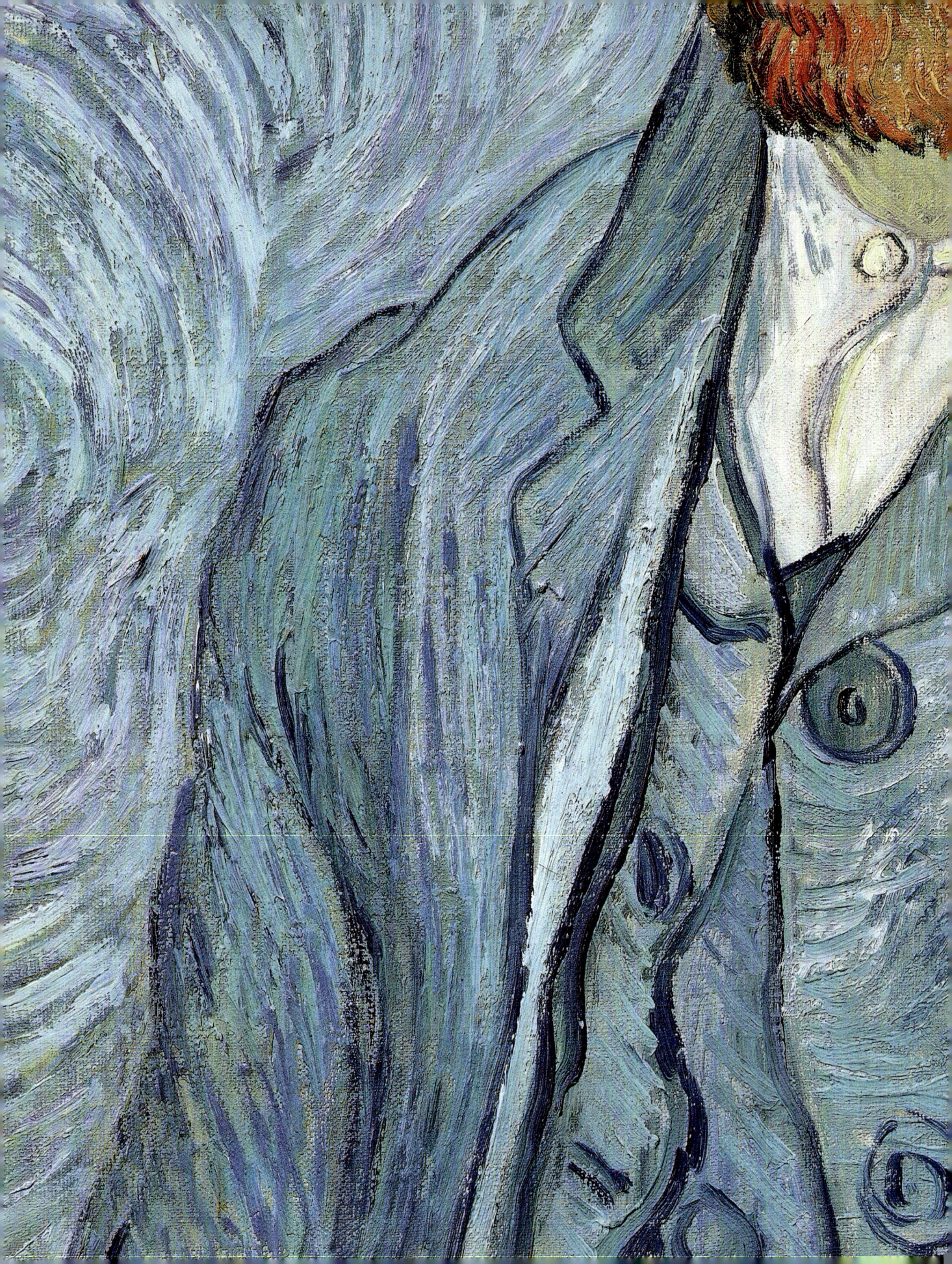

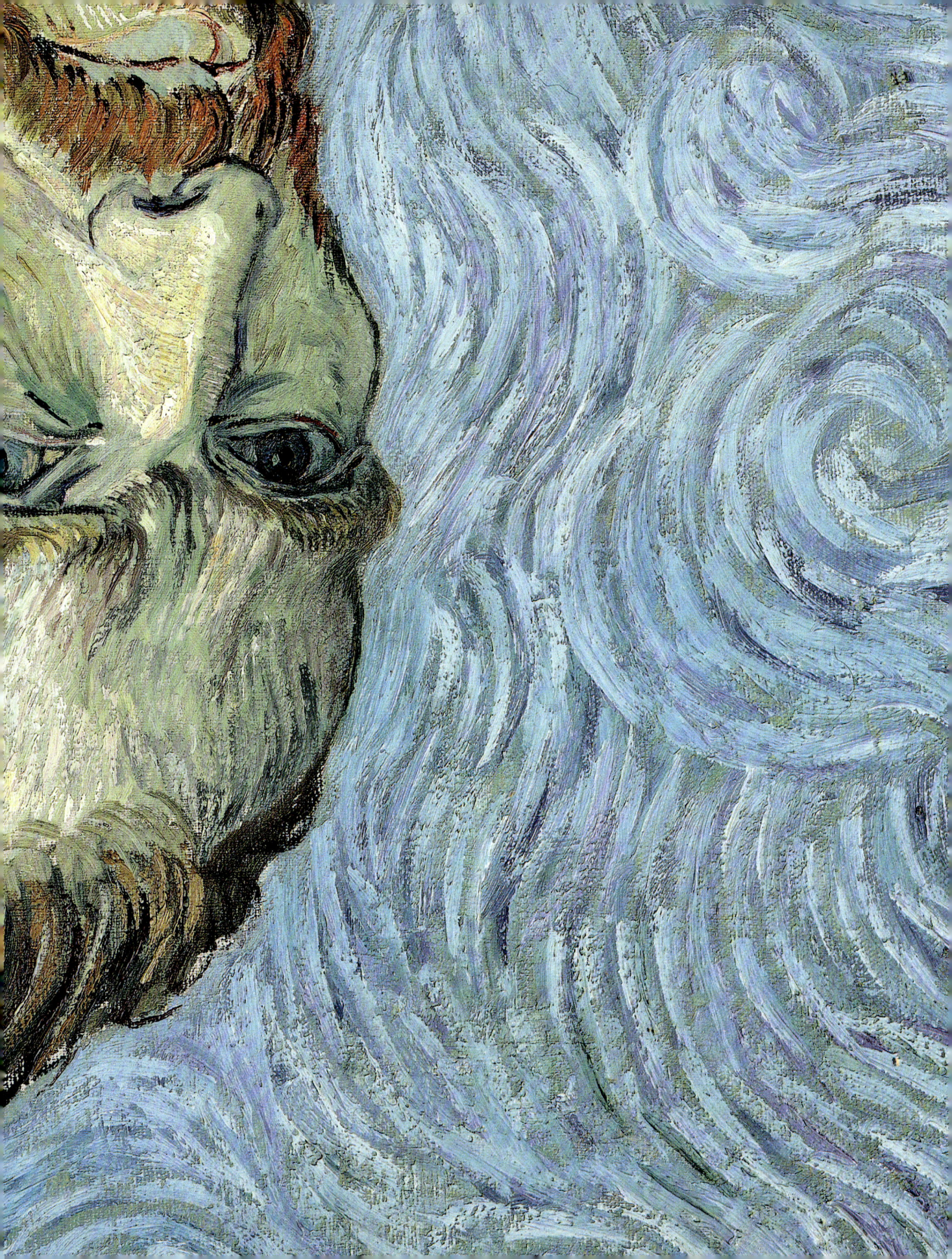

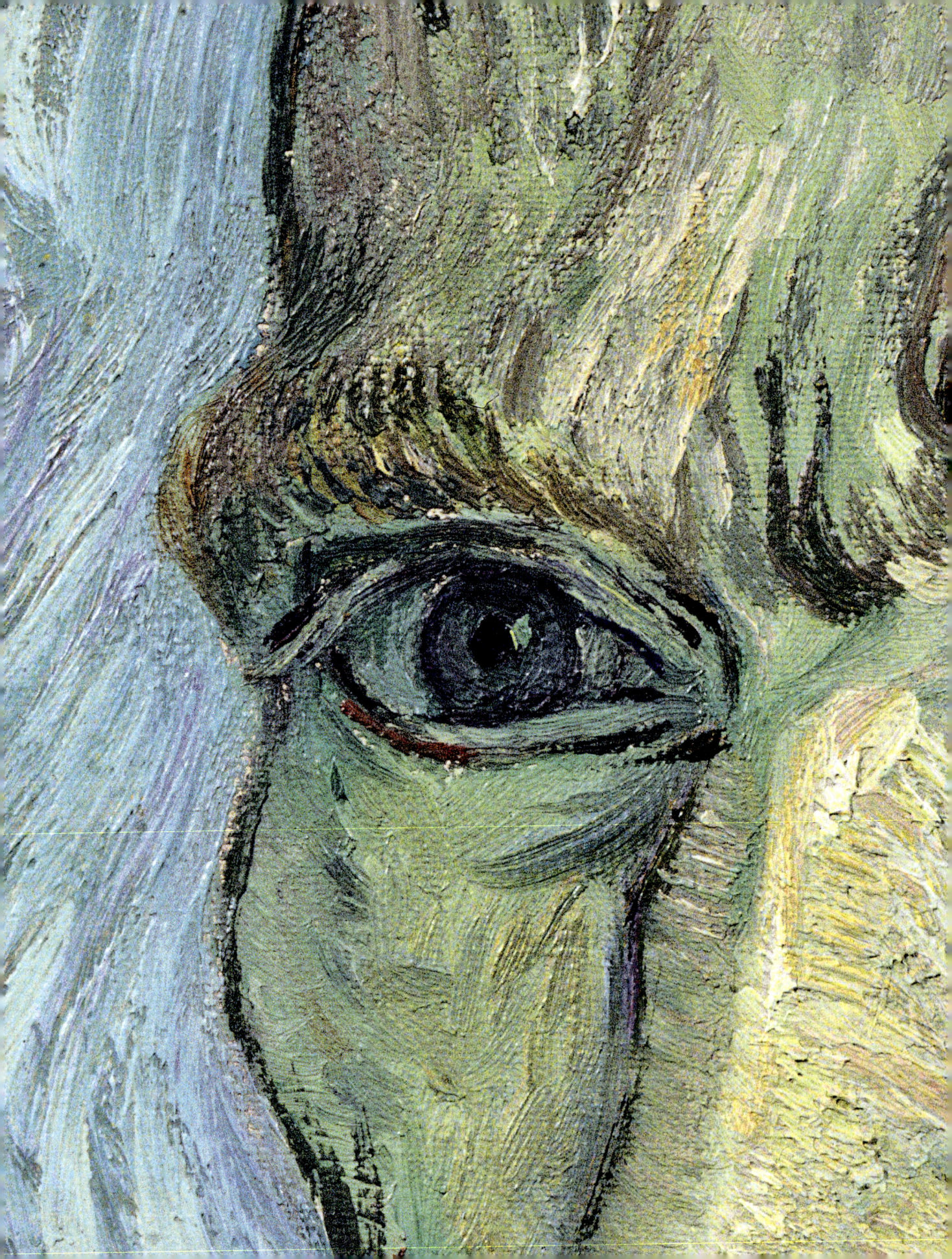

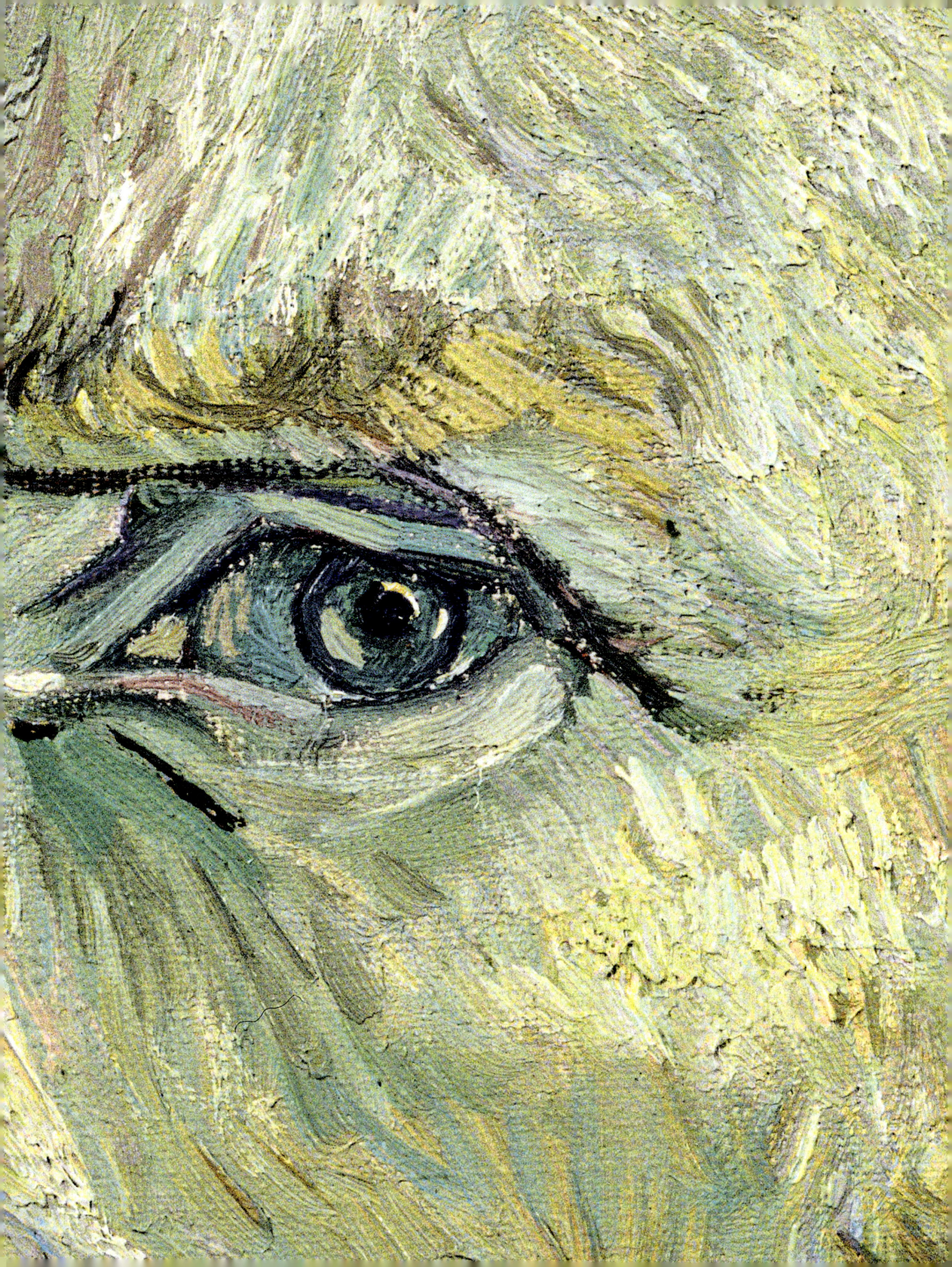

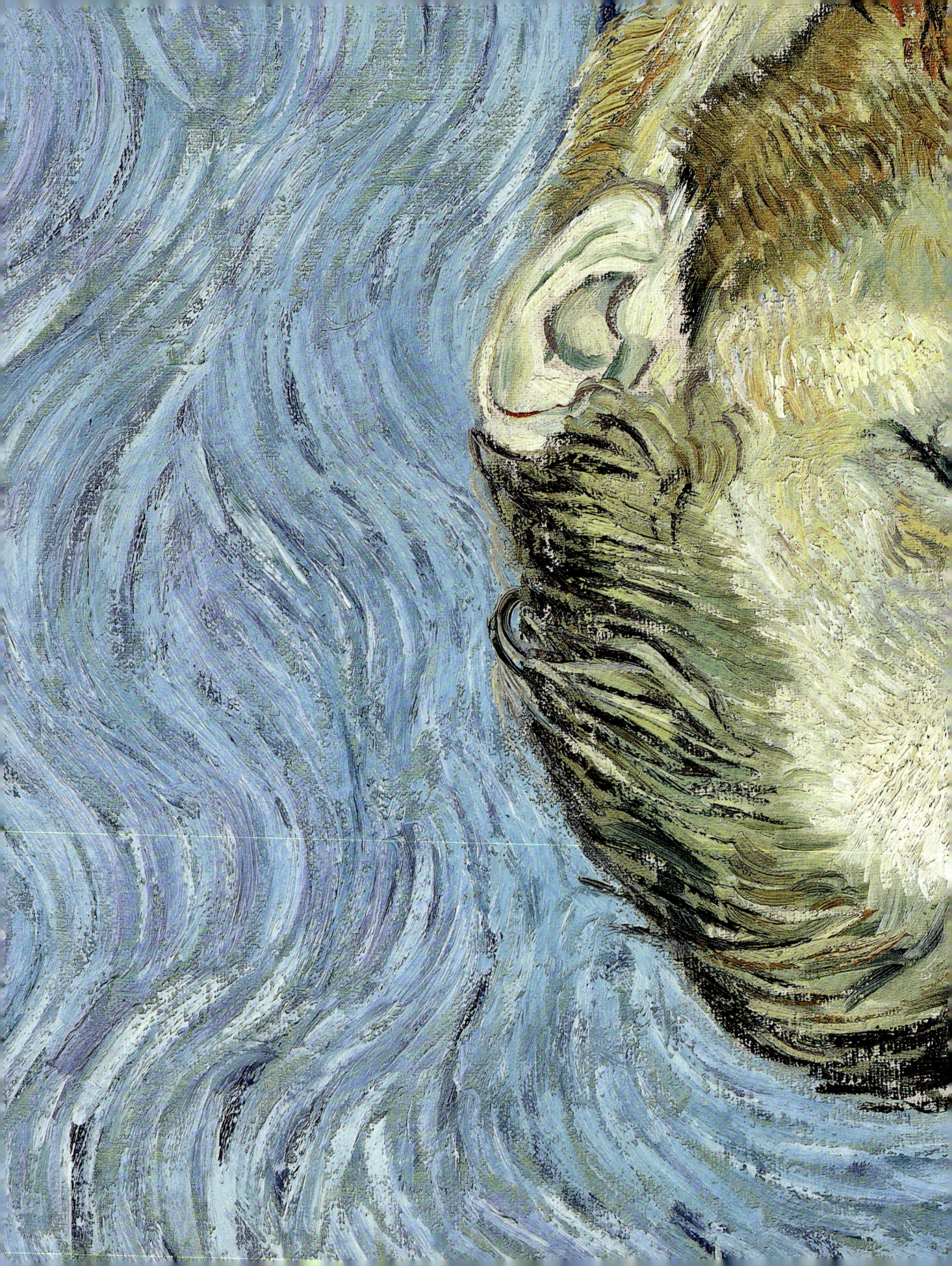

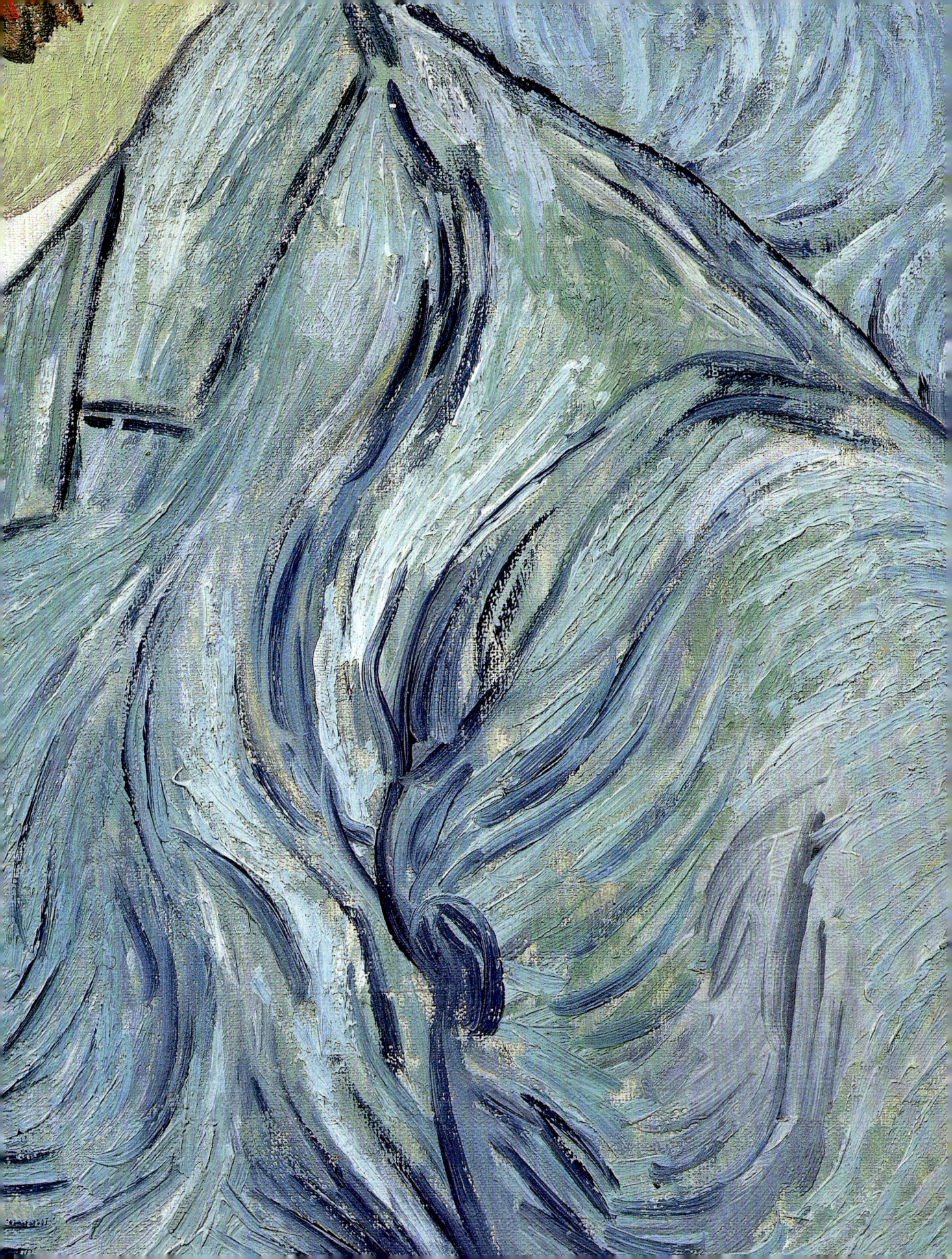

"People say, and I'm quite
willing to believe it, that it's
difficult to know oneself
– but it's not easy to paint
oneself either."

Vincent Van Gogh
Letter to Theo, summer 1889

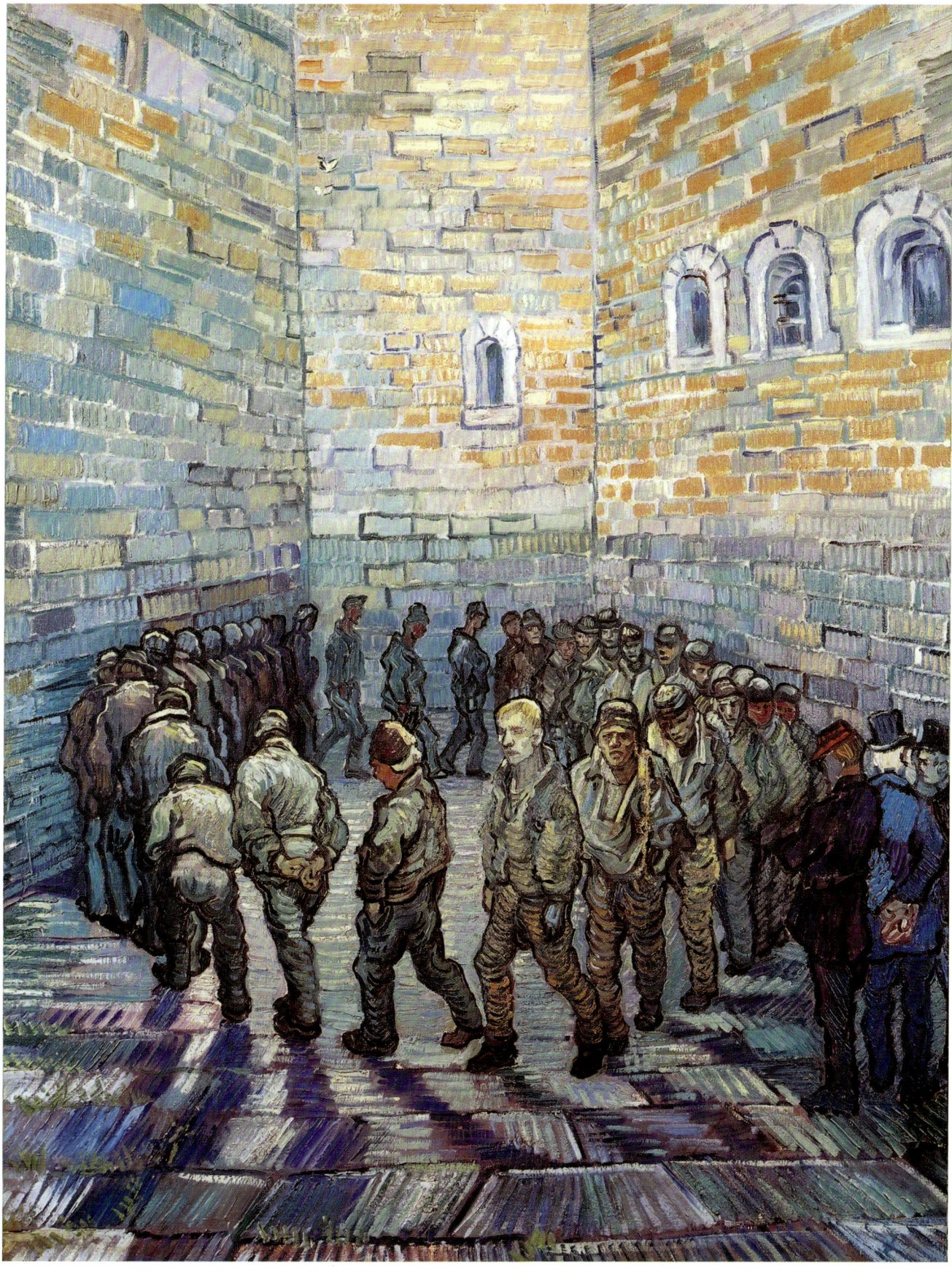

**Prisoners Exercising (after Gustave Doré),** February 1890, oil on canvas, 80 × 64 cm, Moscow, Pushkin Museum

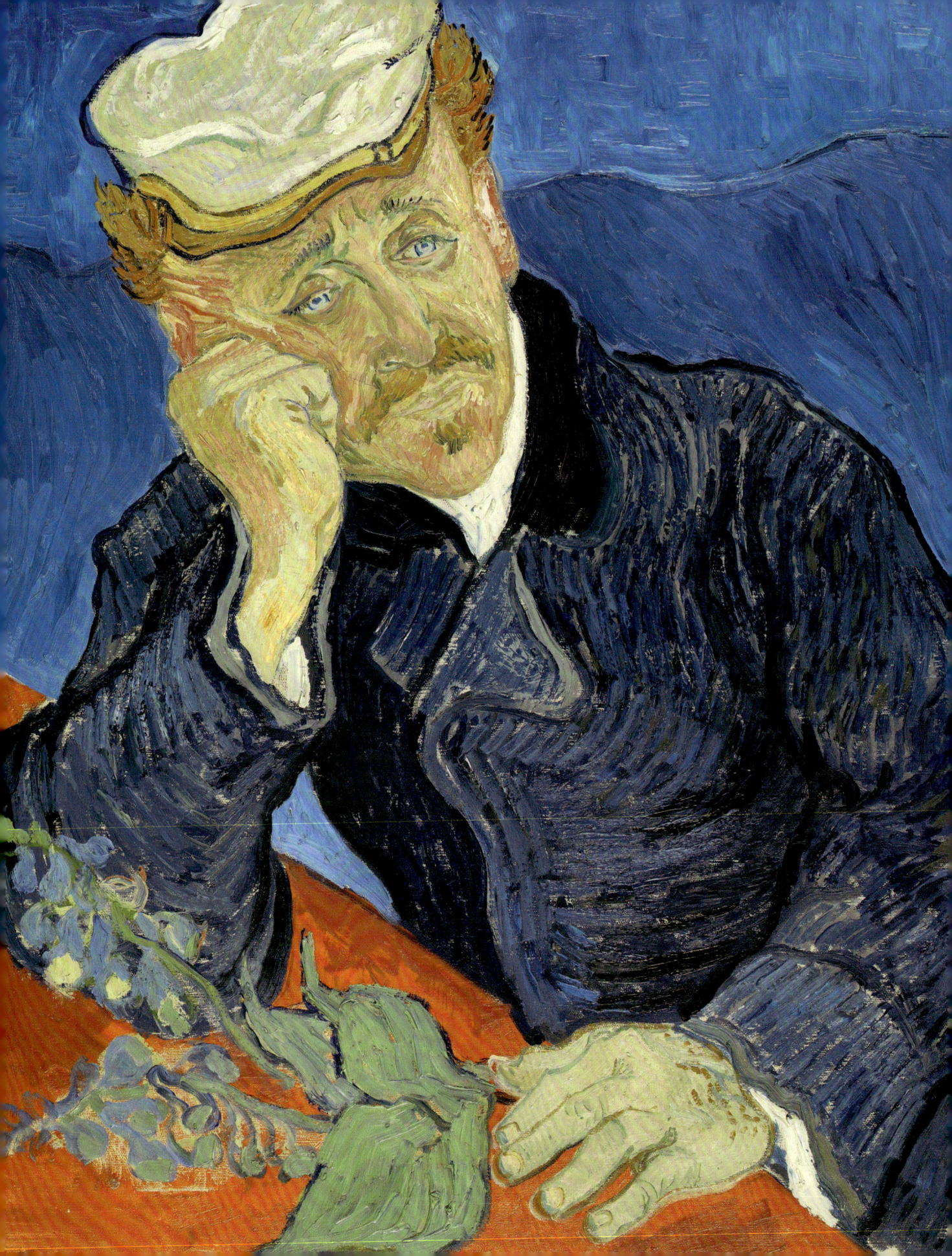

# Auvers-sur-Oise

## The last journey

Welcomed by Theo at the Gare de Lyon, Vincent spent three days in Paris with his brother, his wife Johanna and their newborn baby. Moving family moments, the rediscovery of numerous paintings stored in Theo's home – of which the artist felt that some needed to be retouched – and visits from friends; after many months of solitude, this all proved too much for Vincent, who was once again consumed by the desire to take up his paintbrushes in the peace and quiet of the countryside. Thanks to Camille Pissarro's intervention, Docteur Gachet, the artists' friend, was waiting for him in Auvers-sur-Oise.

Van Gogh immediately got on with Docteur Gachet: "He looks like a man who understands things well," Vincent wrote to Theo, although the character did seem "rather eccentric" to him. He liked the countryside, "[...] among other things, many old thatched roofs, which are becoming rare [...] It's gravely beautiful." The first motif that he tried his hand at was that of thatched cottages, from which he drew an important conclusion about colour: "And I already feel that it did me good to travel to the Midi, the better to see the North. It is as I thought, I see more violet hues wherever they are."

Lodging at the Ravoux Inn, on Place de la Mairie, Van Gogh was welcomed into a family atmosphere, where he led a regular life: he got up at five o'clock, went to bed at nine and spent his days at his easel, painting continuously. In the mornings, he worked on his chosen motif; in the afternoons, he worked in the back room of the inn. During the seventy days that he remained in Auvers, he would produce some seventy-five paintings and sixty drawings.

He first depicted the village, which struck him as very beautiful, as well as its streets and inhabitants (p. 111), and its town hall. Docteur Gachet's presence, even only a few days a week, allowed him to have a semblance of a social life, while also providing him with a number of motifs. He would paint his portrait (p. 106), which he commented on in a letter to his sister Willemien: "I've done the portrait of Monsieur Gachet with an expression of melancholy, which might often appear to be a grimace to those looking at the canvas. [...] Compared to the calm ancient portraits, how much expression there is in our present-day heads, and passion and something like waiting and a shout." The doctor's daughter, Marguerite, also appears in his paintings, depicted in front of their piano or in their garden (p. 117). Another garden in Auvers also caught the artist's eye – that of Charles Daubigny, who died in 1878, and whom Vincent greatly admired. Flowers also blossomed under his brush, whether as sumptuous bouquets of roses, irises (pp. 112 and 113) or simple field flowers.

One of Van Gogh's masterpieces during his stay in Auvers is undoubtedly the village church (p. 119), which he painted in the early days of June. In this boldly chromatic painting, he exalts the complementary colours, describing the work himself in a letter to his sister: "[...] the building appears purplish against a sky of a deep and simple blue of pure cobalt, the stained-glass windows look like ultramarine blue patches, the roof is violet and, in part, orange. In the foreground, a little flowery greenery and some sunny-pink sand."

Vincent did not either deprive himself of the joys of colour, despite painting in tones that were more muted than in the Midi when he depicted the surroundings of the village, the banks of the Oise (p. 120-121) and, above all, the fields stretching to the horizon in the rolling plain (p. 118). The famous *Wheatfield with Crows* (p. 122-123), which he painted in July, depicts three diverging paths cutting through the wheat, with black birds against a stormy sky. It was long considered, without proof, to be his last painting: it gave rise to many interpretations, with many commentators reading in this work a premonitory vision of his imminent death.

At the beginning of July, Vincent went to spend a day in Paris, at Theo's house. Despite the friendly presence of Émile Bernard, Henri de Toulouse-Lautrec and Albert Aurier, the atmosphere was heavy. For the first time, Van Gogh's brother, who was himself in conflict with his employers, alluded to the financial weight that his upkeep represented; also, Johanna told him that they were going to spend their holidays in Holland, instead of the stay that they had planned in Auvers.

At this time, Vincent also became aware that he could not rely on Docteur Gachet. Despite the reassurance that his family would later attempt to offer, he was once again confronted with his tragic solitude; and, as the days went by, he felt beset by the terror of a new crisis. Without telling anyone around him, Vincent went to a gunsmith in Pontoise, where he purchased a revolver. Three days later, on 27 July, he shot himself in the heart. After several long hours in agony, he passed on 29 July, with his faithful brother Theo at his bedside.

**Portrait of Doctor Gachet** (detail, p. 106)
June 1890, oil on canvas, 68.2 × 57 cm, Paris, Musée d'Orsay

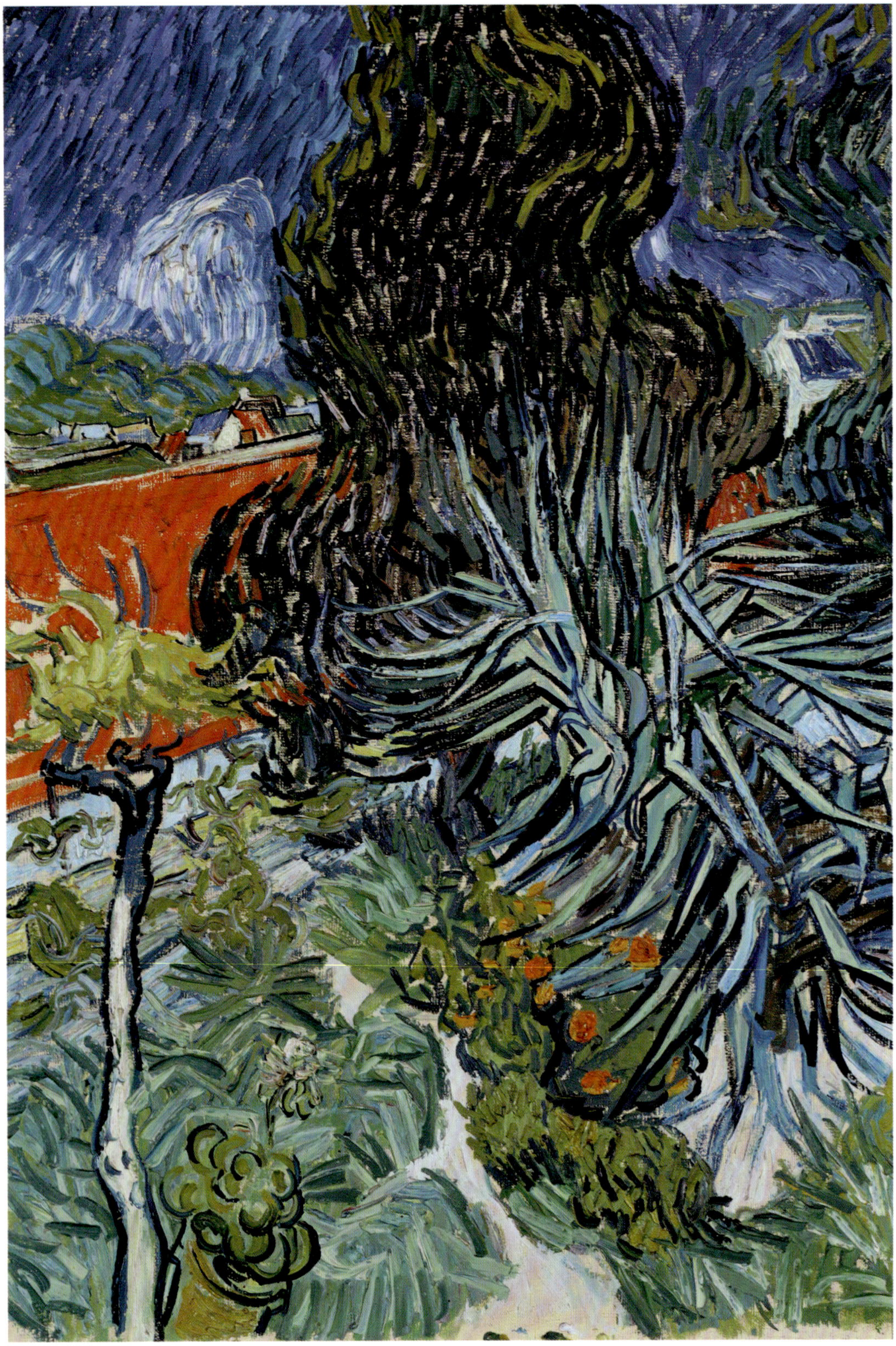

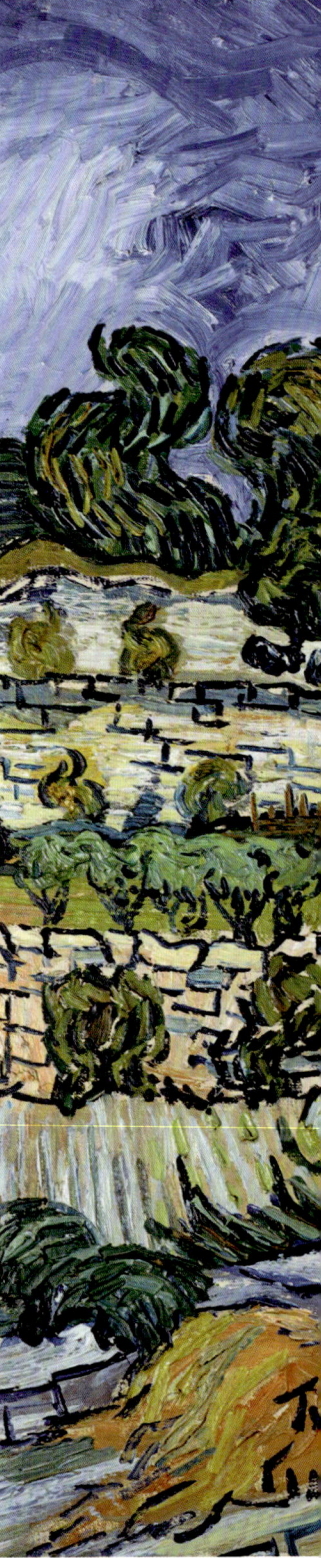

**Doctor Gachet's Garden in Auvers,** May 1890, oil on canvas, 73 × 52 cm, Paris, Musée d'Orsay

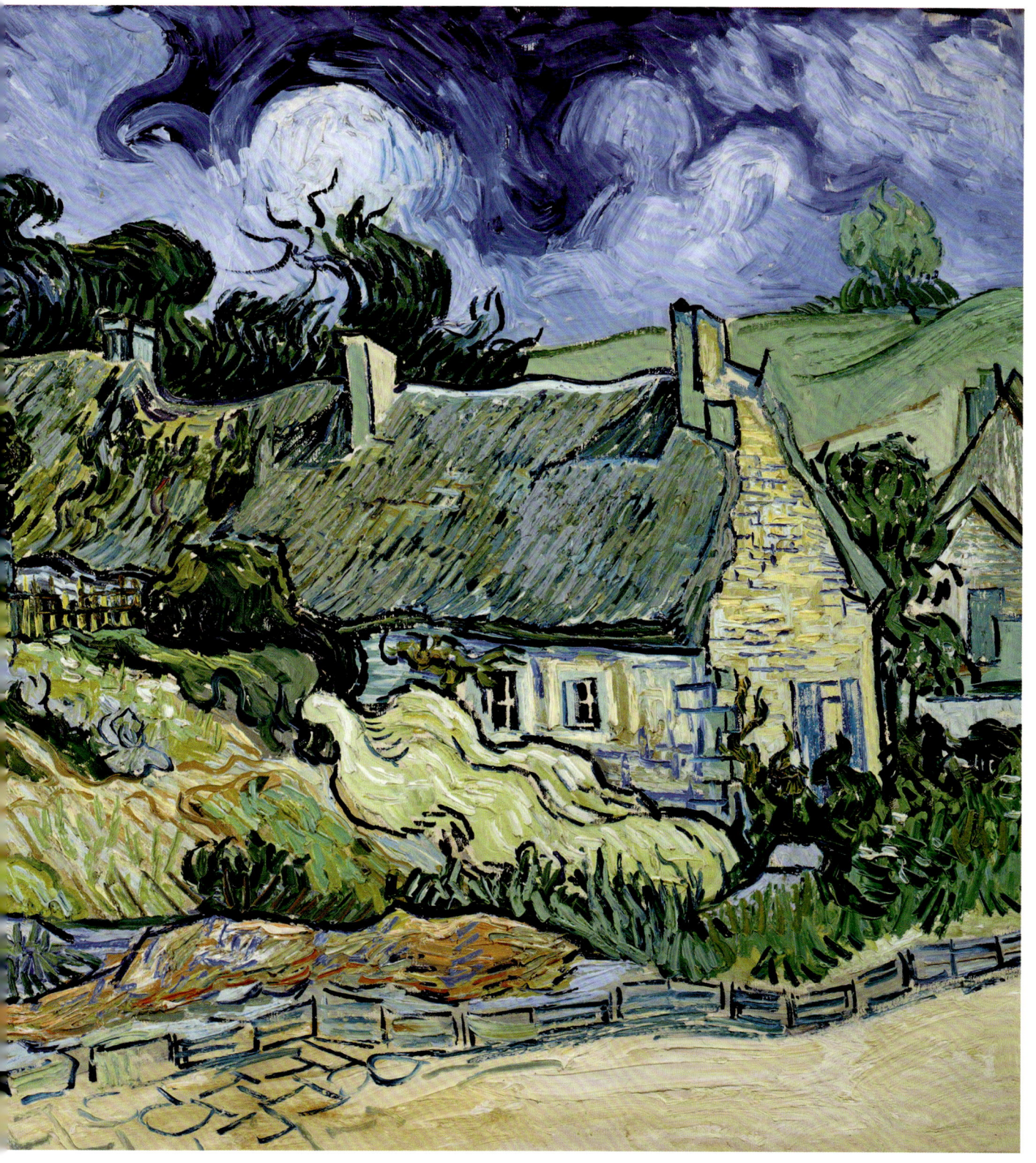

**Thatched Cottages at Cordeville,** June 1890, oil on canvas, 73 × 92 cm, Paris, Musée d'Orsay

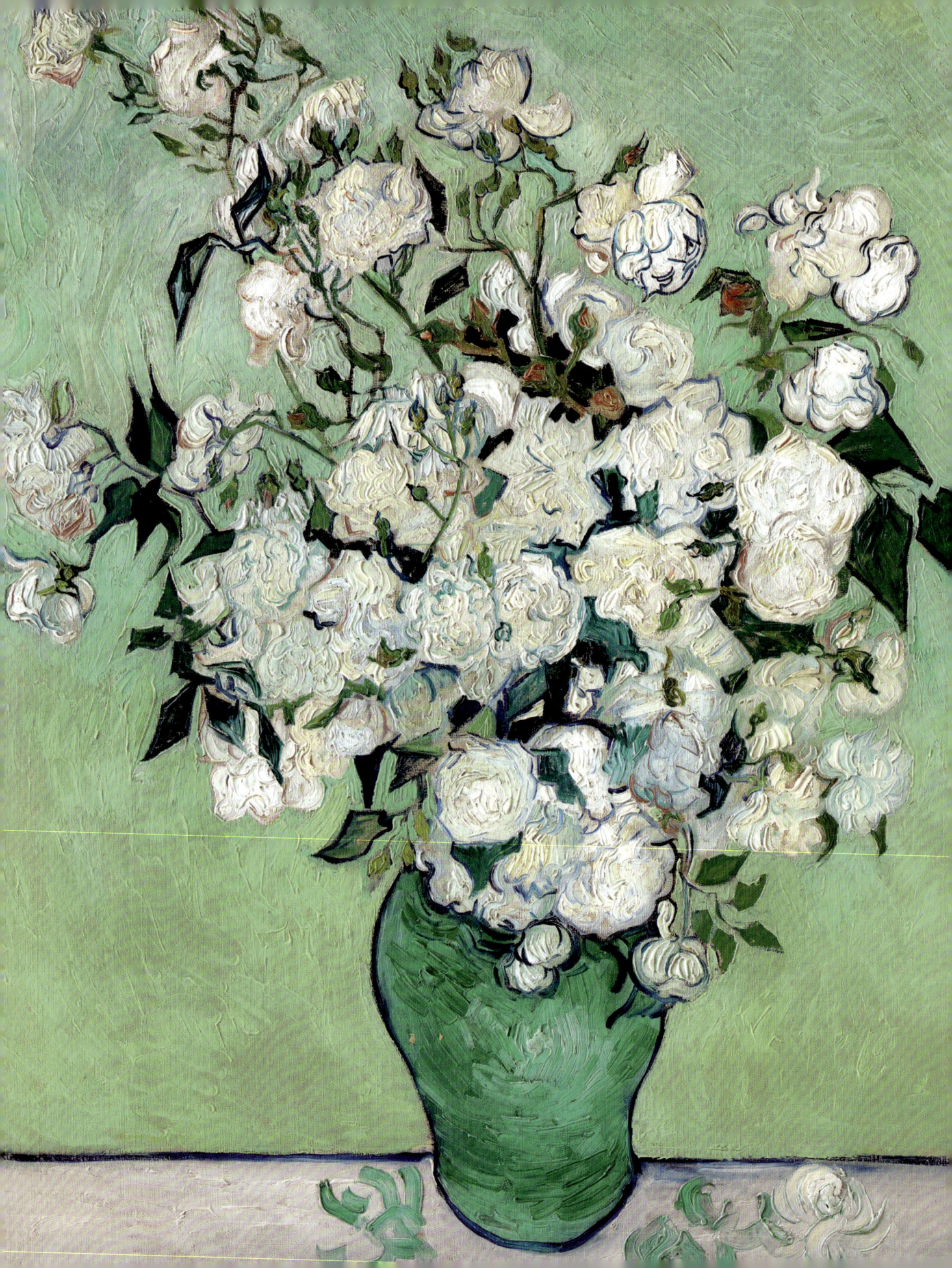

# Almond Blossoms

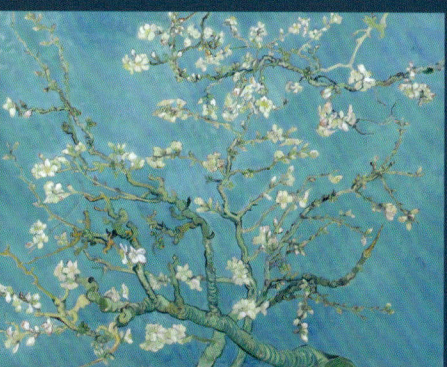

This very fresh painting was produced by Van Gogh in Saint-Rémy-de-Provence, in February 1890, to celebrate the birth of his nephew and godson, his brother Theo's son, born on 31 January. He chose to symbolise this new life with a painting of a blossoming almond branch, a metaphor for spring and the renewal of nature. The delicate petals, which have now turned white, were originally pale pink. The composition is remarkable in its originality: the trunk is not visible, and the flowering branches appear to float in the sky. Inspired by the Japanese prints that he admired, Van Gogh adopted a style that was both realistic and synthetic, depicting flowers with great precision, against a flat blue tint. In July, the same year, Van Gogh would see this painting hanging in baby Vincent's bedroom in Paris.

*Almond Blossoms*, February 1890, oil on canvas, 73.3 × 92.4 cm, Amsterdam, Van Gogh Museum
*Roses*, 1890, oil on canvas,
93 × 74 cm, New York, The Metropolitan Museum of Art (left, detail)

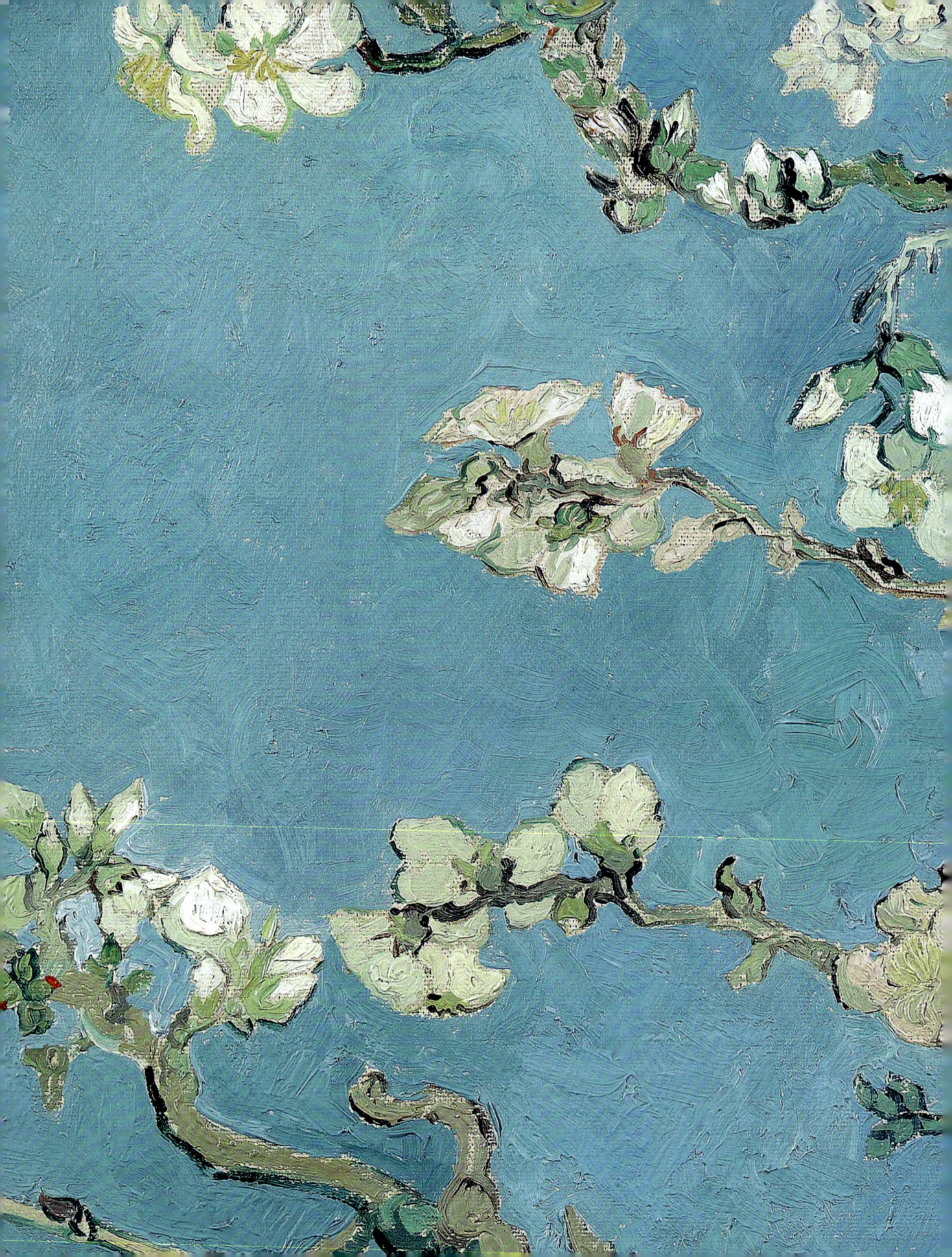

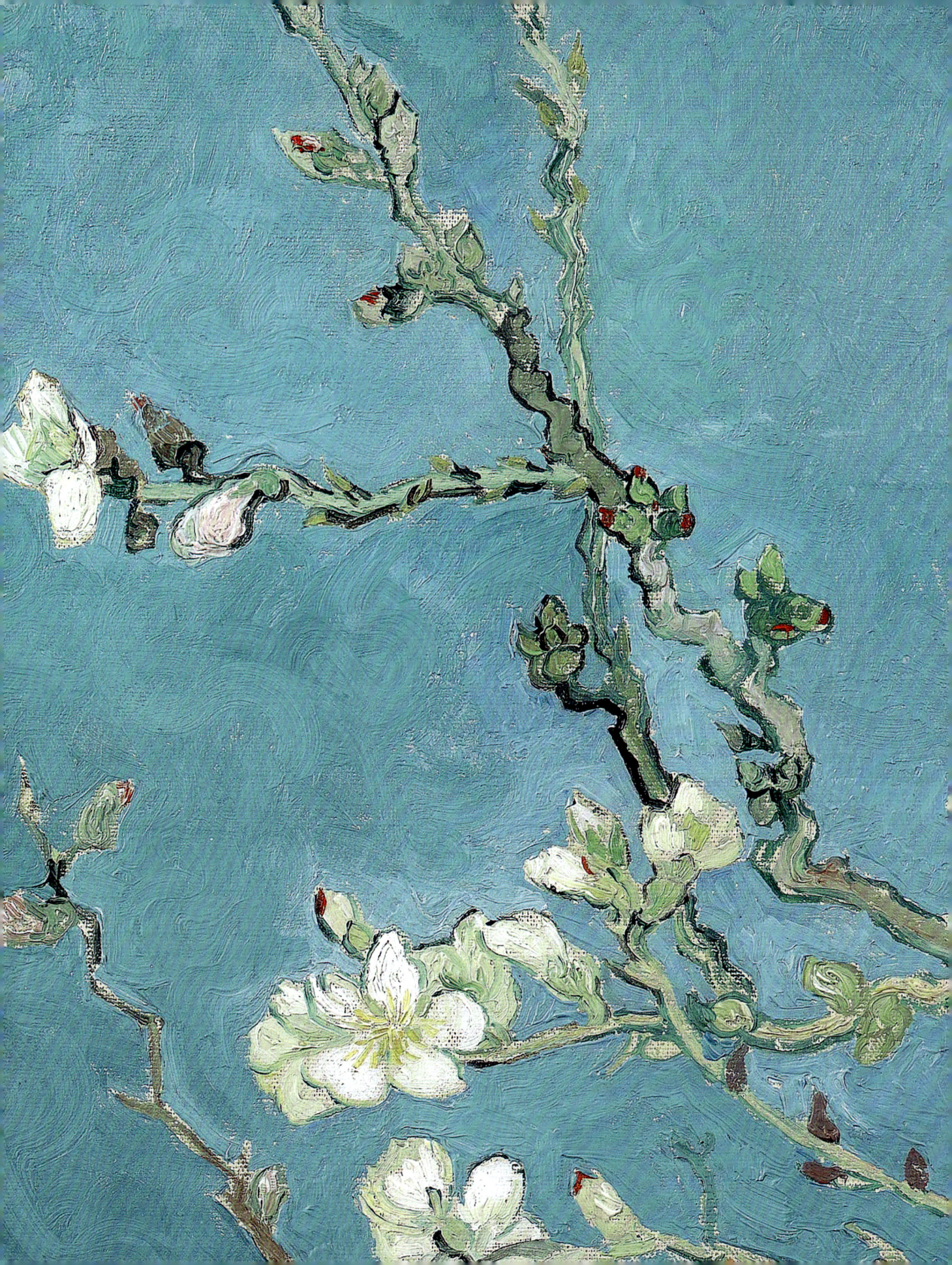

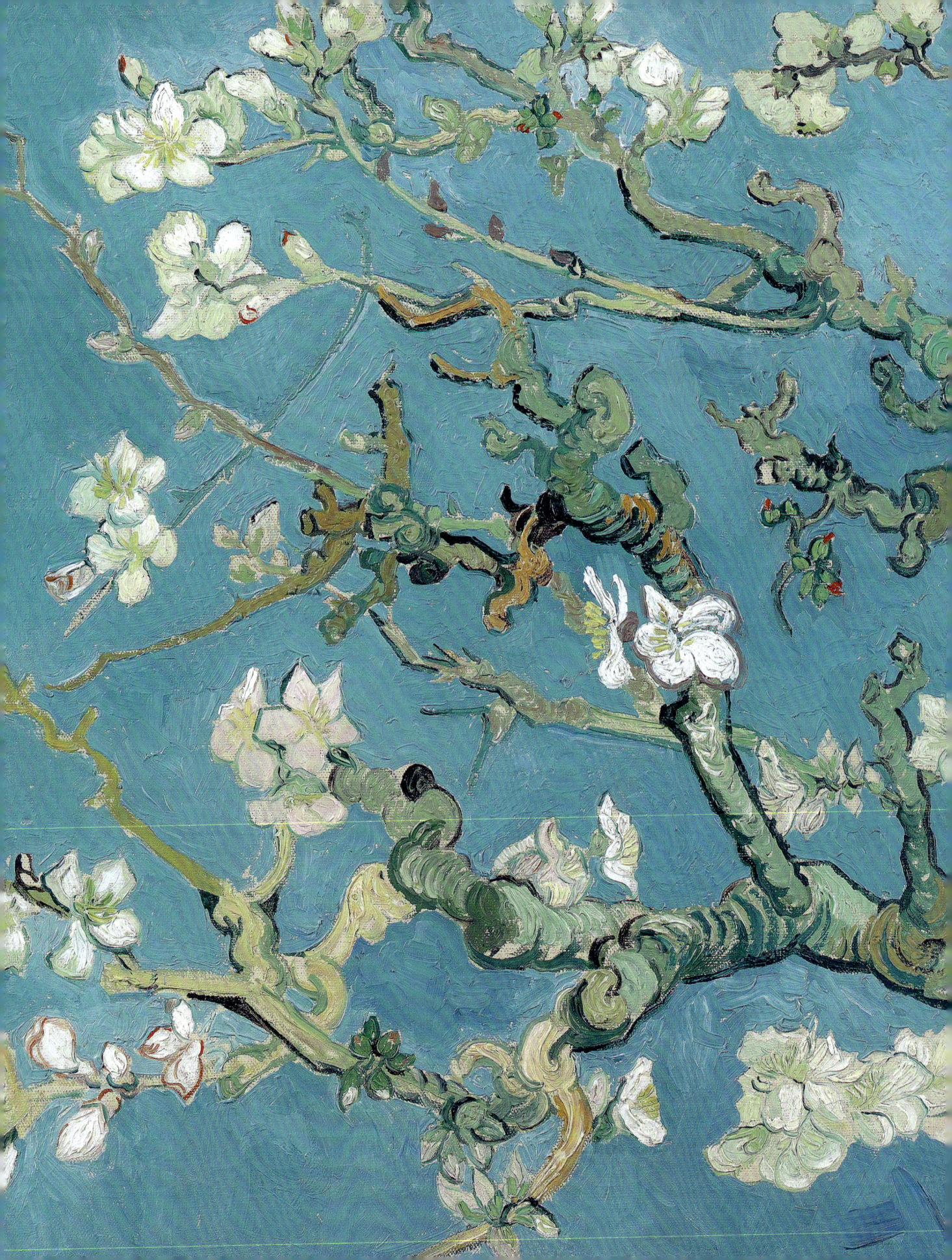

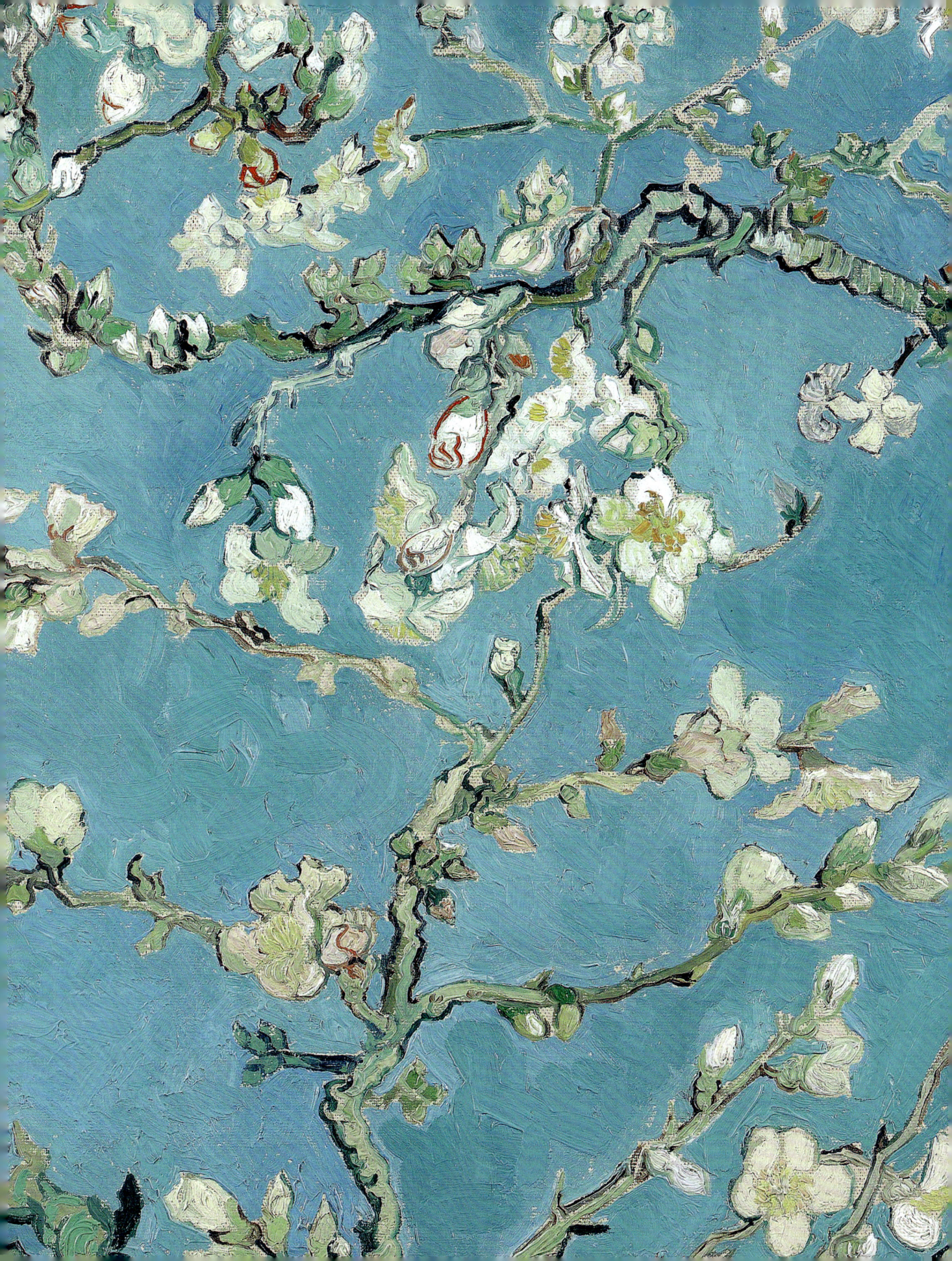

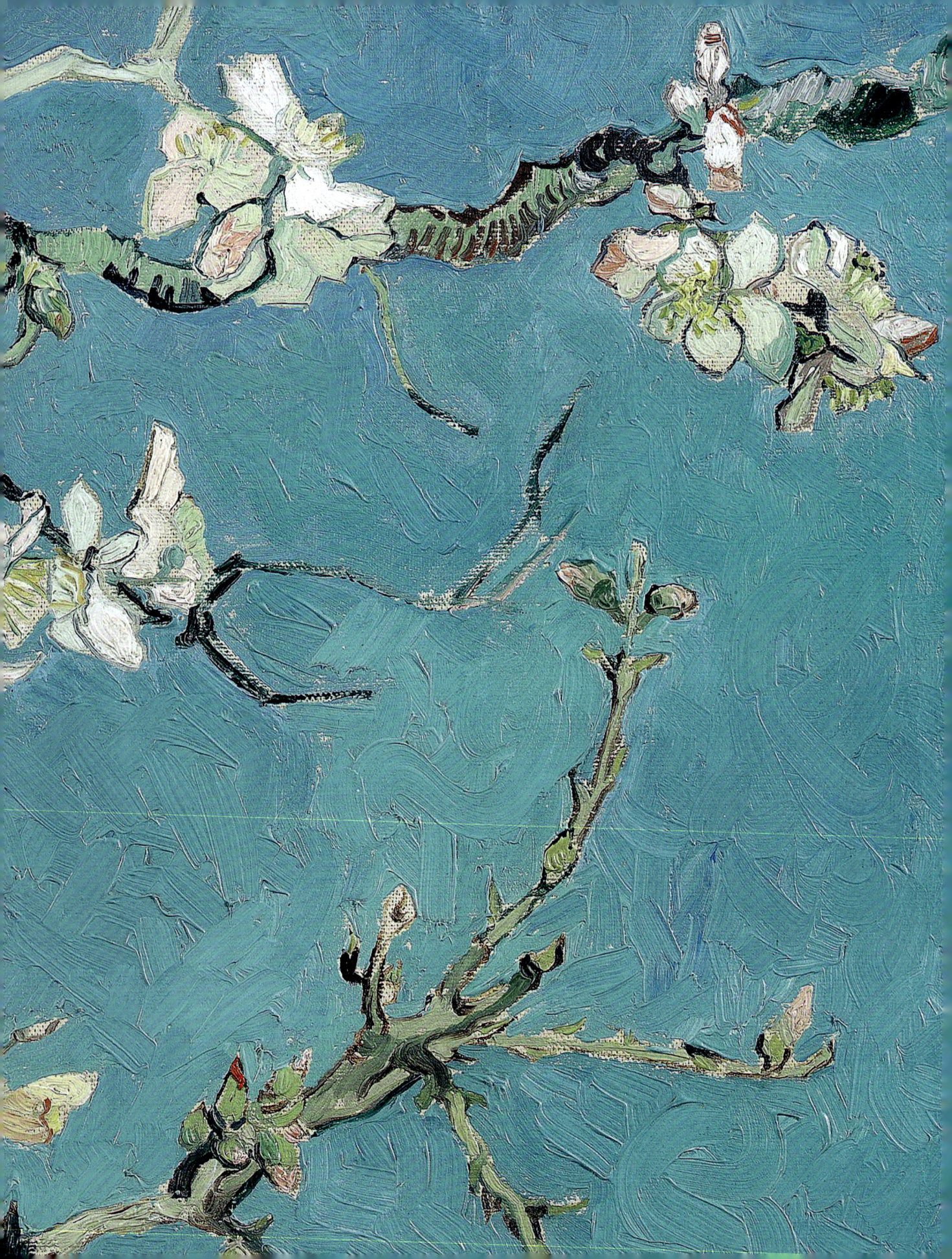

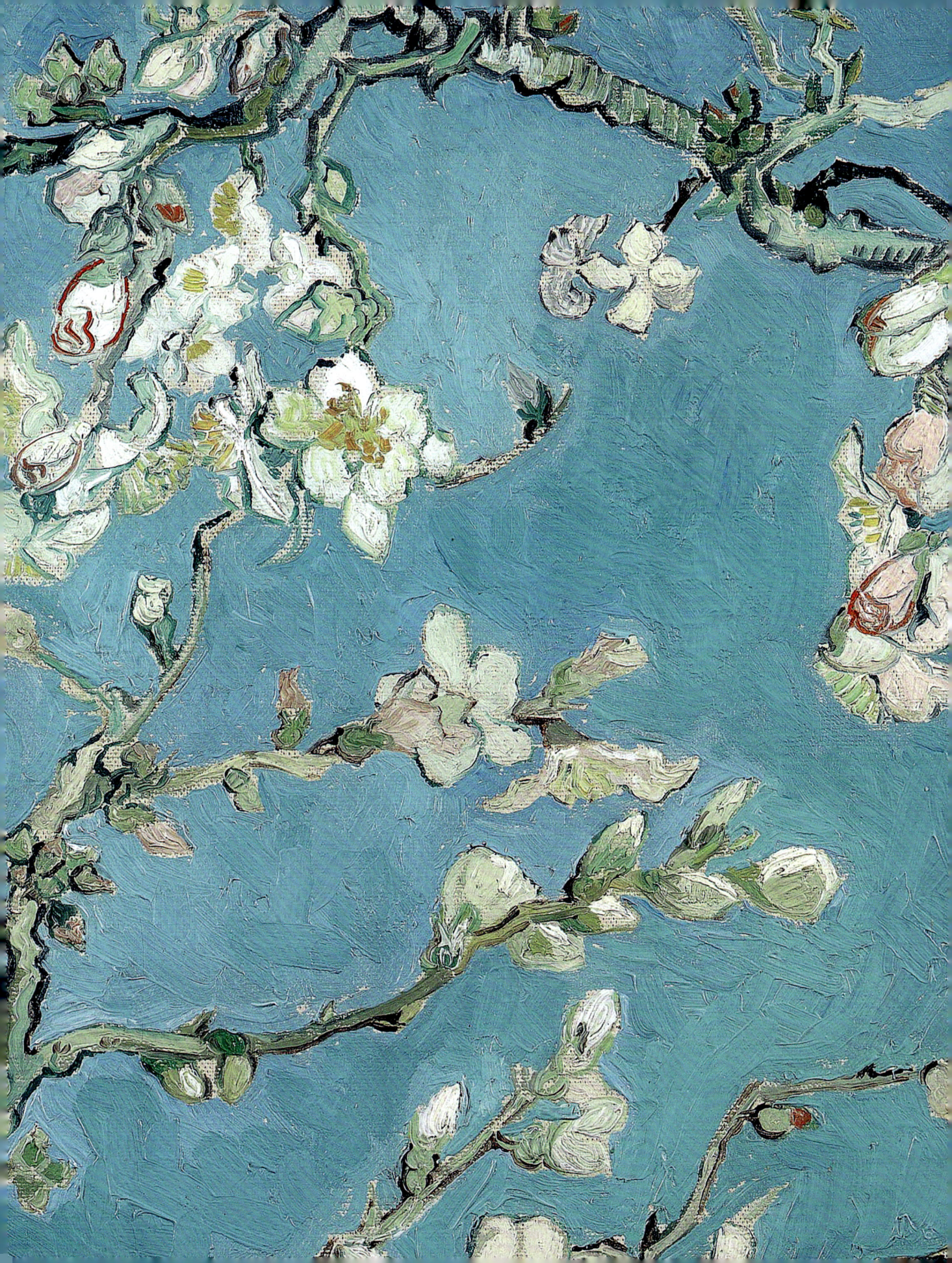

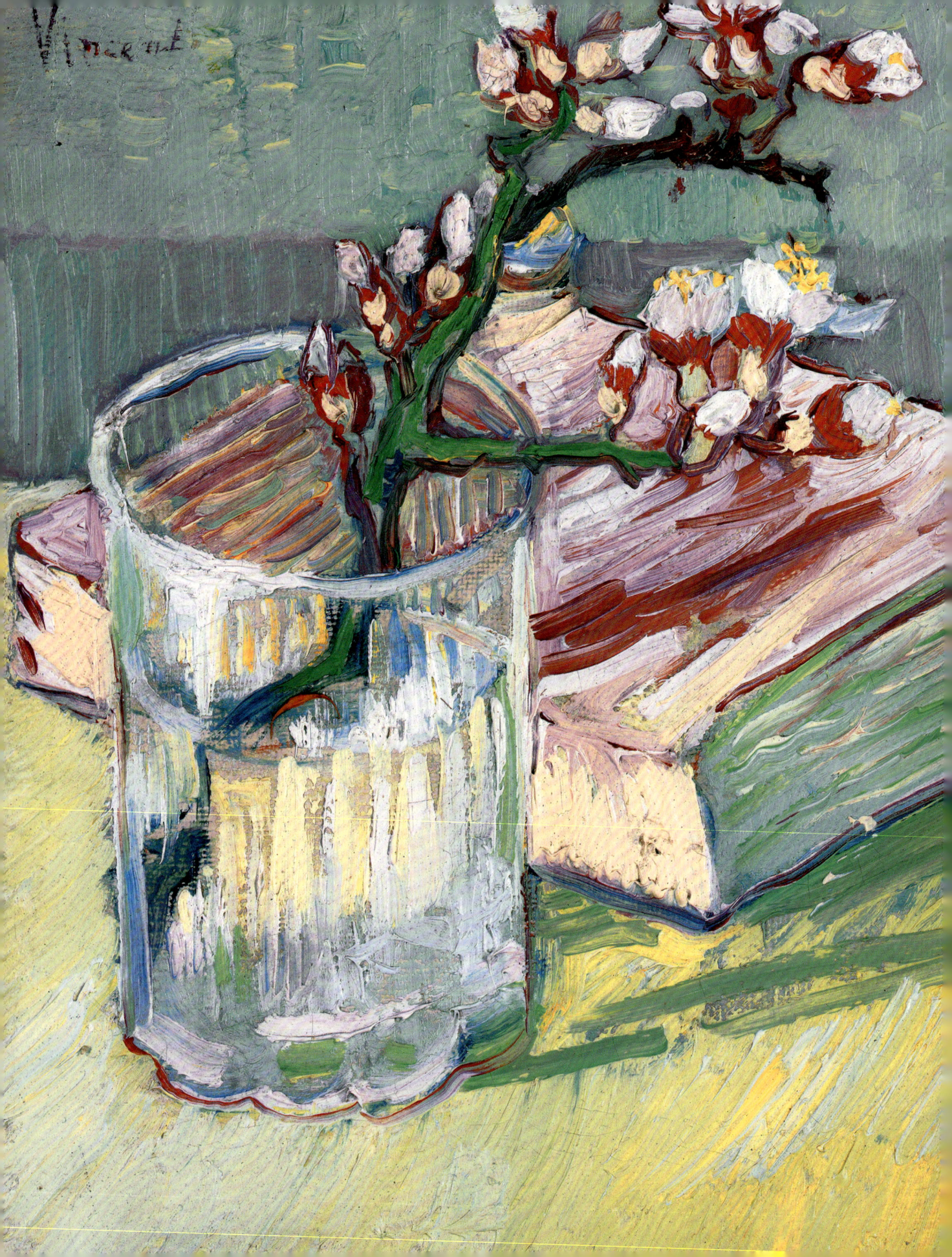

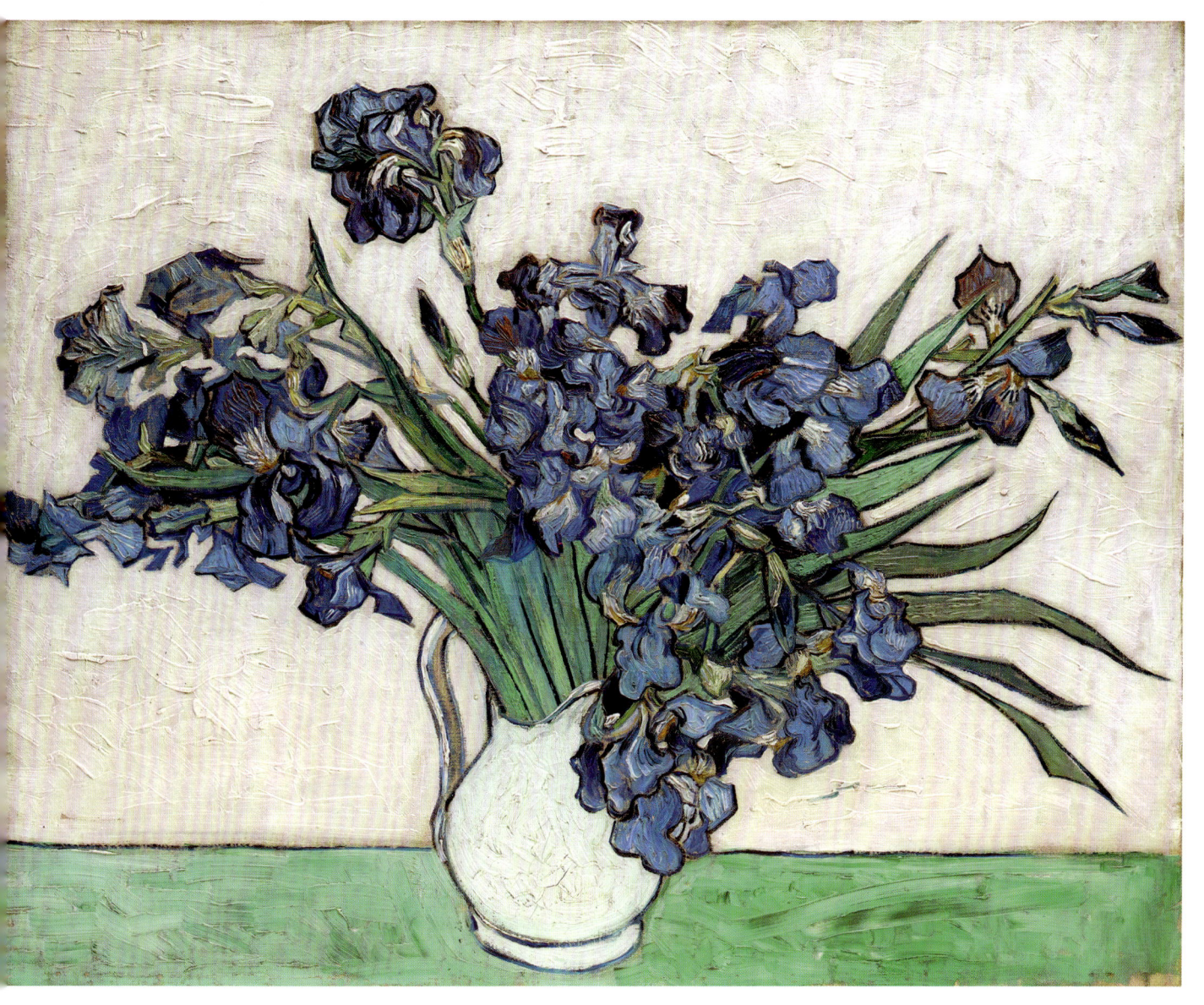

**Irises**

May 1890
Oil on canvas, 73.7 × 92.1 cm
New York, The Metropolitan Museum of Art

**Blossoming Almond Branch in a Glass with a Book**

February-March 1888
Oil on canvas, 24.2 × 19.1 cm
Private collection (left, detail)

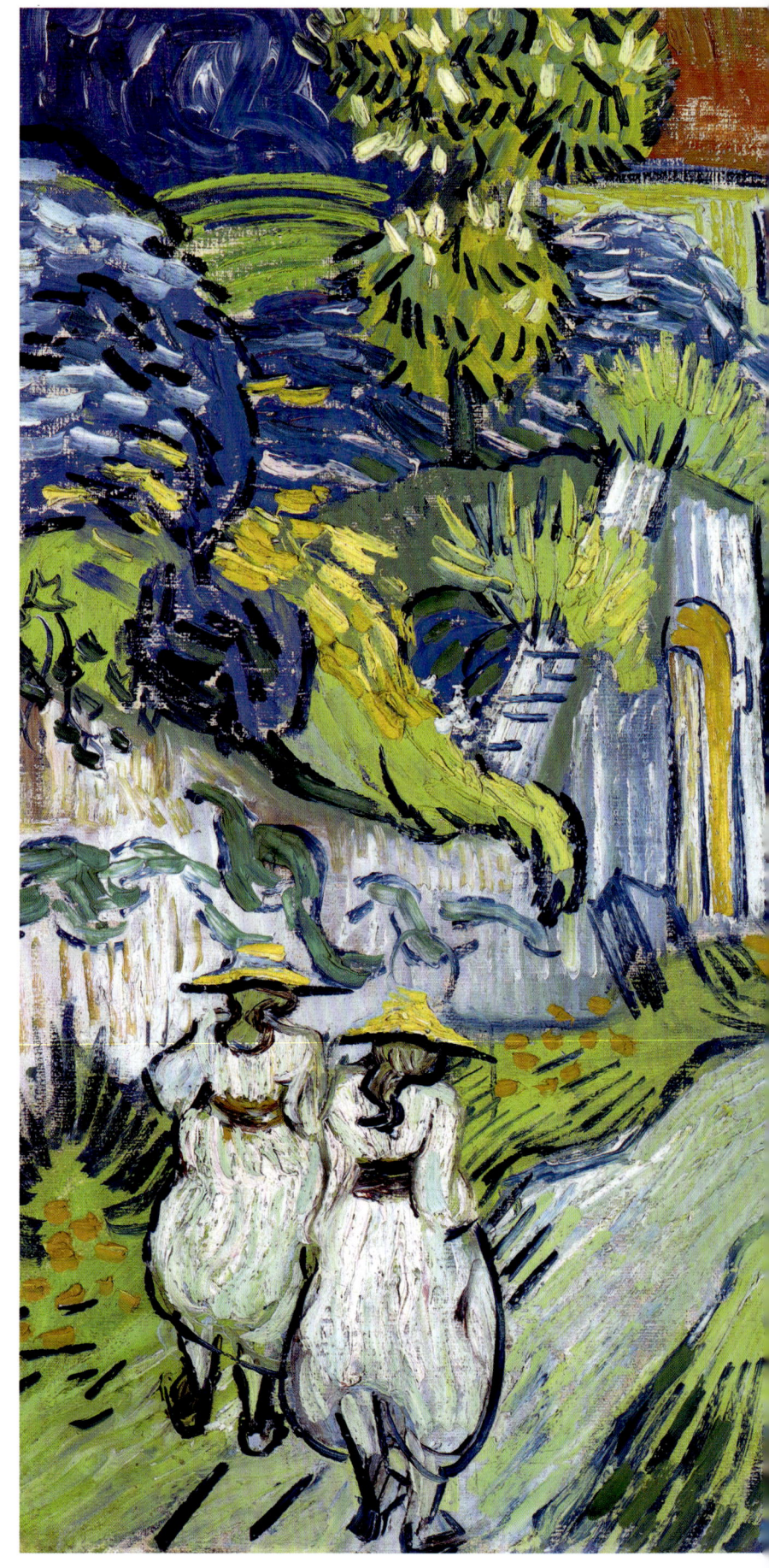

**Stairway at Auvers**

May 1890
Oil on canvas, 50 × 70.5 cm
Saint-Louis, Saint-Louis Art Museum

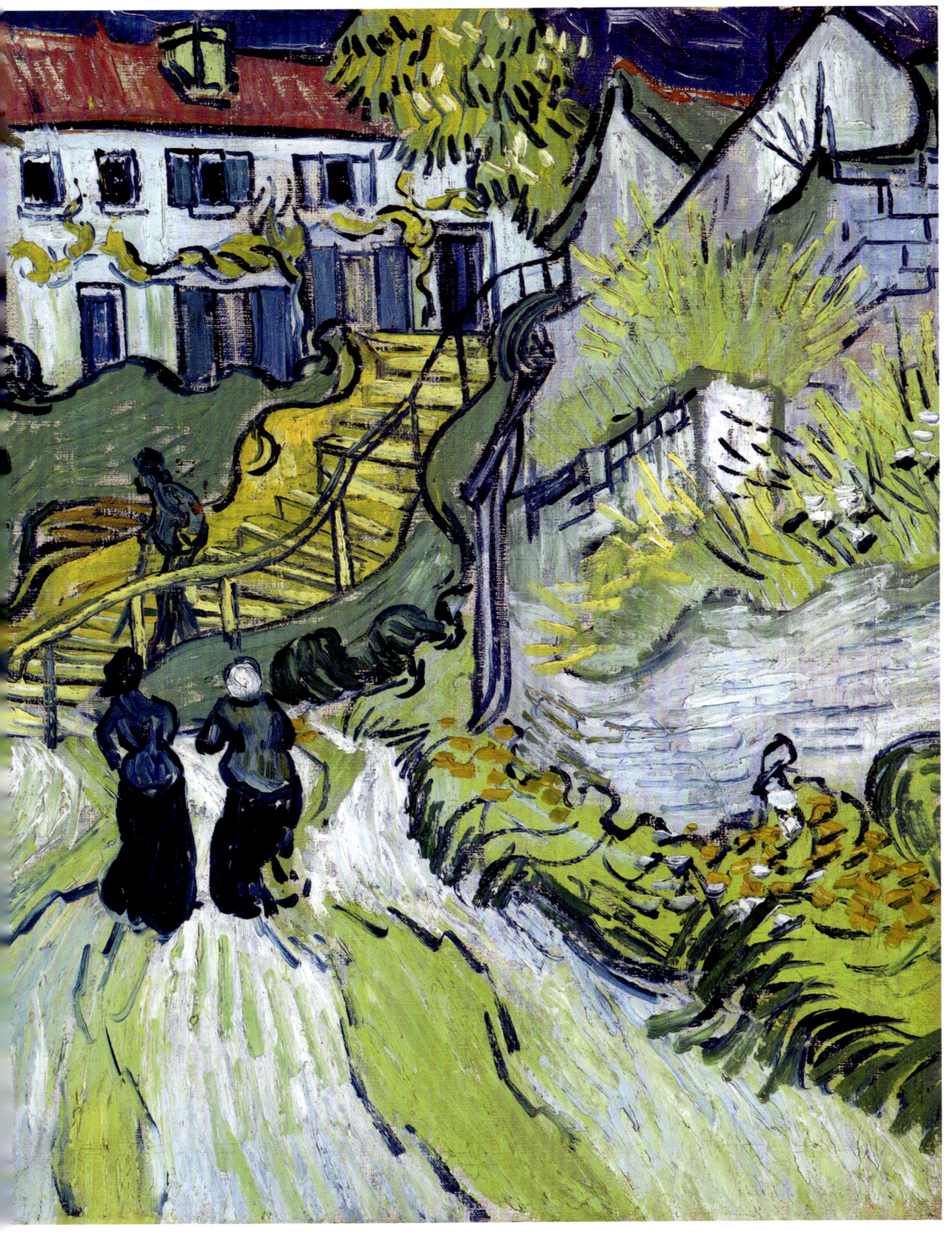

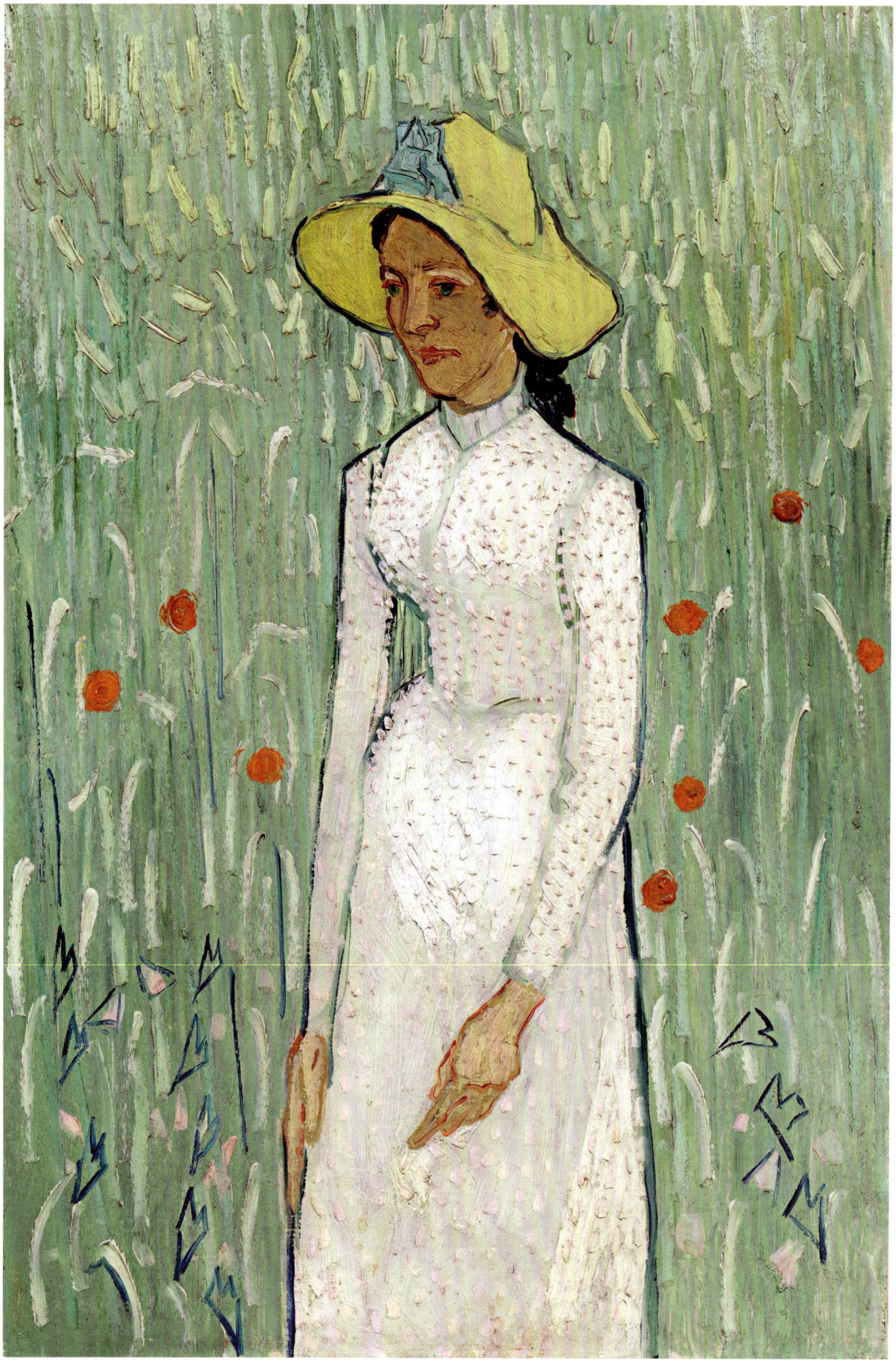

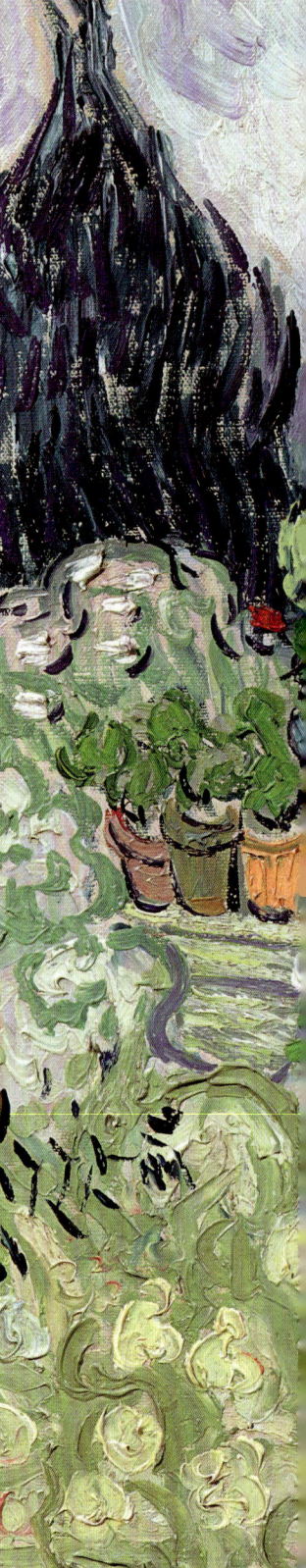

**Girl in White,** 1890, oil on canvas, 66.7 × 45.8 cm, Washington, National Gallery of Art

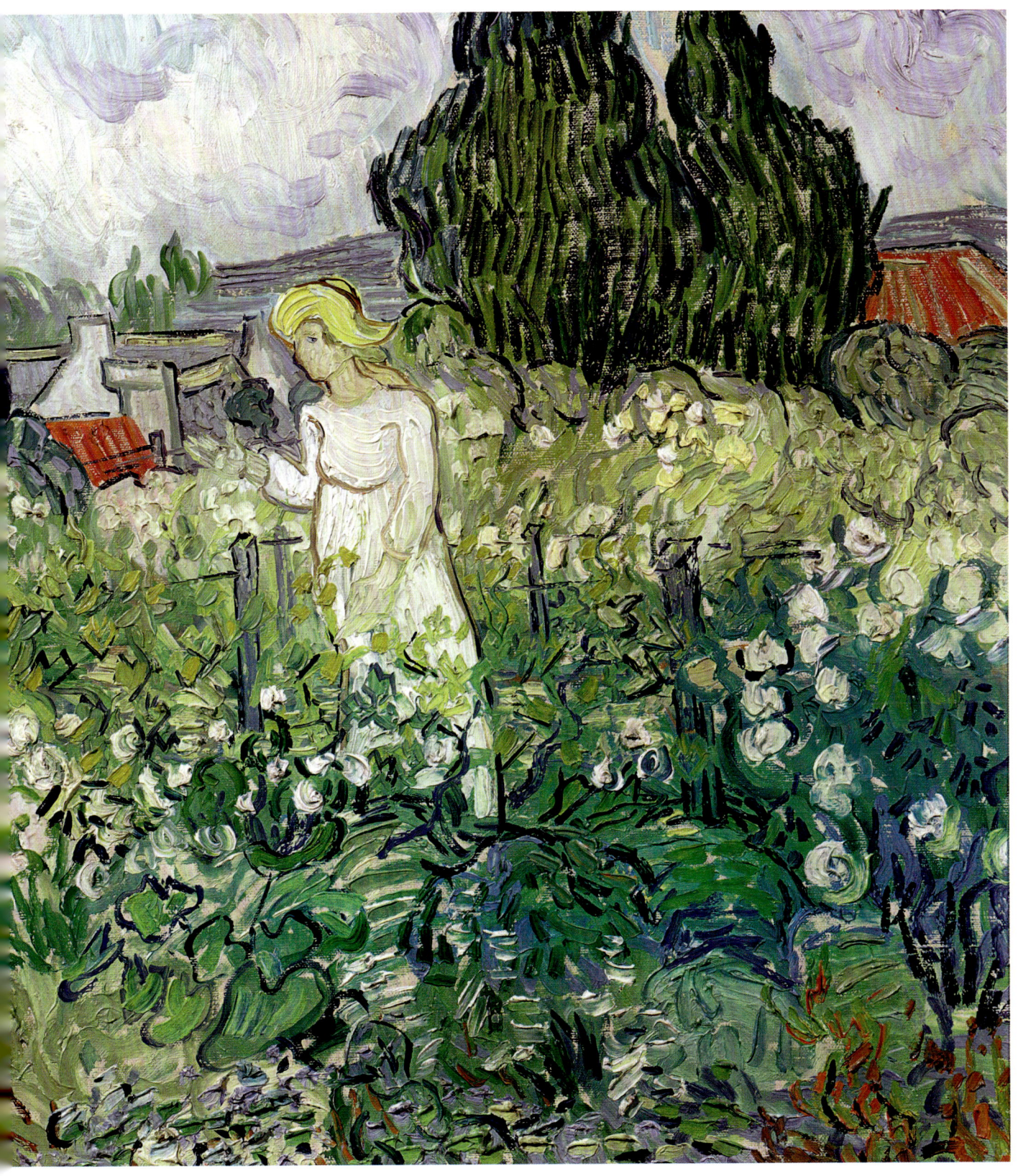

**Doctor Gachet's Garden in Auvers-sur-Oise,** June 1890, oil on canvas, 46 × 55.5 cm, Paris, Musée d'Orsay

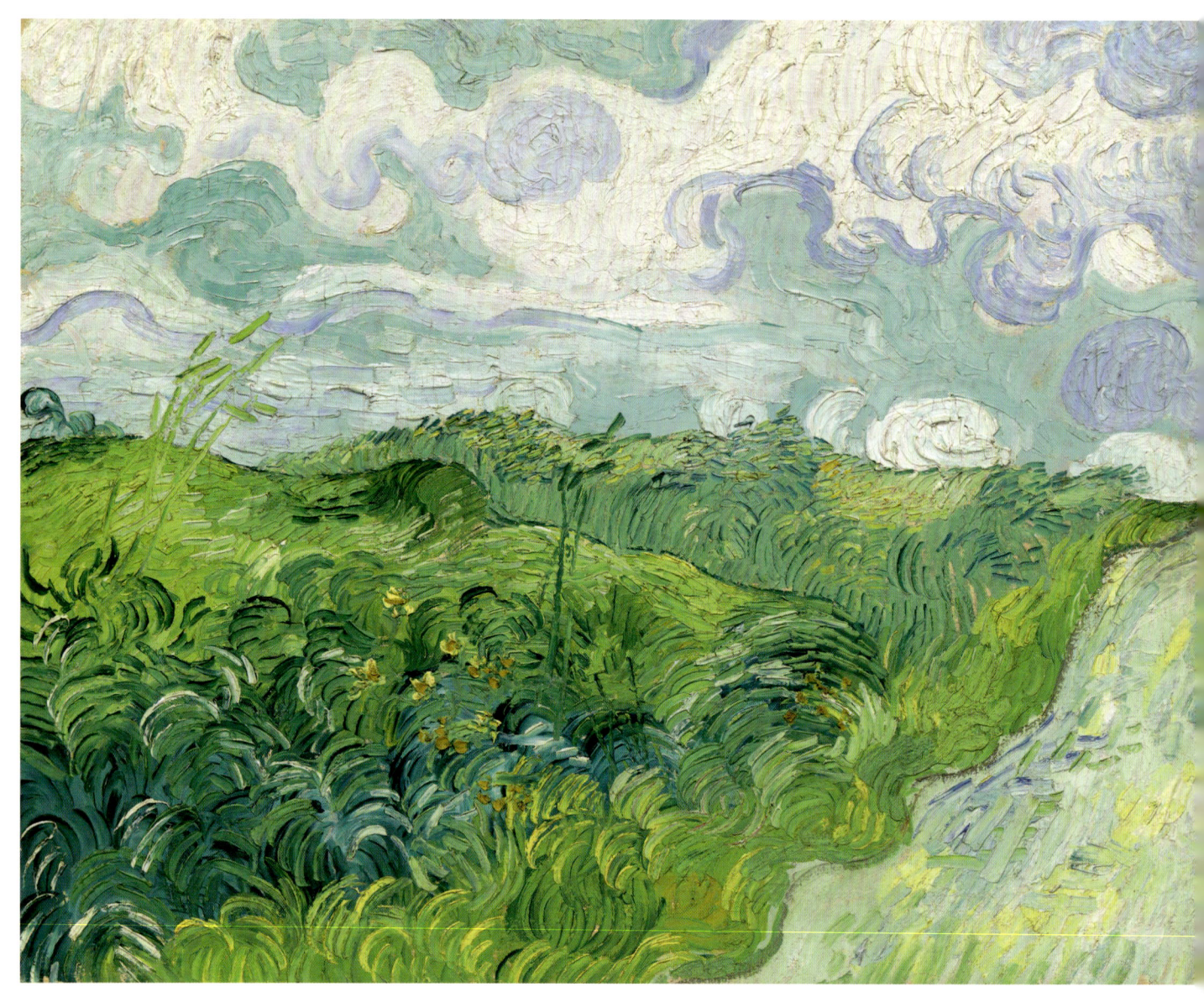

**Green Wheat Fields, Auvers**

June 1890
Oil on canvas, 72.4 × 91.4 cm
Washington, National Gallery of Art

**The Church at Auvers**

1890
Oil on canvas, 93 × 74.5 cm
Paris, Musée d'Orsay

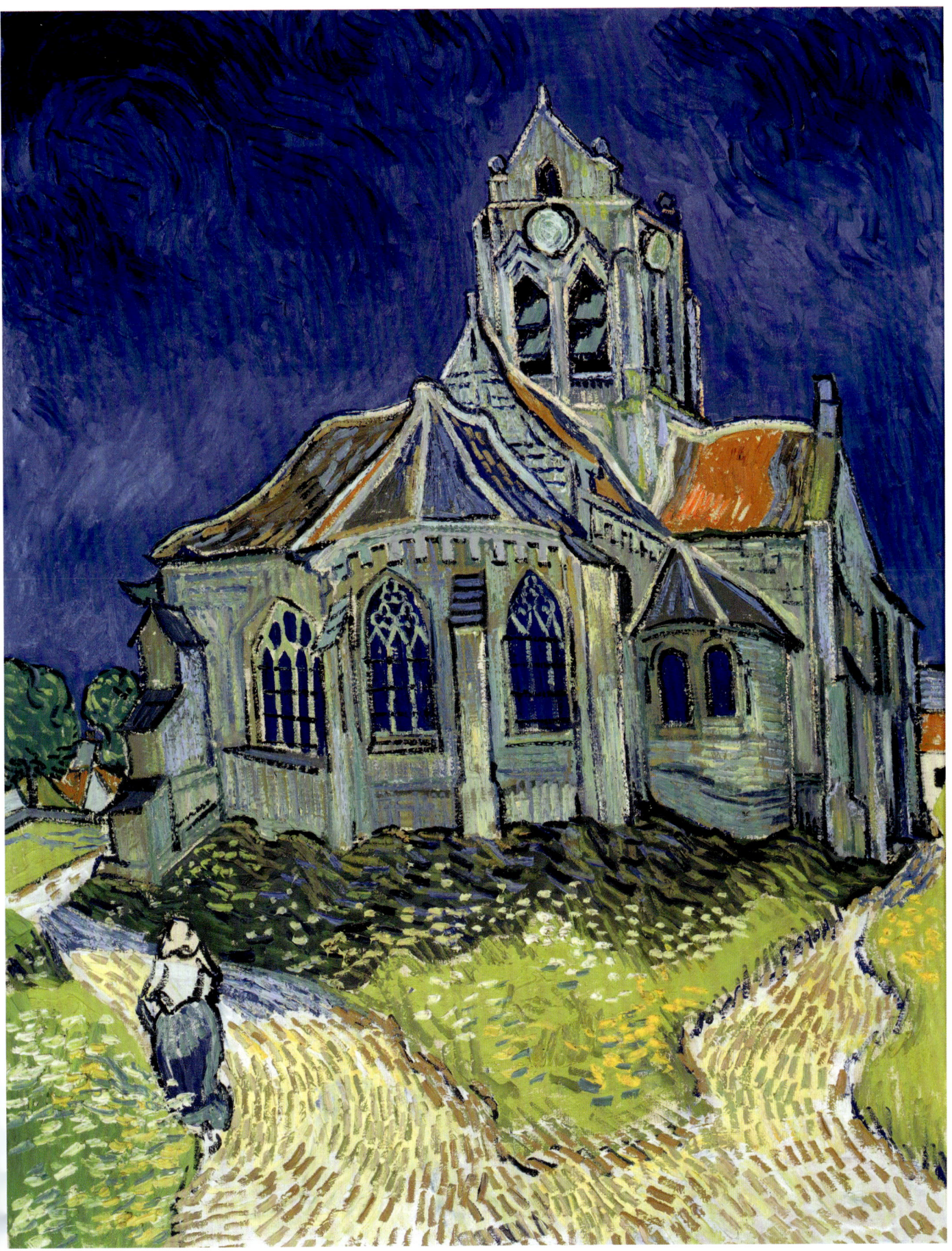

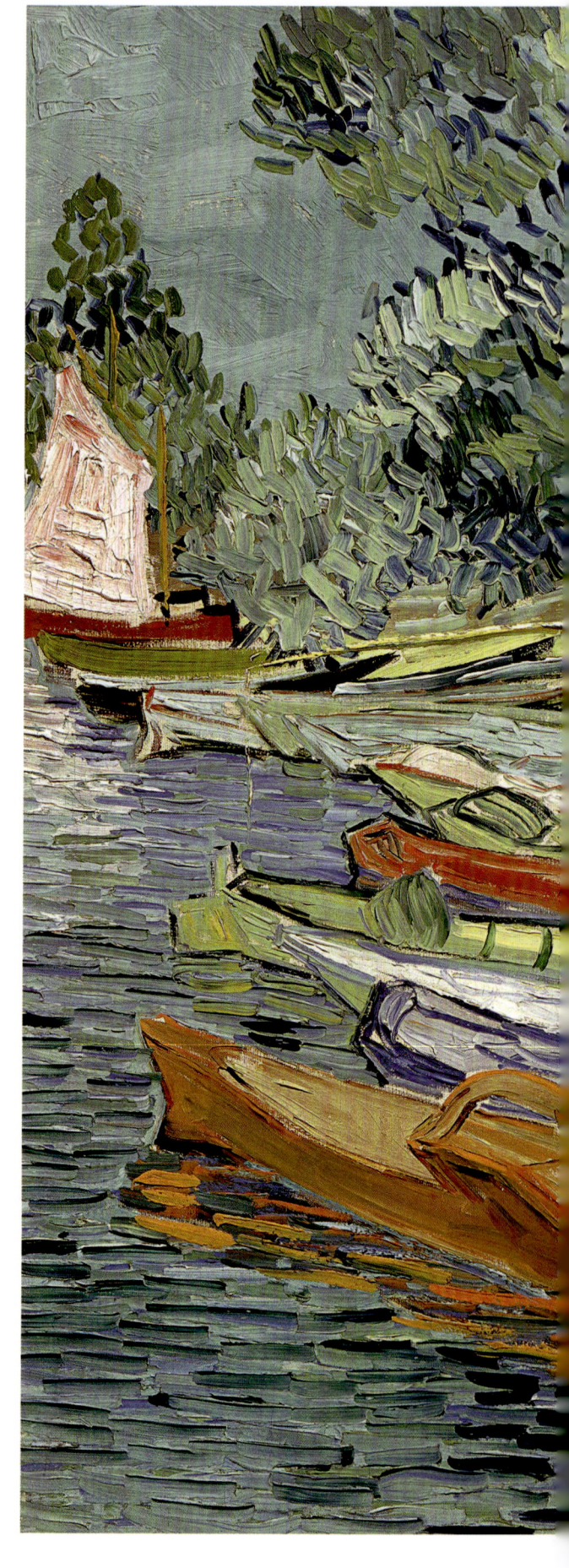

**Banks of the Oise at Auvers**

July 1890
Oil on canvas, 73.3 × 93.7 cm
Detroit, Detroit Institute of Arts

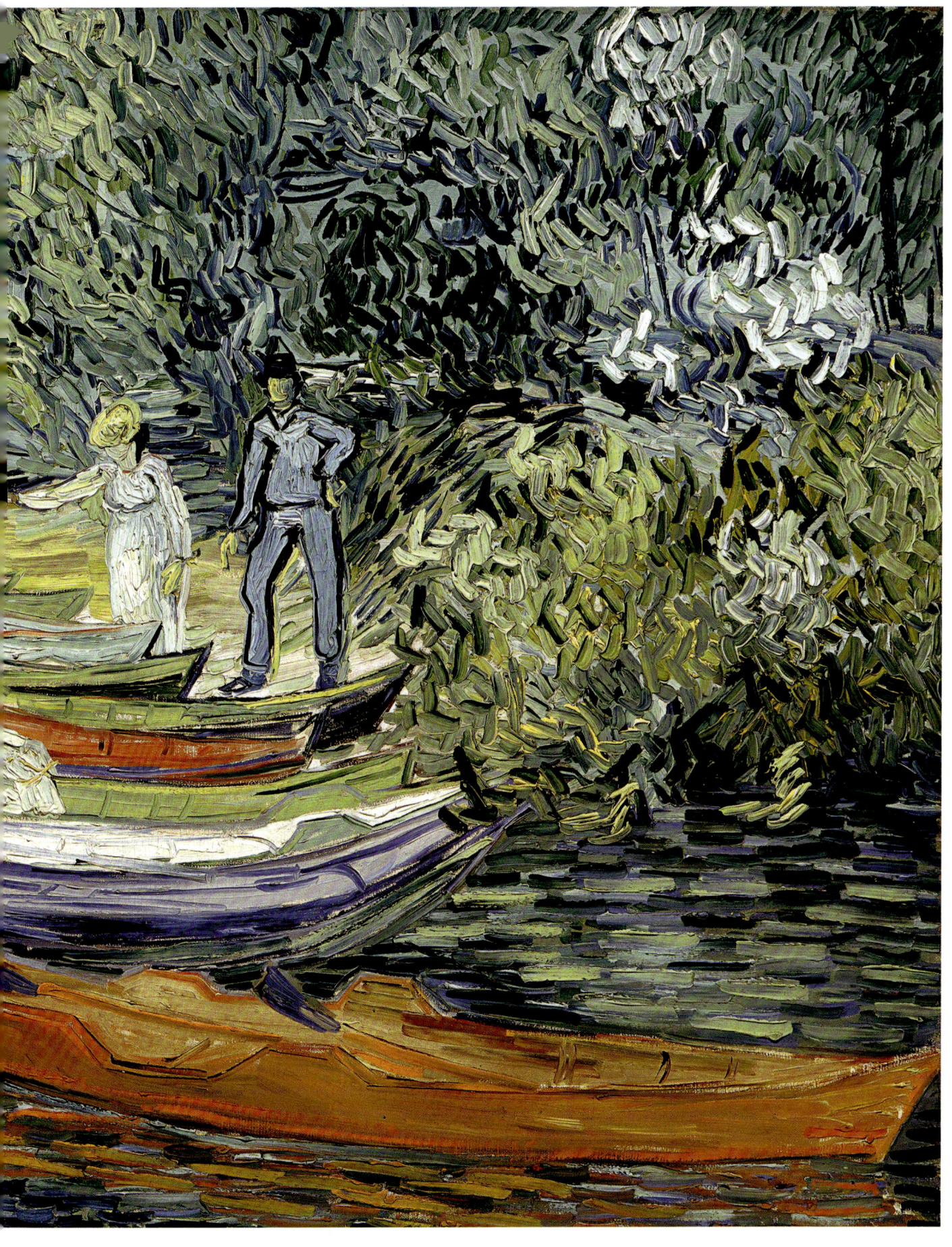

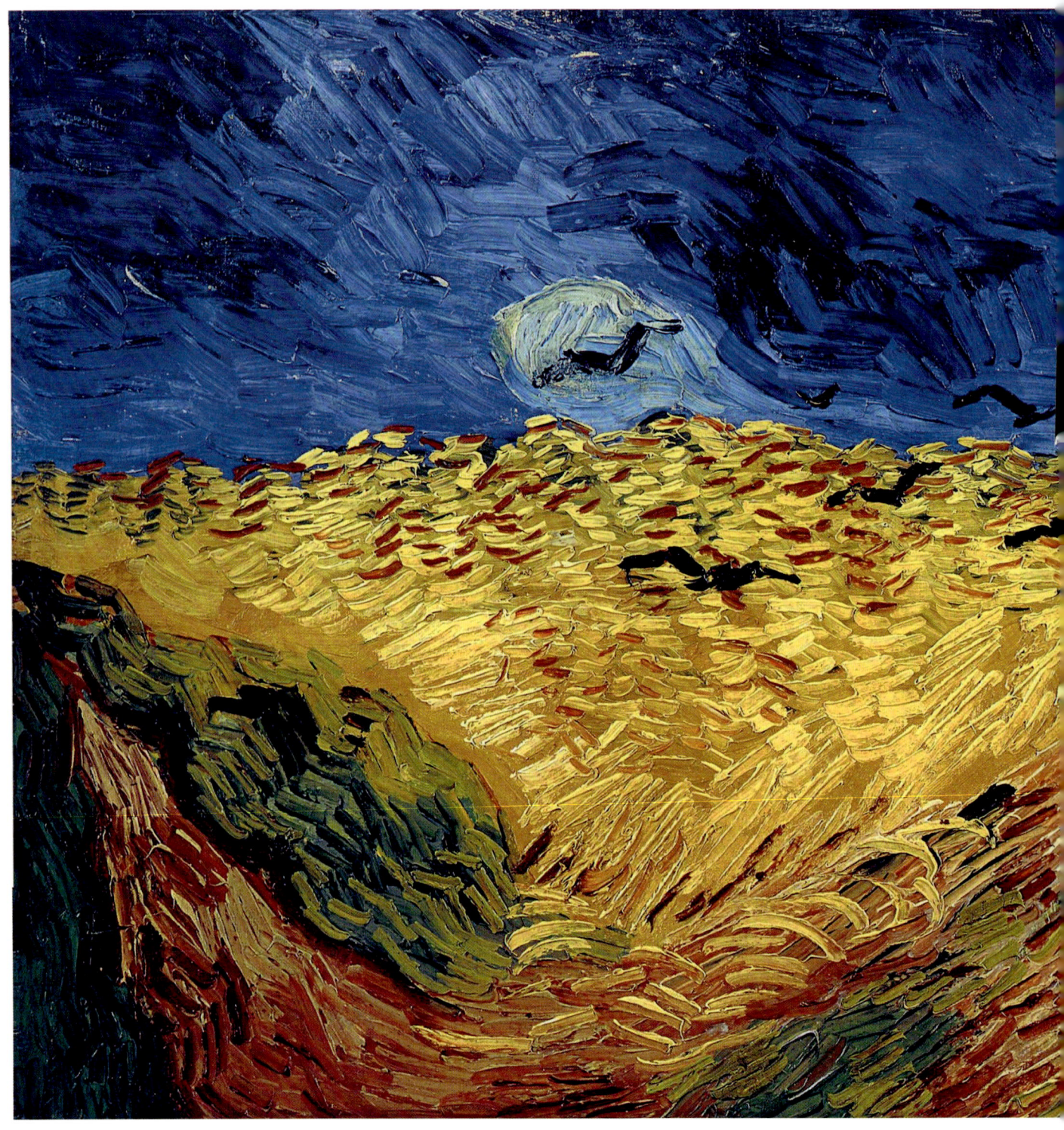

**Wheatfield with Crows,** July 1890, oil on canvas, 50.5 × 103 cm, Amsterdam, Van Gogh Museum

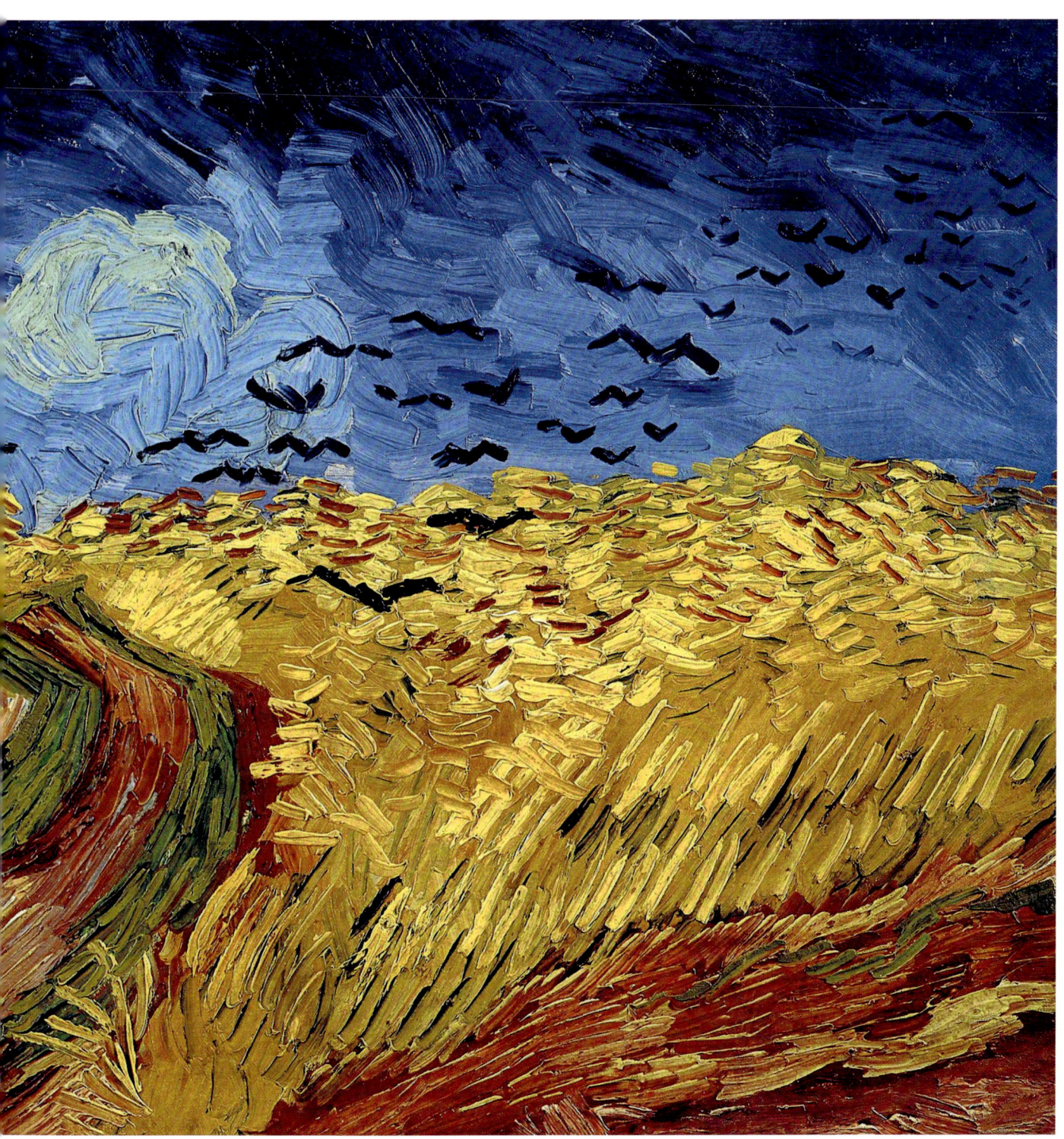

© Prestel Verlag, Munich, London, New York, 2024, 3rd edition 2026
A member of Penguin Random House Verlagsgruppe GmbH,
Neumarkter Strasse 28, 81673 Munich
produktsicherheit@penguinrandomhouse.de
(The above information is mandatory information according to GPSR and
should be used for all queries relating to the safety of our books)

First published in French
Van Gogh. L'art plus grand
© 2023 Éditions Hazan

A CIP catalogue record for this book is available from the British Library

Translation: David Rocher
Copy-editing: John Stilwell
Editorial direction Prestel: Katharina Haderer
Production Prestel: Martina Effaga
Typesetting: Weiß-Freiburg GmbH — Grafik und Buchgestaltung
Separations: Hyphen Group
Printing and Binding: C&C Printing

Printed in China

ISBN 978-3-7913-7759-9

www.prestel.com